Thomas M. Dixon

TOMMY MACK:

Unsettled Years

Craig & Betty,

If you enjoyed my first book – you'll have no problem with this one...

Best of luck, always

Tommy M.

Dec, 2011

ALSO BY

THOMAS DIXON

TOMMY MACK: An Appalachian Childhood

TOMMY MACK

Unsettled Years

A Memoir

and

Family History

The 2nd book in the Tommy Mack series by:

THOMAS DIXON

TOMMY MACK: Unsettled Years

Printed in the United States of America on acid-free paper.

First edition May 1, 2014
Second Edition September 12, 2014

Hardcover ISBN: 978-1-63263-128-2
Paperback ISBN: 978-1-63263-129-9

www.tommymackbooks.com

Please visit www.tommymackbooks.com for special requests, news of upcoming books, and other communications.

The events and times herein are all true, gathered from the best of memory and written record. All photos were taken by the author or a family member unless otherwise stated. Permission to use family photos has been granted in writing. The names of some people and places have been changed for privacy reasons.

To the offspring of the Dixon Clan:

Patricia (daughter of Daisy)
Chester Jr. (son of Daisy)
Ramona (daughter of Wesley) and her children, Cody and Selena
Melissa (daughter of Wesley) and her daughter Alicia
Anthony (son of Wesley) and his children: John, Brittany, Ryan, Shadoe and Anthony Jr.
Ronnie (son of Ronnie)
Donald (son of Ronnie) and his daughters Alexa and Natalya
Pamela (daughter of Virginia) and her daughters Lacey and Courtney
Mark (son of Virginia) and his son, Justin
Wanda (daughter of Virginia) and her children Ashley and Tyler
Paul Jr. (son of Paul) and his sons Paul III and Noah
Cindy (daughter of Donna)
Carol (daughter of Donna)
Victoria (daughter of Tommy) and her daughters Avery and Emma
Andria (daughter of Tommy) and her daughter Sydney
Colleen (daughter of Gary) and her daughter Victoria
Brandi (daughter of Gary) and her children: Anthony, Mikeya, and Jayla
Heidi (daughter of Gary)
Kevin (son of Debbie)
Erika (daughter of Debbie) and her children: Aiden, Gianna, and Ethan
Amy (daughter of David) and her daughters Piper and Sadie;

Love wholeheartedly, forgive honestly, learn well, and never stop reaching.

ACKNOWLEDGMENTS

This year, 2014—and it's by coincidence only—the month of May hails the 50th anniversary of the family journey to Delaware.

To all my brothers and sisters: David, Debbie, Gary, Donna, Paul, Ginny, Ronnie, Wesley, and Daisy; thanks so much for your support and encouragement.

I am particularly grateful for Debbie and Gary's candid contributions. Talking so freely about their lives and the choices they made has provided a much-needed balance to the story. I'm sure it was difficult at times. Our wish is for the truth to be told and certain hard-earned lessons to be revealed. And so it will be.

I'm happy to express the most sincere appreciation to my editors: Al Desetta, for his uncanny knack for brevity and frank assessment of my early manuscript; Orlo Otteson, for his inspiration; and Myrle Bowe, for her keen eye and sincere interest in my project. Also, there's Todd Engel (cover design) along with Angela Hoy and the rest of the fabulous crew at Booklocker.com publishing. All of your assistance has been invaluable.

Finally, I would like to thank the Delaware Public Archives in Dover, the Delaware Historical Society in Wilmington, and the Killeen Area Heritage Association in Killeen, Texas for their contributions. Select photos from these organizations prove that a picture can say a thousand words, and that means less you'll hear from Tommy Mack.

God is just:

*He will pay back trouble to those who trouble you
and give relief to you who are troubled,
and to us as well.*

2 Thessalonians 1:6-7

CONTENTS

INTRODUCTION

My first memoir, *Tommy Mack: An Appalachian Childhood,* described the joyful, carefree, but often dark and tumultuous years our family spent in southern coal-mining towns in the 1940s and 50s. With an alcoholic and abusive father as villain, we moved frequently throughout Virginia and West Virginia, surviving on welfare and pickings from our gardens, and finding solace in each other.

When my father's violent behavior could no longer be endured, my mother Myrtle packed up seven of her ten children for a one-way trip out of Appalachia, the only part of the country she'd known for more than four decades. We loaded our most important worldly possessions into a small U-Haul trailer, hooked it up to my brother's 1956 Oldsmobile, and drove from Tazewell County, Virginia to Wilmington, Delaware. The year: 1964. I was twelve years old.

Just two weeks earlier, emotionally distraught and not knowing where else to turn, I promised the Lord I'd never ask for anything again, if only He would rescue us from my father's evil clutches. To my surprise, a plan was put into motion almost immediately and within days the family had been delivered. This planted a few powerful questions in my mind: could this be a mere coincidence, or had God really answered my prayers? And if He had, would He hold me to my promise to never ask for His help again?

In many ways our lives in Delaware were better, even if we were still poor, lived in crummy apartments, and survived on public assistance. Heck, at least we had indoor plumbing. We didn't have to feed chickens or slop hogs and were hundreds of miles from our father.

My siblings and I went to school, held summer jobs, discovered the opposite sex, played sports, and generally adapted to life "up north" as we traveled on the path to adulthood. But the anger and violence that had been pervasive during my early childhood—their roots go deep within the family, sometimes erupting when least expected—didn't magically disappear.

Back in Appalachia, school bullies had pursued me—that is, until they saw my big brother Paul looming before them, coming to my defense. Now I was stuck in a suburban public school system alone, my big brother's protection gone. So I had to make a decision: allow myself to be bullied or fight back. I generally chose the latter, but at the risk of becoming a bully, too.

Soon after arriving in Delaware, I faced still more questions. Would we really be free from poverty and my father's alcoholic violence? Would we be able to stay "delivered" and stick together as a unit? Would the family problems that took root back in coal country now surface in new and ugly ways in the city streets and suburbs of Wilmington? Had I used my one-and-only bargaining chip with God too soon?

Tommy Mack: Unsettled Years contains a number of violent episodes, as I stand up for myself (and sometimes others). In trying to understand my actions, I can only provide motive and rationalization, not justification. But I now know that when someone does you wrong, retaliation does little to change that person. Instead, it changes you in very uncomfortable ways.

The ugly specter of racial conflict also shows itself in this book. Segregated Appalachian schools gave me little exposure to other races. Then fate (or divine intervention) deposited me into desegregated territory north and east of the Mason-Dixon Line in the 1960s, a time of great racial tumult and upheaval. I learned that great distrust and animosity can exist between people of different races, but also great understanding and friendship as well.

During my formative teenage years in Delaware, I was in need of healthy adult role models. But no such luck! My older siblings were busy working on families of their own, with little time for the four youngest. I had to settle for the next best thing: my mom and a couple of oddball "big brothers" who were not related to me. My mother did the best she could, relying on old-fashioned morals and discipline. While she abhorred most forms of violence, she didn't spare the rod. There are moments in this book when some of her children take a stand. I loved and still love her deeply, but the time had come to put an end to a form of discipline that had outlived its usefulness.

Our family lived through some wonderful, strange, sad, and hectic times, when personal, family, and national issues seemed troubling and sometimes overwhelming. We wondered if we'd ever graduate from junior high, let alone high school or college. Some of the baggage from the past was, indeed, unpacked in Delaware. Some of my siblings went astray, testing our love and patience. And our father resurfaced in our lives in totally unexpected ways.

But we also enjoyed happy times, as all families do: lazy summer days at swimming holes, sports, friendships, parties, and the music of the times, of course—Elvis, The Rolling Stones, The Beatles, The Beach Boys, The Supremes, and many more. Through love, perseverance, and God's graces, we survived the bad times, savored the good moments, and ultimately prospered as a family. *Tommy Mack: Unsettled Years* is my record of how we did it.

Krebs Chemical & Pigment Company, Newport, DE, Oct. 31, 1932. Note the building by the river at lower right: that's #10 Water Street. (Courtesy of the Delaware Historical Society.)

I

OUT OF APPALACHIA

1964

The house where Aunt Katherine lived, 50 years later (2014).

Close Quarters

My mother had called ahead from a payphone to announce an approximate time of arrival, and our little family caravan arrived at Aunt Katherine's, or Kitty's, house in Delaware around eleven the next morning. It had been a 500-mile drive that spanned more than two days.

As we pulled into the driveway, I took note of the huge house looming before us. *This must be the place*, I thought. We exited Ronnie's Oldsmobile in time to avert another bout of motion sickness. While stretching out the travel kinks, we spotted my aunt and her six-year-old son Edward coming out to meet us.

"Gracious be the Lord!" she said. "How is everybody?"

"A little worn and ragged," Mom said, "but we're all safe and sound."

"Myrtle, it's so good to see you," she said, smothering Mom with a big hug.

"It's good to see you too, Kitty. How long has it been, two or three years?"

"I'd guess about that, but it seems more like eight."

We spent several minutes milling about the yard, getting acquainted and talking about the long and uncomfortable trip. Then Kitty asked us to come inside for refreshments and to discuss storage and sleeping arrangements. As we moved from the sunny outdoors to the cool shade of our aunt's front porch, I felt relieved to be freed from vehicle confinement and to have safely reached our destination.

The journey had been an adventure for some and pure torture for others. Numerous detours, various stops, and the heavy load—which included two adults, two teenagers, four children, and 500 pounds of belongings, packed into an eight-foot U-Haul trailer—had slowed our progress. Many of the mountainous interstate highways were in various stages of construction. Hundreds of workers, together with dozens of huge, powerful earthmoving machines, were parting mountains to form the freeway that would become Interstate Highway 77.

Except for my big brother Ronnie, none of us were aware of the massive amount of federal and state spending, all in the name of progress. These highway projects had been going on for months and months, while the family had been eking out a simple hand-to-mouth existence in the small Virginia coal mining towns of Boissevain, Pocahontas, and Falls Mills. We didn't fully understand the ways of the busy, complicated world outside Bluefield, West Virginia.

Highway construction had caused detours around and north of Washington D.C. and Baltimore, a route that added fifty miles to our journey. Most of us had rarely ventured out of the Boissevain-Bluefield area, and we initially enjoyed watching the oh-so-beautiful mountains, rivers, and valleys fall away behind us. Soon, however, the heat and close quarters began wearing on us. At about the two hundred mile mark the younger kids began quarrelling and smacking each other, behavior that required Mom to place Paul in the back seat to squelch potential free-for-alls and keep the peace.

"Now listen!" Mom shouted. "If Paul catches another one of you kids pinching, kicking, or even touching someone else, I'm gonna have Ronnie stop this car and spank your behind right here in front of all this traffic going by! Do you hear me?"

We rolled our eyes, wondering how this could possibly work, since we were packed together like sardines. We got Mom's message, however, and we soon calmed down.

Every now and then I'd look back to see the U-Haul trailer zigzagging back-and-forth as we barreled along the country roads and highways. At any moment I expected it to break free from our bumper and collide with the nearest object—another car, the guardrail, or one of the many tidy ranch houses decorating the roadside. If that happened, I thought we'd really be homeless. Amazingly, it never did.

* * * * *

Aunt Katherine's house, at 507 North DuPont Road, was located just outside Wilmington in a community called Richardson Park, or simply "The Park," a well-established blue-collar district.

Employment opportunities were plentiful. About a mile away on Boxwood Road, the General Motors Corporation and its Wilmington Assembly Plant were rolling cars off the line at a steady rate. A Chrysler production plant sprawled down the road in Newark, adjacent to the bustling University of Delaware campus. The DuPont Experimental Station, the largest research and development facility of E. I. DuPont de Nemours and Company, sits high above the

Brandywine River just north of the city limits. A pigments plant occupied the banks of the Christina River in Newport, and the company's corporate headquarters was (is) located in Wilmington.

Minutes after entering the house I watched two cousins stroll warily in, looking us over. They had dashed home during the school lunch period, hoping we had arrived. Carl, about fourteen, was the oldest. He stood taller and stockier than me, and more tanned than Paul. Next came eleven-year-old Marlene, Aunt Katherine's second-born, or middle, child. Mom had shown us pictures of these cousins and, amazingly enough, Marlene looked even prettier in person.

The house was a three-story post-war design, with a full basement. Unfortunately for us, the landlord had divided the building into two apartments, with the ground floor space leased to another young family—an arrangement that created some discomfort for our extended family.

After some initial chitchat, Cousin Marlene showed my sisters Debbie and Donna where they'd be sleeping; and Cousin Carl showed us boys (Paul, Gary, David, and me) our sleeping arrangements. My excitement grew as we explored the house.

They had an indoor toilet that actually flushed. The kitchen contained a large enamel sink, a fairly new working refrigerator, and pantries for food and linen storage. We were tickled to death to see our very own telephone, resting on an end table in the living room. I felt like a blind man who'd regained his sight and stepped out of the dark ages. Half of my siblings had never used a phone, and Gary, Donna, and I gazed at the contraption, wondering if we could even dial a number correctly.

Marlene and Carl finished lunch and said goodbye, returning to school six blocks away. Little Edward stayed, complaining of some illness, an excuse he'd given his mother that morning. I'm sure he'd faked it. His mother knew it, too, but had relented and was quite willing to grant him time to spend with his aunt and cousins.

Early that afternoon, we moved our personal items from the U-Haul into the house. Ronnie unloaded the remaining furniture at our cousins' place, three blocks away on Schoolhouse Lane. Our Aunt Pauline had three adult sons: Reds, Cherry, and Van. They had invited Ronnie to bunk with them at their place until we could find a suitable apartment of our own. Van, the youngest, would join them there in a few weeks. Ronnie would spend his nights sleeping in a worn-out recliner chair, an uncomfortable arrangement that lasted for several weeks.

The days following our arrival proved to be pleasant times. My cousins were finishing up the school year, and I began looking forward to spending more time with them, especially Marlene, who seemed so genuinely sweet and considerate. We also met some of the neighborhood kids and began to work our way into one or two cliques. Eleven-year-old Tommy Miller was in good standing with one particular group—The Park Skateboarding and Bike Club. When I saw these boys riding their bikes and skateboards, I swore that I would do whatever it took to be part of the team.

I approached my mother with a rare request. "Mom, can I have two dollars?"

"Two dollars! For goodness sakes, Tommy, do you think money grows on trees around here? What do you want with two dollars?"

"Tommy Miller has two used roller skates, and he's asking a dollar each for them."

"You'll break your neck using roller skates around them streets."

"No I won't. Besides, I'm gonna bolt them to a piece of wood and make myself a homemade skateboard. Tommy Miller's gonna help me."

"Roller skates or skateboards, it doesn't matter. You're still gonna break your neck."

"Ah, Mom, come on, pleeease," I begged, following her into the living room. "Just two dollars, and I won't ever ask you for anything again."

"Tommy, you shouldn't make promises you can't keep. Now I know you'll be back here next month asking me for something else. So, I'm not gonna hold you to such a ridiculous promise." She sat down on the sofa and reached for her purse.

"All right!" I shouted, watching her dig through its contents.

Aunt Kitty must have heard my pleading. "Here, Myrtle," she said, and handed Mom a dollar bill. "Let me split that with you."

"Thanks Kitty, that's nice of you. It'll help."

Shocked and elated, I bellowed, "Thanks Mom! Thanks Aunt Kitty!" and headed for the door, clutching the money.

"Now you be careful with those things!" Mom shouted after me. "If you get hurt, I'll take a switch to ya!"

That week, with Tommy Miller's help, I built my first skateboard. Tommy also offered me several used parts to build a bicycle—but at a cost. You see, Tommy Miller was a businessman. He said he couldn't let me have the parts for a penny less than seven dollars. Knowing how scarce money was, I wouldn't dare ask Mom for any more dollar bills. So I got pretty good at skateboarding over the next two weeks. The bicycle I so badly wanted would have to wait.

Getting Acquainted

Our family relations began to fray that first Sunday morning together. Aunt Kitty marched into one room and out the other, demanding that all the Dixon children attend Sunday church services, just like her own children. Mom thought we could try Aunt Kitty's church at least once, but she was concerned about the way her sister kept pushing the issue.

"Myrtle," Kitty said, "why don't you come to church with us? I'm sure the Lord has been waiting to have a nice conversation with you."

"Humph," Mom replied, "if the Lord wants to talk to me, then He should talk to me. I don't need a second person relaying His message."

I heard brother Paul snicker, perhaps thinking that Mom had put Kitty in her place. As it turned out, however, everyone except Paul and Mom attended church services that first Sunday. I didn't mind. I was always looking for a new adventure, but nothing could have prepared us for what we saw—that is, people clapping, swaying, and shouting in crude and confusing ways, and my Aunt Kitty and a few others sprawled about on the floor, kicking, speaking, and screaming in such a strange manner, I found myself breaking into a cold sweat. The language sounded especially bizarre, unlike anything I'd ever heard. And as I watched Kitty kicking and rolling around in the aisle, I saw her dress inch up past her big behind, exposing her bloomers. Thankfully, a gentleman in the congregation took the initiative and kindly covered her with his suit coat.

A few weeks later my sister Donna was baptized and became a member of my aunt's church. It wasn't long before Aunt Kitty noticed Donna roaming about the house and yard dressed in a pair of modest walking shorts.

"What are you doing wearing those ungodly things?" she asked.

"Oh, you mean my shorts?" Donna said. "I've always worn shorts in the summer."

"Well, things are different now, Donna, and I expect you to wear something appropriate, something more ladylike. Now go in the house and put on something decent."

"No, I'm not taking them off. It's too hot!"

"Look here young lady," Kitty said, "if you don't practice your religion, you'll forever be called a hypocrite. You don't want to be called a hypocrite now, do you?"

"Well … nooo."

At first Donna didn't understand the definition of the term hypocrite and she pictured something akin to a water buffalo. Whatever the meaning, she knew it wasn't pretty, but she refused to change her shorts and Mom wasn't about to force her. Aunt Kitty continued to nag Mom and to criticize Donna for the way she dressed, repeatedly calling her a hypocrite. Donna soon learned the meaning of the term and, had it not been for Kitty's nagging, she might have remained faithful to the church. She greatly appreciated Aunt Kitty's help and wanted so much to please her. She thought getting baptized might be one way to do it, but would soon come to regret that decision.

* * * * *

By the second week, both natural and man-made problems began to invade our new dwelling. The third floor bedrooms became unbearably hot, forcing us to move to the second floor and sleep on the carpeted living room floor. Even with the windows open, we were barely able to tolerate the heat. With nine children and two adults taking showers, the hot water would run out before the third shower. Aunt Kitty insisted that we all take lukewarm showers to stretch out the hot water supply. And the toilet kept plugging up. It overflowed several times before we were informed that an adult had to be present to flush it. Heck, we never had any of those problems with our outhouses back in Appalachia.

Cousin Carl proceeded to give some of us a crash course on the inner workings of a toilet, but the engineering continued to baffle me. I think everyone except Paul bailed out early on the lesson. But one day, as Carl explained the functions of the float and flush valves, Donna noticed a brown paper bag with something hard inside, wedged behind the tank. They opened the bag and discovered a half-empty bottle of whiskey. This finding embarrassed Aunt Kitty, since her boyfriend had placed it there, sure that it would stay hidden. Hypocrites come and hypocrites go, Donna thought, but some are occasionally exposed.

Arguments between my siblings and our cousins were becoming more frequent. Paul and Carl had an arm wrestling match, which Paul easily won. Carl and I arm-wrestled, too, and after some struggle he defeated me. Now king-of-the-hill, Carl began to bully and annoy his smaller cousins when Paul wasn't around. Soon after that, Gary and I were standing in the front yard when Carl told us to do something ridiculous, and totally out of line. I can't remember what, but at the time I knew it was something that went against my budding moral compass.

I said, "Nooo, I don't have to do that."

Carl walked over to me, puffing up his chest like a rooster, and said, "You'd better do it."

"I don't have to do what you tell me. You're not my father."

He pushed me, saying, "It's my house and you'd better do it."

I stood my ground. "No!"

He pushed me again, shouting, "Do it—hillbilly!"

Well, believe it or not, that was the first time I recall being called a hillbilly. And although I knew it to be true, it stung—especially coming from Carl, my cousin. To me, these had to be fightin' words. Without warning, I tackled him to the ground. We wrestled around the front yard, finally rolling down a dirt bank and ending up jammed against a sturdy row of hedges. We were stuck. Carl had me in a powerful headlock—my first—and I began to wonder if I could possibly break free. Meantime, Gary had rushed into the house and told everyone that Carl and I were fighting. Just when I thought I was about to squirm free, Paul appeared, staring down at us.

"Carl, let him go."

"If I do, you're not going to let him hit me, are you?"

Paul said, "Tommy, you promise to leave him alone if he lets go?"

"He started it," I muttered, my voice practically smothered by Carl's cotton shirt. *I should bite him*, I thought. Then I noticed Mom and Aunt Kitty standing behind Paul.

Aunt Kitty said, "Carl, you let Tommy go now, or I'm going to take a switch to you."

At that instant, Paul pried Carl's arms from around my neck and pulled us to our feet, wedging his body between us. Kitty grabbed her son and led him toward the house, smacking him repeatedly on the back of his head.

Mom said, "Tommy, what in tarnation was all that fightin' about?"

Overheated and sweating, I stood there petrified, expecting Mom to wallop me good. But she didn't. I thought of how embarrassing it would be to get a good switchin' right in front of my cousins, especially Marlene. I hesitated, trying to formulate an excuse that would save me from a painful and embarrassing whipping.

"Well, the cat got your tongue, young man?"

"Uh—Carl was bossin' and pickin' on Gary and me," I cried, "and—and—and he called us a bunch of hillbillies, Mom."

Mom's eyes got real big, and after swallowing the lump in her throat she said, "Tommy, just you remember sticks and stones the next time someone says that." Walking back to the house, Paul brushed away the dirt and grime from the back of my clothes, just like he'd done so many times before.

Banished

A couple of days after my scrap with Carl, Mom called me into the living room and told me that Debbie and I were going to spend the rest of the summer in Texas with brother Wesley and sister Daisy. Daisy had given birth a month earlier to a healthy baby girl, Patricia, my first niece. Now, in addition to the newborn and three-year-old Chester Jr., Daisy was about to play nursemaid to her baby sister again. Debbie would be staying with Daisy and her budding family in San Antonio, while I would live with Wesley and his wife Kay in Killeen, Texas. My sister Ginny had arrived there a few months earlier.

I didn't object to the plan. *Is Mom trying to get rid of me because Carl and I aren't getting along*? "Why me and Debbie, Mom?"

"Tommy, I asked Wesley and Daisy who they wanted. Wesley and Kay wanted you. Daisy and Chester picked Debbie. We thought that would be best for everyone. You'll be riding the bus all the way, so I'll feel better having you there to look after Debbie."

With that, I began contemplating a new adventure. Sensing that our two families were trapped in a crowded and uncomfortable situation, I went along with the decision easily. Debbie, on the other hand, wasn't exactly thrilled. We all knew how much she hated being away from home and family. Her previous attempts at living with Daisy had caused her to cry and cry, until she finally became sick and had to be returned home. This time it took a lot of explaining by Mom to placate my little sister.

At the bus station in Wilmington, Mom and Ronnie huddled with a Greyhound representative to discuss the logistics of transporting a twelve-year-old and an eight-year-old halfway across the United States without an accompanying adult. The representative pointed out that the bus company transports children all the time. "Each bus driver will be responsible for handing them over to the next terminal representative, ma'am, and they'll be delivered safely to their destination." These remarks were intended to reassure us.

Mom placed a lot of trust in the bus company's system and its employees. At the time, she didn't think she had a better choice. Greyhound was celebrating its fiftieth anniversary that year, and Mom couldn't resist taking advantage of the super low travel packages. Airline tickets were out of the question.

Mom and Ronnie stayed with us at the stop until we were loaded onto the bus. As the bus pulled away, Debbie and I looked back at our mother and brother walking across the street to the car. It took only a moment for them to fade away into the city traffic. We remained calm, but our pain was palpable.

Our major stops and changes went something like this:

South: from Wilmington to Baltimore, Maryland; Washington D.C.; Richmond, Virginia; Charlotte, North Carolina.; Atlanta, Georgia; and Montgomery and Mobile, Alabama.

West: from Mobile Alabama to Baton Rouge, Louisiana; Houston, Texas; and finally to Austin, Texas.

For three days and two nights my sister and I felt trapped and unable to stretch out for more than a few minutes of rest or sleep. And I spent the entire trip watching after Debbie, making sure she was comfortable, sometimes joking and acting silly in an effort to cheer her up. The trip seemed to last forever, and just as much a blur then as now. If you don't take pictures, write it down; otherwise, the best is lost forever. We saw more strange sights, sounds, human attire and behavior, than we ever had—skyscrapers, multi-lane highways, street musicians and performers, panhandlers, drunks, and bums—all plying their so-called trades on city streets and within bus terminals.

I can sure vouch for the efficiency and professionalism of the Greyhound and Trailways companies at that time. They catered to my sister and me, always seating us directly behind the bus driver, who kept an eye on us when we visited the cafeterias and restrooms and made sure that we boarded the proper bus.

Around seven o'clock on the third evening we pulled into Austin. A terminal employee placed us in a confined area near a payphone. I had Wesley's and Daisy's phone numbers and addresses stuffed into one of my pockets, but I had used Aunt Kitty's phone only once to call Wesley from Delaware. Now, as I approached the payphone to call my brother, I felt nervous and unsure of myself. I read the directions, dropped a dime into the machine, and dialed the numbers. The operator told me I had to deposit more money, so I put more change into the phone. Seconds later I heard a ringing, followed by a voice on the other end.

"Hello?" I said tentatively, not sure I recognized the voice.

"Hello? Who's there? Can I help you?"

Yes! It was Ginny. I felt so relieved to hear her familiar voice.

"Ginny, it's Tommy. Debbie and I are at the bus stop in Austin."

"Oh my," Ginny said. "Are you alright?"

"Yeah, we're fine."

"Did you have a good trip?"

"It was too long. We're tired, Ginny. How long will it take for you to get here?"

The town of Killeen, seventy miles away, awaited our arrival.

"Sit tight," Ginny said, "it might take two hours to get there."

Debbie and I ate a hearty dinner in the terminal cafeteria, then returned to the main waiting area and sprawled out on the big wooden benches, still under the eye of a terminal representative. I spotted Ginny and Kay around dusk, walking toward us from the parking lot across the street. We were thrilled to see familiar family faces, and we hugged and hugged. After our long trip to Texas, the ride to Killeen seemed easy.

Paul, 16, Donna, 14, Gary, 10, and David, 6, taken in Richardson Park, while Debbie and I were away, basking in the hot Texas sun.

Deborah Sue (Debbie), 8 years old.

Tommy Mack, 12 years old.

Having delivered Debbie safely to Daisy in San Antonio, Wesley wasted little time showing me around Killeen. We visited the Fort Hood military facilities and stopped at the Post Exchange (PX), where he bought me pants, t-shirts, swimming shorts, and two oh-so-important hats to prevent sunburn. Dressed in his uniform, he also took me into one of the barracks. I guess he wanted to introduce his little brother to a few of the men. He may also have wanted to impress me with a small dose of military protocol.

A soldier said, “Good morning, Sergeant Dixon,” as we walked into the dorm.

“Good morning,” Wesley replied firmly.

“Sergeant Dixon, who’s the kid?” another soldier asked.

“This is Tommy,” he replied, placing his hand on my shoulder, “one of my little brothers.”

Two recruits said, “Hey Tommy, nice to meet you.”

“Hello,” I said shyly, noting that some of the men were in various stages of dressing.

We continued down the long building, passing cots on both sides of the aisle, greeting soldiers and receiving greetings. As we approached the latrine and shower area, I heard someone whistling and humming. We paused at a table just as a naked man burst into the open room, singing at the top of his voice. Holding a towel in one hand and a can of shaving cream in the other, he headed straight for Wesley and me. I had never seen a grown man naked before, and certainly never one so eager to expose his nakedness. The scene was making me increasingly nervous and I looked away. But the man continued his strutting and musical performance, until he saw the two of us blocking his way. I didn’t know whether to move or wait for Wesley to move me.

“Good morning, Sergeant Dixon,” the man said, finally placing the towel over his private parts.

"Morning," Wesley said. "Specialist Lawrence, I'd like for you to meet Tommy, one of my little brothers. He'll be spending most of the summer with me."

"Hi, Tommy," the man said.

"Hello."

Lowering his voice, Wesley said, "Hey Pete, I was showing Tommy here around town, and thought I'd stop by to see if we're still on for the double date this Friday night."

"You bet," Pete said. "I wouldn't miss a chance to get to know your sister better."

"Good, is eight o'clock at my place alright?" Wesley asked.

"Sure. Eight it is," Pete said. As we turned and began walking away, he said, "Nice to meet you, Tommy."

"You too," I said.

* * * * *

Friday night arrived and we enjoyed the dinner hour, complete with loud but pleasant conversation. I wasn't feeling homesick, maybe because I hadn't really called a place home since we'd left Falls Mills. Even so, I began to wonder what a twelve-year-old would do in a small military town like Killeen. Wesley must have been reading my mind.

"Hey, Tommy, now that school is out, you'll begin to see more kids your age around the neighborhood. I think you should walk up to one of them tomorrow and introduce yourself."

Ginny said, "Yeah, Tommy, you'll have more things to do when you make some new friends."

"The summer could get kind of boring without some friends your own age to play with," Kay added.

"What do you think, Tommy?" Wesley asked. "Are you up to making some new friends?"

"I guess so," I muttered, remembering another time when I was the "new kid" and the target of bullying.

It was almost eight o'clock when Kay, a big Elvis Presley fan, turned off the television and started playing some of his rock-and-roll hits on a small portable record exchanger, awaiting Specialist Pete Lawrence's arrival. I'd had few opportunities to listen to a record player, but I recognized some of the tunes and lyrics, and soon began to groove with the beat. Wesley and Kay seemed to enjoy my enthusiasm.

A loud knock interrupted the music. Kay turned down the volume and answered the knock. Pete stood tall crowding the doorway. Dressed in civilian clothes, he sported the biggest and cockiest grin I'd ever seen.

"Come on in and have a seat, Pete," Kay said, "Ginny is still getting ready. She'll be out in a few minutes."

A minute later, Ginny stepped into the living room wearing a brightly colored skirt and a fitted white blouse. What a knockout! Pete seemed more than pleased with his Friday night date. While Ginny and Pete chatted, I watched Kay place a collection of Presley's hits on the record player. "It's Now or Never" led the way, and Wesley and Kay began to slow dance. Their mutual affection captivated me, and for the first time I began to wonder about my own future. *When will I dance with my first girlfriend? What will she look like? Pretty. I'll make sure of that. When will I get married, and what will my wife look like?*

One song later, Ginny and Pete joined them with a spin of "Fame and Fortune," which became one of my all-time favorites. Since the two had met only briefly before my arrival, I surmised that it might be their first real dance. I watched them, awestruck. Three songs later, Ginny flipped the album.

"Here, Tommy," she said, reaching out and pulling me to my feet, "come and dance with your sister." The 1960 hit "Are You Lonesome Tonight" was a fitting tune, and we danced until Kay interrupted:

"Ginny, don't be selfish now, let me have my first dance with my little brother-in-law." With that, Ginny stepped aside and I finished the song dancing with my new sister-in-law. Everyone looked amused, especially me. These were my first attempts at slow dancing and I found it quite to my liking.

The grownups stayed out well after midnight, and I spent the evening watching television and playing records. I listened repeatedly to several of Elvis's songs that night and began to learn the lyrics. I found myself wanting to dance and moving to some of Elvis's faster songs, making sure the curtains were closed. I especially liked his 1962 hit, "Good Luck Charm."

I was awakened around one or two o'clock by the returning double-daters. They tried to be quiet, but the alcohol was showing its effects. When I awoke again, around breakfast time, I saw Ginny and Pete—fully clothed—asleep within the twisted sheets on the floor beside my foldout cot. After a cool shower, a good breakfast, and a strong cup of coffee, they seemed ready for yet more weekend excitement.

Pedro

"Hey Tommy," Wesley said, pulling the car to the side of the road, "have you ever driven a go-cart?"

"No."

"Well, today's your big day, little brother. We're all going to ride the go-carts."

My heart fluttered. *Oh crap*!

Looking around, I noticed that Wesley had parked the car near a small amusement center. The sign read: "Big Dan's Off-Road Go-Karts." The place had a quarter-mile, oval-shaped dirt track with bales of hay and old tires scattered about. I noticed two kids a little smaller than me whisking their carts around the course. I could feel my blood pressure begin to rise as we walked through the entrance and started looking at the available rental carts. Odors of rubber, engine exhaust, and gasoline permeated the air. I listened as Wesley told Pete and Ginny that he and Kay had ridden there a couple of times, and he promised it would be a lot of fun.

Again, my heart skipped a beat as I fought against the fear of driving a motorized vehicle. *I can do this. How hard can it be? I've heard about kids younger than me driving these things. Yeah, that man over there will show me how to do it.* As I ran that thought over and over in my mind, I began to convince myself that driving a go-kart was a piece of cake, something any 12-year-old boy could do blindfolded. And even if it wasn't, I stood ready to bluff my way through this because I didn't want anyone to think I was afraid of something new.

After paying admission, an attendant matched the adults with an appropriate cart. I told the attendant my age and he asked if I'd ever ridden one. Since I hadn't, he matched me with what looked like a less powerful model. I listened as he told Ginny and Kay how to work the gas pedal and brakes. It sounded easy enough.

The attendants were timing our take-offs to limit the number of carts on the course. Ginny went first, then Kay. I was to go next, followed by Wesley and Pete, but I ran into an immediate problem—my cart wouldn't move. The attendant checked it and noticed that I was simultaneously depressing the gas and brake pedals.

"Look kid," he said "remember now, you only have to use your right foot. Just keep your left foot away from the pedals and everything will be fine. Okay?"

"Okay, I got it."

I bolted from the starting gate and all seemed fine down the straightaway. But as I approached the counterclockwise curve I couldn't slow down. I was unable to focus on the road and at the same time properly brake the cart. Realizing this, I instinctively headed for the hay bales on my right. I took out two bales at fifteen miles per hour before slamming head first into the tire barrier. Wesley, Pete, and an attendant rushed to the accident scene and found me sprinkled with hay and my lip bleeding, the consequence of having banged my head into the steering wheel. My embarrassment trumped any pain I felt.

"What happened," someone asked.

"I don't know. I couldn't stop it."

Attendants checked my go-cart for damage and took it for a spin, trying to discover any possible malfunctions. Finding none, they banished me. For the next twenty minutes I sat in the car, massaging my swollen lip with an ice cube and watching the others enjoying themselves.

On the way out, I heard one of the attendants tell Wesley, "Don't bring the kid back here until he gets his driver's license."

"I don't think you'll have to worry about that," Wesley replied.

* * * * *

Days later, while sitting on the front stoop, I saw two young boys hanging around the entrance to our driveway. One of them waved and said hello. Remembering what I was told, I took this as an invitation to walk over and introduce myself.

"Hi! My name's Tommy. What's yours?"

"Hi. I'm Timmy and this is Duck."

With a slight accent, Duck said, "Hi Tommy. My real name ez Pedro, but my friends call me Duck. That's because of my feet, chu know."

"Yeah," Timmy said, "they're huge. Show him your feet, Duck."

Watching Pedro kick off his sandals, I guessed him to be mostly of Mexican descent and around nine years old. Timmy appeared about my age, with a freckled and slightly tanned complexion.

"Holy cow," I shouted. "Look at those feet!"

"I told you," said Timmy, laughing.

I marveled at this kid's feet; they really did resemble a duck's. When I placed my sneaker next to Pedro's well-tanned foot, I almost choked. Duck was about three years younger, but his foot already surpassed the size of my sneaker. However, I decided then and there not to call him Duck. Out of respect, I would call him Pedro.

Pedro, Timmy, and I wasted no time getting to know one another. I stuck my head in the house and told Kay we were going to the local park to play.

"Put on your hat," she said, "and be back in a couple of hours."

At the park Pedro looked pumped-up and full of energy, running here and there as fast as he could. I said, "Man, look at that boy run! Don't he ever get tired?"

Timmy said, "With those duck feet, he can run faster than anybody I know. I'll bet he's faster than you, Tommy."

I didn't buy it. Someone with feet *that* large—duck feet at that—couldn't possibly outrun me.

"I can run pretty fast," I boasted. "I'm three years older, too. He can't be faster."

Timmy yelled, "Hey Duck, come here! Tommy wants to race you!"

Pedro sprinted over to us. "Okay!" he shouted, his eyes gleaming with excitement. Then he leaned over and began taking off his sandals.

"He always races barefooted," Timmy warned.

"That's okay with me," I said, "it won't do him any good."

Pedro and I lined up, ready to race from a telephone pole to the nearest tree, about a hundred yards. Timmy would start us. I stood a head taller, but as I looked down at Pedro I noted a devilish grin and sparkling eyes—and a look that seemed to exude confidence. Being three years younger, perhaps he felt he had little to lose. For some reason, I started to doubt myself.

I heard Timmy yell "Go!" and we shot forward. I had no idea how badly he wanted to win, but I knew that I had to; my reputation and a great deal of pride were on the line. For thirty yards we were dead even. Then Pedro pulled away with the ease and grace of a beast, the four-legged kind, built for speed. I finished about four yards behind. I had never seen anyone so young, run so fast. Duck—no, Pedro—had blown me away. Pedro was his name, and running was his game.

Before that day I had lost very few foot races, and I'd never lost to someone so young and so small. Pedro had shattered one of my deeply held (and grossly wrong) beliefs: that small kids weren't supposed to best older and bigger kids—in anything. After a day or two of licking my wounds, I gathered something positive from my loss and disappointment: if I worked hard enough at it, maybe I could best an older, bigger, and stronger person at something, too.

A week or so later, Pedro left Killeen to spend the rest of the summer with his relatives in Mexico. For years afterward I watched the track events at the Olympic Games closely, half expecting to see Pedro running for the gold. I think of him often, but I never saw him again.

Looking north along Killeen's Fourth St. on left, Sixth (or Gray St.), and Eighth Street at right. Fort Hood is located about 1.6 miles northwest of the railroad depot (at forefront), c. 1964. (Courtesy of the Killeen Area Heritage Association.)

Looking west: the south side of Avenue D intersects with Gray St. in Killeen, c. 1974 (Courtesy of the Killeen Area Heritage Association).

Looking west: the north side of Avenue D intersects with Gray St. in Killeen, c. 1974 (Courtesy of the Killeen Area Heritage Association).

Killeen Days

From there on, I spent most every day cavorting with Timmy. We always seemed to find something to do to pass the time. Many kids around the Killeen area talked about hunting wild pigs in the rough Texas brush and mesquite trees. At first this sounded entirely unexciting, but then I had a change of heart. *If that's what 12-year-old boys do for thrills in Texas, then I want a piece of the action.* Well, that's what I thought at first. After several days of bow hunting in the hot sun, we hadn't heard the oink or snort of a wild pig—but that didn't stop us from firing-off an arrow or two. Eventually I wised up and quit the sport.

In no time we created another dangerous pastime. Simply by accident, Timmy and I stumbled upon the sport of ice pick throwing. Yes, ice picks, that super-pointy—and dangerous—tool, common to most households in hot southern states like Texas. Timmy's older brother, Sergeant Gastoff, had left a couple of picks lying around outside his trailer, and we started throwing them at the wooden planks that littered his front yard. After several throws, I was thrilled to see my picks sticking about half the time. *Wow! I seem to have the knack for this. It sure beats sweating away the day hunched under a mesquite tree waiting for wild boar.* I soon learned that timing and balance were the keys. Timmy wasn't quite as successful, but we kept at it that first day, throwing until the wooden handles cracked.

The next morning I took my last three dollars and headed out on foot to Killeen Hardware, located somewhere around Avenue D and Gray Street, about eight blocks away, and bought six ice picks at twenty-nine cents each. After lunch I met Timmy on his front porch. He was holding four new picks.

"Hey, Tommy," he said, "the manager at Killeen Hardware said some other kid just stopped in and almost cleaned him out of ice picks." He laughed, adding, "I figured it was you."

I snickered. "Yeah, it was me."

We reinforced the wooden handles by wrapping them with black electrical tape we'd found in one of his brother's toolboxes. We also filed down the needle-like points to help them stick and lessen the chance of them breaking. Then we spent the better part of an hour making a target out of several wooden planks. We painted the figure of a human on it and practiced, aiming for the heart, for an hour or more each day in the Texas heat. I saw the sport as the perfect pastime for that heat; we just stood in the shade, throwing and retrieving the picks. No sweat!

The Fourth of July came, and Kay and Ginny informed me that we were going swimming at Belton Lake, a rather large body of water about 16 miles east of Killeen. The man-made lake had grown out of a project designed to prevent flood damage. It also served to conserve water and provide a habitat for fish and wildlife. General recreation just happened to be a lucrative side benefit.

I saw only the recreational aspect, which for me meant learning to swim. The weather was sunny and hot, with a slight breeze, low humidity, and temperatures close to ninety-five degrees.

Wesley drove the vehicle, or should I say—the machine: a 2-door, white, 1962 Pontiac Catalina, in good condition, with a 389 cu. in. "Trophy" V8 engine—rarin' to go. Kay was up front, Ginny and Pete and me in the back. Zipping down the highway, I listened to the radio blasting popular songs and watched Ginny and Pete trying to sneak in an affectionate kiss or two. All the windows were down, allowing fluttery gusts of wind to whip the girls' hair into a frizzy, tangled mess. Everyone was joking. Pete began teasing Ginny about her hair and me about this and that, mostly girls.

"Tommy, you got a girlfriend back home wait'n for ya?"

"Of course not," I said, "I'm only twelve years old."

"I had my first girlfriend at twelve," Pete boasted. "Don't you think it's time you started working on a girlfriend?"

Kay said, "Oh, leave him alone, Pete. He'll find a girlfriend when he's ready."

"Well, okay. Tommy, when you're ready and you need a couple of tips, just let me know."

We pulled into a large parking lot filled with cars. Each of us grabbed something and headed for the beach. Right away I noticed the beach's enormous size. I thought, *no one should be kicking sand into our picnic baskets here.* The sand and beach seemed to roll endlessly along the water's edge. Seeing all this made me eager to run ahead and smack water, but I held back and just removed my t-shirt, waiting for the others. I noticed Pete staring at my chest.

"My eyes must be playing tricks on me," Pete moaned, "because I think I see a ghost—right before my very eyes."

I thought: *What the heck's he talking about?*

"Oh my!" Ginny shouted. "Tommy, you're as pale as a ghost. Here, let me put some lotion on you."

We all greased up and then plunged into the cool water. For the first time in my life I felt comfortable frolicking in water deep enough to drown me. The water temperature seemed perfect and the sand and small pebbles soothed my feet, far different from the freezing water and sharp rocks back in Falls Mills.

After several plunges I was actually swimming and learning to tread water. We had lunch, and the two couples pitched their blankets and settled down for a soak in the sun. I, for the life of me, couldn't understand the pleasure associated with lying around in the sun. It seemed like a cruel, downright deviant, form of torture.

By the time I got my t-shirt back on, my back felt like one giant, barbecued pork rind, if you can imagine that. I sat on the beach for an hour, a towel draped over my head and shoulders. I no longer resembled a ghost; I looked more like a lobster. Wesley (and everyone else) finally noticed that my color had changed, so they decided to head back home. Wesley, Kay, and Ginny were a little sunburned, too. Pete carried a natural tan and hadn't burned. But I had the worst case, especially on my back and shoulders.

That night, as I was about to fall asleep, Ginny applied vinegar to my skin in an attempt to soothe me, but the pain soon returned. I awoke to a house that, at first, seemed entirely dark and quiet. Then I heard them.

"Pete, stop," Ginny whispered, "he'll hear us."

"No he won't," Pete mumbled. "He's pickled out from all that sun and vinegar."

For a few short moments I could hear low murmurs and quiet stirrings coming from the foldout sofa next to me. I pretended to be asleep. My pain and discomfort were distracting, and I had little interest in the two lovebirds. I had never experienced such severe pain, nor had I ever suffered so much. I continued to toss and turn throughout the night, my pain interrupted by soft whimperings nearby.

Troubling thoughts broke through my tears. *If Mom saw me now, she'd take a switch to Wesley and Ginny. Shouldn't they have protected me from the sun? Was that too much to expect from an eighteen-year-old sister and twenty-two-year-old brother? Shouldn't they have known better? Should I have known better?* I slept very little that first night.

For three days I rarely left the house. When I did, it was only to make a quick dash to the street to fetch the mail or a newspaper. Even then the sun seemed to burn through my t-shirt, leaving me squirming in pain. Timmy would relieve me by coming over and playing cards and board games. He also loaned me several issues from his skimpy comic book collection. It had been several weeks since I'd read a comic book, and digesting the latest (June) issue of *The Amazing Spider-Man* and *The Hulk,* just happened to be what the doctor ordered. A week later I was back to where I wanted to be—hanging out with my buddy at his place—early in the morning or late in the day, when it was cooler and the trees and buildings could provide ample shade.

* * * * *

Late one night I sat at the kitchen table as Ginny peeled dead skin from my back. She was doing a great job and enjoying it, too. After she had finished the task, we decided to make our beds and get some sleep. So, just as I'd done many times before, I marched into the master bedroom (the only bedroom) to gather the linens from the closet. When I opened the bedroom door, I saw Wesley's naked body lying on top of Kay's. In a flash he rolled away from her and they quickly covered themselves. At the same time, my jaw fell off my face. "Oh, excuse me," I said, before dashing away.

I stopped in the living room to think about what I did. Ginny sat at the table going about her business, unaware of the mess I'd stumbled into. *Why didn't I knock before I went in?* Anger welled up in me. I walked in a circle around the living room, fuming and ready to pop my cork at any second. I walked to the front door and stared out into the black night. *Why didn't they lock the door?* Those were the two questions I asked myself over and over that night. Near tears, I slammed my fist into the doorjamb and stormed from the house. I had witnessed something private, something taboo. Emotionally distraught, I circled the block several times, until I was able to calm down and gather my thoughts. *Why didn't I knock before I went in? Why didn't they lock the damn door?*

An hour later I returned to the house and saw that Ginny, now in bed, had made both our beds. I closed the door and removed my shoes.

As I crawled under the sheet, Ginny asked, "Where have you been for the last hour?"

"Just thinking."

"Do you want to talk about it?"

"No, it's personal," I replied. "Goodnight, Ginny."

"Goodnight, Tommy."

The next day I gathered my courage and apologized to Wesley and Kay for my trespassing error. It must have sounded like the most embarrassing apology ever uttered. My face, already sunburned, must have turned beet red in color.

"Wesley, I'm sorry I barged into your bedroom."

Making light of the issue, Wesley said, "Oh, don't worry about it. No harm done."

Kay said, "Yeah, don't let it upset you, Tommy. I told Wesley to get up and lock the door."

"I think we all learned a good lesson," Wesley added, "I'll remember to lock the door next time I want some privacy, and you'll remember to knock on closed doors. Won't you?"

"You bet," I said. With that, I breathed a sigh of relief and walked away, feeling reassured.

Summer's End

July passed, and I tried even harder to make the most of my final two or three weeks in Killeen. Mom had written twice, informing me that they had moved into an apartment in Newport, Delaware, and that I would be starting school there after Labor Day. No one had offered a plan for my transportation back to Delaware, and I was dreading another long bus trip.

On another hot day in that scorching summer, Wesley and Pete took us to the Fort Hood Open House Air and Ground Show. It was a huge event. In addition to an awesome air show with dozens of parachutists, the program featured a massive "mock" display of tanks and other armored vehicles. Two hundred acres of rough terrain were crawling with dozens of tanks and hundreds of foot soldiers advancing toward the viewing stands. The mass then veered off to our right and began firing live ammunition that exploded in the distance. It reminded me of the toy soldier wars my brother Gary and I had conducted only a year or two earlier. Now we were witnessing real maneuvers, with real soldiers and equipment, and on a scale I never would have dreamed of. I wished so much that my little brother could be with me.

Since that day, I've learned a little of the history of Fort Hood. In 1942, Camp Hood (re-commissioned as Fort Hood in 1950) was tasked to meet the ever-increasing demands of World War II. Killeen became a boom or bust town during the 1950s, depending on the number of troops stationed in the area. Their success being tied together, Killeen and Fort Hood began to thrive when the First

Armored Division returned in 1959. Fort Hood now holds two full divisions, the First Cavalry Division and Fourth Infantry Division/Mechanized, as well as the largest active duty armored (tank) post in the U. S. armed services, taking up about 340 square miles.

* * * * *

Wesley's 1962 Pontiac Catalina (minus a good set of wheel covers) rests beside the off-base military housing in Killeen, Texas. I wonder how much, or if, I noticed the sky that cloudy day in August, 1964.

I stood on the sidewalk next to the driveway facing Pete. He was dressed in his military police (M.P.) uniform and leaning against the trunk of Wesley's sweet looking Pontiac, sipping on a cold beer. I began bragging to him about my ice pick throwing skills, when suddenly the young girl from two houses away appeared.

"Hi, Tommy," she said, the corners of her mouth curling up in an exaggerated smile.

A little red-faced, I said, "Hi, Lisa."

She was cute, about thirteen or fourteen years old. I had met her once, but we'd hardly exchanged more than a friendly hello or two since. Before I could say another word, Pete said, "Well, Tommy, aren't you going to introduce me to your friend?" Until then I had rarely introduced someone, so I jumped at the chance for some practice.

"Oh yeah," I said. "Lisa, this is Pete. He's dating my sister."

A subtle frown flickered across Pete's face. I took that to mean something went wrong with my introduction.

Shaking Lisa's hand, Pete said, "It's a pleasure to meet you, Lisa."

"It's nice to meet you, too."

Pete paused, glancing back and forth at the two of us, waiting for me to say something. I stood mute, unsure of what to say next.

Lisa broke the ice. "Well, I have to be going. See you around, Tommy."

Pete and I said, "Bye."

Watching her sashay down the sidewalk, I could see that she looked a bit sharper and dressier than usual.

"That's some nice stuff you're letting get away," Pete whispered. "Tommy, you and I really need to have a talk. Hasn't Wesley taught you anything?"

"Oh, she's too old for me."

"I don't think so, Tommy. But you may be too young for her."

"What do you mean? I'll bet she stopped by to flirt with you, Pete, not me."

"Nooo—not at all! Tommy, the girl likes you. I could see it in her eyes when she looked at you, boy."

"You really think so?"

"You bet she does," he said. "But you gotta start taking the bull by the horns, man. A good way to start is by practicing some bullshit lines to feed the girls."

"Okay. Will you write some down for me?"

"I'll tell you what. You make a list and we'll go over it later. That way, it'll get ya ta thinkin'."

"That sounds good. I'll start on it tonight. Thanks, Pete."

"There's a couple of other things you need to know, Tommy."

"What's that?"

"Tommy, us men need to stick together." He motioned for me to come closer and whispered, "For one thing, when you introduced me to Lisa, you shouldn't have told her I was dating your sister."

"Oh?"

"You bet. Never slam a door in a buddy's face, Tommy. You know what I mean?"

"Hmmm…yeah, I think so. I'm sorry about that, Pete. I guess I wasn't thinkin'. I'll put that one first on my list."

"You do that." Continuing to whisper, he said, "Now, the other thing…let's keep our lists just between you and me. Okay?"

"Okay, Pete."

Soon after Pete's pep talk, Kay invited a friend to stay at the house while she and Wesley were traveling. She stayed for only two or three nights, but I vividly remember her visit. Connie was a little older than Ginny and Kay, maybe in her early thirties, and very likable. She catered to my needs even more than Ginny, often fixing breakfast and lunch snacks and asking if she could "fetch" me anything. She was attractive enough—for an older woman, that is. As the hours turned into days her physical attributes, especially her bust line, began to increasingly occupy my mind.

I recalled a moment a few days earlier, when Wesley stopped by Timmy's to pick me up and take me home for dinner. Again, he had driven his Pontiac, and it was looking extra sharp that day since he'd just washed and waxed it. Timmy and I decided to show Wesley our ice pick throwing expertise, and I proceeded to stick eight out of ten throws. Timmy stuck about five out of ten. Wesley had to be impressed; he stuck only two, and one of those quickly fell out of the target. Timmy said it should stick for five seconds to count. I said it should be more like a minute. We argued for a while until Wesley straightened us out. He said, "A pick should stick until the next person's turn."

I said, "Oh, that makes sense."

Timmy agreed too, and thanks to my big brother a very important issue had been settled.

I said goodbye to Timmy and climbed into the car. Wesley and I were about to drive away when Timmy's sister-in-law Betty dashed out of the trailer waving her arms.

"Hey, Wesley! Wesley!" she yelled.

Wesley stopped the car and we watched her walk up to the driver's window. I grew curious, seeing that she still wore her nightgown.

"Wesley Dixon!" she shouted, "I thought I heard your voice. You weren't trying to sneak away without saying hello, were you?"

Betty was a very attractive blond with a slight German accent. She usually slept late while her husband performed his duty at the Army base. She had even fixed lunch a few times for Timmy and me. From their conversation, I learned that she and her husband knew

Wesley from frequent partying at the NCO (noncommissioned officers) clubs. She also knew Wesley and I were brothers.

As she continued to converse with Wesley, she rested her forearms on the car door and leaned forward, her ample breasts almost completely exposed. Although Wesley's front row view was making him a little nervous, I also noticed him leaning back, trying not to block my view, a gesture that I appreciated. This show continued for several minutes, until Wesley realized the time and tore himself away.

"Well, Betty, Tommy and I really have to be going. My wife and sister are waiting for us. We'll be seeing you guys at the club, okay?"

"Okay, Wesley," Betty said, stepping back and throwing an alluring smile. "See ya later," she purred. "You too, Tommy!"

"Bye, Betty!"

On the way home, Wesley says, "Well, Tommy, I think we got an eyeful today, don't you?"

"We sure did! You know, she never left herself uncovered like that when she fixed me and Timmy our lunches. I think she really likes you, Wesley."

"Oh, you think so, huh?"

"Yeah, but don't worry, I won't tell anybody."

"Thanks, little brother. It'll be our little secret."

I'll never forget those few short minutes. They sparked a young man's curiosity—and hormones as well.

Anyway, as I was saying, Wesley and Kay were away for the night, and our new guest had been given the use of their bedroom. At about ten o'clock in the evening, Connie, dressed in a fluffy cotton bathrobe, excused herself to take a shower. I watched a summer rerun of something on television while Ginny hunched over the kitchen table playing solitaire, a game I found boring after playing it one time too many. There it was. I could hear the sound of the shower as I watched the TV show. The devil inside me began to speak: Hmmm, the bathroom window curtain might be open.

"Ginny," I said casually, "I'm going to take a walk. I'll be back in a few minutes."

"Okay, Tommy."

All was quiet behind the house. A small weedy backyard adjoined a few acres of undeveloped land, with rain-washed ditches, brush, and a few small trees scattered about. I stopped in the middle of the yard, turned, and faced the house. I could see the bathroom window flooded with light, the curtain pulled aside.

Oh my goodness. The adrenaline began to surge, and I marched forward glancing left then right, looking for any out-n-about neighbor. The window was too high for me to peer into directly, so I stood with one foot on the outdoor water spigot directly below and pulled myself up. Again, that damned devil's voice: *Connie should be lathered up real good by now*. From my tip-toe I could see through the window and down into the shower and tub.

There she stood, just as I had imagined—eyes closed, her face, neck, and bosom coated with bubbly soap. Then, almost on cue, she turned to face me. In that instant, water washed away enough suds to reveal exactly—no—much more than what I wanted to see.

Due to the sudden overload of stimuli, my eyes bugged out of their sockets. At the same time I lost my grip on the windowsill. My foot slipped too, turning on the outside faucet and breaking the stillness of the night. Like a cat I landed feet first and fumbled with the valve, turning off the water real quick. I looked wildly about, trying to determine if anyone had seen or heard me.

I walked around the block a couple of times, mulling over what I had done. Although I had witnessed a marvelous sight, I felt deep remorse. Once again, as with Wesley and Kay earlier, I had invaded someone's personal space. But this was no accident. A wave of shame washed over me and I thought I'd never be tempted to repeat such a deed. Oddly enough, I was surprised the next morning at how easy I kept a straight face when chatting with Connie. She gave no hint of suspecting anything.

By the middle of the month the logistics of my return to Delaware had been worked out. Wesley's commander just happened to know a Mrs. Martin, who was planning a trip to the Philadelphia area. A very nice lady, she jumped at the chance to take Debbie and me all the way to Delaware. Ginny decided to come along, too, to help with the driving and expenses.

A day or two before our scheduled trip Ginny and Pete had gone out on a date, leaving Wesley, Kay, and me to ourselves. Wesley had prepared a nice spaghetti dinner, but when Kay began setting the table, the two started to argue. As Wesley served us, Kay grumbled about the size of her portion.

"It's too much. Wesley, I can't eat all that!"

Angry and frustrated, Wesley said, "Just eat it, Kay!"

Wesley joined us at the table and we began to eat. Hoping to calm the situation, I asked him several questions and he eagerly responded.

Then Kay said, "This spaghetti tastes funny."

"There's nothing wrong with the spaghetti, Kay," Wesley said. "Tommy, how's the spaghetti?"

"Tastes good to me," I mumbled, shoveling a forkful into my mouth.

While Wesley and I continued our conversation, Kay picked at her food and complained. She had lost a lot of weight during the summer and Wesley was concerned. *Why didn't Kay just eat what she could handle? Then maybe Wesley wouldn't mind if she left some on her plate*. Fifteen minutes later Wesley and I were done eating and began placing our dirty dishes in the sink. Kay had hardly eaten a mouthful.

"Kay, if I have to treat you like a kid, then I will," Wesley said. "You need to eat. I'm not letting you leave until you eat something!"

"I don't have to eat this crap!" she screamed, tears rolling down her cheeks. "You're not my mother!"

Oh boy, this is starting to sound bad. Maybe I should take a walk and visit Timmy.

On my way to the door, Kay continued to whine and pout, and I heard Wesley snap, "If you won't eat it, you can wear it!"

Oh oh! *That doesn't sound good*!

Then, a second before ducking out the door, I saw Kay sporting a new spaghetti hair-do and Wesley smearing the run-off noodles and sauce into her face.

"Wesley, stop it! Leave me alone! I can't breathe!"

"Now, little Miss Ungrateful! What you don't eat, you can wear!"

Right away, I freaked out, remembering other not-so-long-ago family skirmishes. I recalled these two lovebirds slow dancing to Elvis a few weeks earlier. *How sweet they looked. How wonderful it must be to have someone that special*. Now look at them.

I stayed at Timmy's until dusk, figuring that would give them plenty of time to repair things. But when I came back they were gone. They had cleaned up the mess and left the door unlocked. A note on the table grabbed my attention. It read, "Tommy, I'm sorry that you had to witness our fighting. It won't happen again. We'll be out late, so make yourself at home. Wesley."

The honeymoon for these two had officially ended. Naïve about the complexities of relationships, I swore I'd work hard to forge more affectionate unions of my own.

* * * * *

I had mixed feelings about leaving Killeen. I knew I would miss Timmy, Pedro, Connie, Wesley, Kay, and the military lifestyle at Fort Hood. I would not, however, miss the weather or the fighting. I regarded Texas as a nice place to visit, but only under the best of circumstances. My thoughts and hopes were centered on returning to Delaware and the rest of my family.

Daisy and Chester had delivered Debbie to us the day before. Mrs. Martin, a pleasant gray-haired woman in her early fifties, arrived at the house in a late model Plymouth station wagon with fake wood-grain side panels. The most notable thing about her was her limp from an artificial leg. Ginny had cautioned the two of us earlier: "Don't say anything about her wooden leg unless she brings it up."

I said, "You don't have to worry about that, Ginny."

We were able to fit our luggage into the back of the station wagon. Joy washed over me; we had avoided a bus ride and had room to move about. We said our goodbyes to Kay and Wesley. For some reason, Pete wasn't there to see us off. I was disappointed; we had not had time to discuss my very short list of "things I would say to girls to get them to like me." Weeks later I would learn the real reason why he'd been unable to see us off.

I have a few memories of our trip back to Delaware. One night we stayed in a motel room so that Mrs. Martin could get some well-deserved rest. Ginny, Debbie, and I watched her that night as she removed her wooden leg. She wasn't embarrassed at all; she just kept talking about this and that while cleaning her stump. I guess I did okay, this being my first experience with a handicapped person.

On another occasion the traffic became especially heavy as we drove through a city, requiring a lot of stopping and starting and sitting with the engine idling. Debbie and I amused ourselves by watching people in other cars. Folks of all ages waved at us and we waved back. When one car pulled up beside us, I found myself face to face with a witch. Yes, a woman so old and so ugly she could have easily played a part in Hansel and Gretel or The Wizard of Oz.

I winced at the sight and quickly turned away. But my curiosity overwhelmed me. Wondering if I had truly seen such a horrible sight, I decided to take another look—and then immediately vomited. Ginny asked me if I was okay. I told her I'd seen a witch, but she just laughed: "Tommy, you're just using that as an excuse for plain old car sickness." It may have been both.

Daisy, 28, caught fishing a few years later in Blanco, Texas, c. 1967.

II

NEWPORT

1964-1968

Donna Marie, 16, ready for the prom at #10 Water St, c. 1966.

10 Water Street

Overdue and a bit weary, we arrived at #10 Water Street in Newport, Delaware in the middle of the afternoon. Thanks and goodbyes were brief and hurried, since Mrs. Martin wanted to make Philadelphia ahead of rush hour traffic. As she drove away I felt a twinge of sadness, followed by appreciation and relief for having been safely delivered to our destination. I don't recall ever seeing Mrs. Martin again.

By the time we lifted our luggage to the sidewalk, many of my siblings were huddled around us, welcoming us home. It had been two months since Mom and the rest had seen Debbie and me, and even longer since they'd seen Ginny.

"Goodness gracious," Mom exclaimed, "would you take a look at Tommy! Tommy, you must have grown a head taller since I last saw you." Her comment came as a pleasant surprise. It seems that hot Texas sun was just as good for growing as it was for burning.

Anxious to catch up on summer events, we hauled our luggage inside and began to check out the new home. The latest family dwelling was a second story street-side apartment, one of four in a building sandwiched between the Christina River and Water Street. The muddy Christina snaked eastward, its northern bank no more than forty feet from the foundation of our new home.

In 1731, a man named John Justice purchased 100 acres and marked off streets for a town that he hoped would become a thriving shipping port. By 1800, grains and goods from northern territories were shipped to Newport by boat via the Christina. Once the mid-1800s rolled around, Wilmington took over as a port when new roads and the railroad arrived. Newport incorporated in 1873 and, by the turn of the next century, was better known as a manufacturing center, home to a glue factory, an iron works, and the Krebs Chemical Company, established by Henrik J. Krebs in 1908. Records indicate that the building at #10 Water St. was built around this time, most likely as housing for the families of upper management, or maybe temporary housing for other V.I.P's. When Mr. Krebs died in 1929, DuPont bought the facilities and it became the E. I. DuPont Pigments Plant. Unfortunately, the plant sat upstream and a block west of the apartment. Its stench, overwhelming at first, would hardly be noticed by the time school started. The plant deposited waste in nearby landfills that eventually overflowed, allowing lead, mercury, and a host of other toxic metals to seep into the Christina River and its bordering wetlands—and into what would soon constitute a portion of the family playground.

The plant's largest employee parking lot, directly across Water Street, dominated the view from both of our street-side bedroom windows. About an acre in size, the lot was normally packed with cars belonging to day shift workers. A few family dwellings were sprinkled along the river side of the street. DuPont and several other businesses lined both sides of Water Street, which faded into a dirt access road for the Penn Central Railroad and ended near the river south of Wilmington. Rail traffic was constant in Newport, some freight but mostly passenger, which flowed east to Wilmington, north to Philadelphia, and south to Newark, Baltimore, and Washington, D.C. Over time we grew accustomed to the sound of the high-speed trains passing by, no more than a city block away.

Mom had furnished the place with a mix of furniture: the scarce pieces we owned, one or two new ones, and some donated. We would later acquire a wringer-washer, but new furniture purchases would be few and far between.

Our apartment building had a main interior stairway entrance at its center that led to my bedroom door, or what would normally be the living room. However, once Mom converted the room into a third bedroom we rarely used the entrance, preferring the porch stairway leading to the kitchen. David, Debbie, Gary, and I slept in this third bedroom using two sets of bunk beds. Mom, Donna, and Ginny shared two beds in the west street-side corner bedroom. Paul and Ronnie had their own single beds in the east street-side corner bedroom.

The first night was a hectic one for Ginny, Debbie, and me. We were trying to situate our belongings and adjust to the new living quarters while being bombarded with visitors and introductions. It seemed as though Mom and Donna had invited half the block's residents to our apartment, which was crowded with adults and kids coming and going. That's when I met Daphnie, our new neighbor, and we instantly locked eyes. Daphnie and Donna had become casual friends while Debbie and I vacationed in Texas. Donna had told her all about me, even showing her a picture or two. We were young and our initial friendship was casual and cautious in nature, but that would change over time.

Later that evening, after friends and neighbors had left, most of us retired to the living room to watch television on a small, used black and white set that Ronnie had bought. I don't recall the specific show, but it might have been *The Beverly Hillbillies*, *Gomer Pyle U.S.M.C.*, or one of Mom's favorites, *The Fugitive*.

Bathed in the glow from the television, we munched handfuls of popcorn, totally immersed in this special family moment. It had been a long time since so many of us had been together to watch TV and we'd never had such a good picture. Gary broke the silence at a commercial break.

"Ho, I'm thirsty!" he shouted, jumping to his feet.

Gary was filled with nervous energy and had developed the bad habit of making loud and startling movements, especially during TV commercials. He seemed increasingly hyperactive and it would take years to break him of this irritating habit. As Gary headed for the kitchen, Paul said, "Wait, Gary, I want to show them our friends."

Gary stopped at the hallway near the kitchen. "What friends?" he asked.

"Gary, you stay put," Paul commanded. "Don't say a word and don't go into the kitchen."

"Yeah, what friends?" I inquired, as Paul led Ginny and me to the kitchen. I glanced at Mom and Donna to gauge their reaction; they were smiling.

"We have to sneak up on them," Paul cautioned, "so be real quiet from here on. I just hope Gary's outburst hasn't scared them away."

Gary struggled to understand what "friends" his brother could be referring to. Once I reached the hallway, I noticed Gary's eyes widen and his mouth pop open. In a hushed voice he said, "Oh…*now* I know what you're talking about."

Ginny and I stood just inside the darkened kitchen doorway. Paul stood behind us, reaching into the kitchen to turn on the light switch.

"Are you ready?" he asked.

"Yeah, I think we're ready," I said, "let's see your sneaky friends."

Paul flipped the switch, flooding the kitchen with light.

"Oh my god!" Ginny gasped.

I stood stock still, my mouth agape, while Debbie ran back to the living room screaming for her mother. More than a dozen ugly brown insects scampered across the sink and kitchen table and disappeared from view.

"What was that?" I asked.

Mom, Paul, and Donna just laughed.

"They're cockroaches," Gary said.

"Holy cow!" I said. "Where'd they go?"

"Into their hideouts and dungeons inside the baseboards and walls," Paul said.

"So," Ginny said, "this is what we get for living in the city?"

Our family had experienced bed bugs, ants, fleas, ticks, spiders, bats, and bees inside our living quarters, but never so many big and ugly insects. Bigger surprises were in store. Mom said she had notified Mr. Metzger, our landlord, and he had promised to address the issue in a couple of weeks. He said he couldn't treat just one apartment; he had to treat all four apartments at the same time.

Mom had always kept a very clean house and she found the roaches especially bothersome. The landlord's treatments never resolved the roach issue; they just slightly reduced their pesky numbers. We placed our own roach traps around the kitchen, but that helped only a little. We knew it would be difficult, if not impossible, to eradicate the pests as long as one or more of our neighbors failed to keep a clean apartment. I never got used to the roaches, but I learned to tolerate them. Fortunately, very few of them resided in the bedrooms, where some of us slept with our mouths open.

The apartment was a big improvement over the shacks we'd occupied. For the first time in our lives we had hot and cold running water. We were connected to a county sewer system, with indoor plumbing: one toilet, one tub, and two sinks per apartment. All great features—that is, when they were working. We had all the basic necessities except for a telephone, which we still couldn't afford despite financial support from Paul and Ronnie. Nevertheless, Mom probably felt like she had been reborn; a fleeting feeling, since the novelty of the modern conveniences eventually wore off.

Looking north: in January of 1929, this early wooden bridge crosses the Christina River at Newport, just a stone's throw from the Water Street apartment at center. Today's steel and concrete drawbridge opened eleven months later (December 1, 1929) and crosses 40-60 feet west of this one. (Courtesy of the Delaware Public Archives.)

An oil-fired boiler in the building's basement provided heat for the four apartments. Apartment #8 (across the hall from us) was the only unit with a thermostat, but it sat vacant until Charlie, the owner's nephew, rented it a year or so later. Thanks to him, the rest of us were subjected to periods of high heat or no heat. The radiators sometimes worked so well that we had to open windows. We dreaded rainy or snowy days when we had to leave the windows completely closed. Then the apartment became stifling hot, almost smothering us.

During that first heating season, Charlie began spying on the three families in units 4, 6, and 10. When he reported that we'd been keeping some of our windows partially open, Mr. Metzger gave us written notice of his disapproval, stating that we were increasing his fuel bill. Mom defended the practice, telling him our rooms were too hot and raising the windows was the only way we could maintain some degree of comfort. Mr. Metzger said he would remedy the situation as long as we promised to keep the windows shut. Whatever he did worked, but only for a while. We got used to the problems that plagued our stay at Water Street.

Baptism at Krebs

Little David started first grade and Debbie third grade at Richie Elementary School in Newport. David had difficulty adjusting to schoolwork and his new surroundings. He surprised Mom and Ginny when he stumbled into the kitchen around eleven o'clock one morning on a school day.

"I'm hungry. What's to eat?"

"Lord Almighty, David!" Mom shouted. "You scared the dickens out of me. Why aren't you in school?"

David wanted to be home with his mother, even if he had to walk six blocks during the school lunch period. He showed up at home a few more times that year, until Mom's switch put a stop to it. By the time he caught on, it was too late; David had to repeat the grade.

Gary, Donna, and I attended grades four, eight, and six at Henrik J. Krebs School, one of the best public schools in the state. In 1926, three years before his death, Mr. Krebs contributed $150,000 to build the school and it opened in September of the following year. To this day I'm amazed at how much this man contributed to making Newport a better place. Kind words followed Mr. Krebs, long before his death, words such as, "If 'Daddy' Krebs hired you, you had a job for life."

Good school or not, dumping two country boys like Gary and me into a city school was a bit like dropping an antacid into a glass of water—it took some time to attain a calm, homogeneous mix. The first day of school is always the most nerve-racking, but especially so when everyone is a stranger. Everyone but family, that is. Gary can attest to that. He was the little one, sandwiched between his big sister on one side and his big brother on the other.

We stood outside the school's main entrance early that first morning, Donna wearing a new blouse and skirt, and Gary and I sporting freshly ironed and starched shirts and trousers that Mom had picked out for us. More than a few eyes were glued to the newcomers, but we did our best not to stare back. We didn't want to start any trouble our first day, especially before the first recess bell.

I made special note of the number of boys and girls munching on something. *What are they eating? Where did they get it?* Then I noticed a store directly across the street. Slicer's Sporting Goods didn't just cater to adults by selling guns, bows-n-arrows, and camping equipment; they also sold a wide assortment of cakes, candies, and soda pop. Kids who didn't spend their allowance there before school often patronized it during lunch, buying soda pop, Zero Bars, Jujubes, Good-&-Plenty, Candy Necklaces, and Sweet Tarts, one of the newer treats. Did their parents know this was going on? If I had the rare pleasure of a weekly or monthly allowance, I couldn't imagine wasting it on such sugary drivel; nope, not with Slicer's also carrying the latest super hero comic books. The Slicer family took advantage of the prime location for a decade or more, until they were forced to move a few years later. Good thing, since cavities among students were probably skyrocketing.

My first day in Mrs. Jester's sixth grade class proved to be an awkward and embarrassing experience, and choosing to sit behind pesky Doug Snitch didn't help. The moment I sat down he spun around and assaulted me with personal questions: "What's your name? Where do you live, Tommy? Where are you from? How long have you lived in Delaware? How many brothers and sisters do you have?"

Wishing to be friendly, I began answering his questions. But then Doug and a few other students quickly picked up on my strong southern accent, and bombarded me with more questions. Mrs. Jester rescued me. She called the class to attention and we pledged allegiance to the flag. When she took attendance, I focused hard on every name and voice, especially the girls.

Although I eventually managed to have some fun, memories of my first week in school still give me jitters. Having to answer questions—too many, too soon, and too personal—created some high anxiety. Once, during outdoor recess, a small group of girls surrounded me.

"Say something, Tommy," Renee demanded.

"What do you want me to say?" I asked.

All the girls giggled and gawked at each other, their eyeballs bulging and goofy looks wrinkling up their faces.

"See, I told you he talks funny."

Gary's experience was much worse. His classmates, and some from one class ahead of him, were relentless at poking fun at the way he talked. One of his teachers tried to smooth over the hurtin' by telling Gary that "all those boys are just jealous." When Gary told me that, we were both thinking: "Bullcrap!"

School bullies were out and about that first year, looking for fresh meat—the new kids. And Gary, two grades lower, seemed like prime pickings. But he only had a problem with one tall, skinny black kid. Gary didn't let the kid push him around any, though. Standing tall, he managed to coerce other bullies to leave a few kids alone.

I was more fortunate; no one really picked on me—at least that first year—although I do recall a certain pecking order. Dodge ball, popular during recess, can be a brutal game. I saw larger and stronger kids clobber weaker kids with the ball. The first time I stepped into the ring I moved fast and quickly learned how to dodge. When my turn came to throw, I concentrated on hitting the biggest kids and the bullies. To the girls and the little guys, I became their equalizer.

Although not regarded as a bully, Jerry Hobbs grew big and stocky for a sixth grader. Eager to size me up, he started a friendly shoving match. Three seconds later he was on his back, staring into my unrelenting hazel eyes. Shooting for the best out of three, he tried once more and again wound up on his back. After a few more playground skirmishes, I had a reputation: don't mess with the new kid.

Durwin Thompson wasn't the biggest kid, but he was one of the toughest and meanest of the sixth grade bullies. He suffered from a birth defect. One index finger had no joints; instead, he displayed a stub of solid bone, hard as a railroad spike. He'd sometimes wave it about in a threatening manner, poking it into the back of any unfortunate kid who happened to turn away from him. Imagine having to sit in front of this kid in class.

By the end of October, I'd become infatuated with a certain dark-haired princess in another sixth grade room. Shirley Dobbins had that special look, stature, and manner that hypnotized young, weak-kneed country boys like me. During lunch and recess I couldn't take my eyes off her. I just loved the way she talked while sipping milk from a straw. If I weren't sitting down while watching her, my knees would surely have buckled. Sometimes I caught her looking my way, too, but neither of us could muster enough courage to start a conversation. On a cool, sunny day during recess, all that changed.

From a distance I noticed Durwin talking to Shirley. He was blocking her way and wouldn't let her pass. I worked my way toward them, trying to pick up their conversation.

"Aw, come on, Shirley, tell me you'll go to the Halloween dance with me this Friday, okay?"

"No, I'm not going with you. Why would you think I'd go to a dance with you, Durwin?"

"Because I asked you," Durwin said, jabbing his stubby finger into Shirley's shoulder.

"Ouch! Durwin, that hurts! Let me by!"

When I saw this happening, I rushed to Shirley's defense.

"Hey!" I shouted. "Leave her alone, Durwin."

"This is none of your business, Dixon."

"I'm making it my business," I said. "Try poking someone your own size."

"Alright, Dixon, I'll see you behind the auditorium after school. Unless you're chicken."

Now I've done it, I thought. I had been challenged and couldn't back away.

"Okay, Durwin. I'll see you there after school."

As Durwin walked away, Shirley said, "Don't fight him, Tommy, you're going to get into trouble."

"Don't worry," I said, pretending to be calm.

During the rest of the day, I thought about the times in Falls Mills when I ran from bullies and my big brother had to protect me. Now I was on my own, preparing to fight a bigger bully to defend a pretty girl's honor. Since I had never been in a real fight, the word *butterflies* began to take on a whole new, and more ominous, meaning. Moreover, I could hear some of my fans whispering, "Dixon's gonna fight Durwin Thompson after school." The word was spreading.

School let out and I started to make my way to behind the auditorium, a handful of supporters accompanying me, including Doug Snitch, Shirley, and her friend Renee Brown. Durwin arrived first, and he didn't look very enthusiastic. That shored up my confidence and chased away some of the butterflies. Durwin and I squared off, circling each other and looking for an opening. My mind flashed back to the spring of 1963 in Falls Mills, when my brothers and I had just finished collecting goose eggs along the creek bank, and Ronnie had gotten into a fistfight with a stranger. The vision of Ronnie throwing jabs and then a right, followed by more jabs and another right, spurred me to take the initiative. *I gotta be quick*, I thought.

Twice in rapid succession I jabbed my left fist into Durwin's face, connecting once. The quick right that followed landed hard near his nose. He covered his face with his hands and turned away, buckling at the waist. Before I could throw another punch, Durwin dropped to his knees and began to cry. Holding up one hand, he looked at me with tears in his eyes. "I quit—I quit," he blubbered.

"Durwin, I think you should apologize to Shirley."

"I'm sorry, Shirley," he said, wiping away the tears.

My emotions surged. I was happy I had won, relieved that neither of us had been seriously hurt, and I felt fortunate that no teacher had caught us. But I also felt sad and embarrassed about Durwin taking a licking. Nevertheless, better him than me. I received some praise for my "good deed," and the word got out that the new, mild-mannered country boy wasn't afraid to stand up for himself—or for others.

That afternoon Shirley asked me if I was going to the Halloween dance. I said I hadn't planned on it, at which point she batted her eyes and flashed her sweetest smile.

"Shirley, do you want to go to the dance with me?"

"Yes, Tommy. I would love to."

The first few minutes of the Halloween dance were awkward, and my nervous butterflies soon dissolved when the DJ played some of Elvis's biggest hits. Yes, those summer practice sessions in Killeen had paid off. Shirley and I danced together the entire night.

But by Thanksgiving we had lost interest in each other and were moving on. Yeah, that's the way these things happen in the sixth grade. After Christmas vacation, her friend Renee Brown started flirting with me. She seemed mature for her age and way too eager, especially for me, to become more than friends. I liked Renee, but only as a friend and nothing more.

* * * * *

Lunch period was a stressful time too. I had to present a special ticket at the cash register in order to receive the free lunches provided to welfare kids. To avoid the embarrassment I eventually began bringing a bag lunch to school. A year or so later, a few sensitive teachers and a key school administrator demanded that all lunch chits be made identical. That's when I went back to consuming the healthier cafeteria food. Just in time, too. Mom's peanut butter and jelly, baloney, and surplus cheese sandwiches were getting mighty old.

Henrik J. Krebs Jr. High School, 234 N. James Street, Newport, DE, Nov. 1933. (Courtesy of the Delaware Historical Society).

My clothes couldn't get much worse. Each summer, Mom took her sons' neck, waist and inseam measurements to Gaylord's and bought our school clothes. I rarely accompanied her. Although the clothes she bought were new, the styles didn't quite match those of the other students. But what could she do? I knew better than to ask Mom for expensive designer clothes. I finally began shopping with Mom at J.C. Penney for clothes that were more stylish and to my liking.

In January 1965, Ronnie took a job at Chrysler's auto assembly plant in Newark. The previous summer he had worked at NVF in Newark, a job he hated. But now his financial assistance, along with the monthly welfare check and government surplus food allotments, allowed us to improve our diet and clothing. Ginny, Donna, and I often accompanied Mom and Ronnie on their weekly grocery trips to Gaylord's. While the women shopped for groceries, Ronnie and I sat at the snack bar in the department store section, sipping coffee or a Coke. Sometimes one of Ronnie's coworkers would join us. About the time the conversation reached full blast, we had to drag ourselves away and help the women load groceries into the Oldsmobile.

Yet Mom still struggled financially to put enough nutritious food on the table. A steady supply of fresh fruits, vegetables, and nuts would have gone a long way in providing proper nourishment for our growing young family, but Mom knew she had called on Ronnie enough. Although I never saw him complain, my big brother may have harbored some resentment about handing over a good chunk of each paycheck. We all love Ronnie, and we appreciate the sacrifices he made. Mom was hoping Paul could get a good job and share some of the burden.

In early March Ginny gave birth to a baby girl, Pamela, fathered by Pete in Killeen. My sister had begun to show six months earlier and that's when she gave up her little secret to the family. Ginny had planned to return to Pete in Killeen, but this sorry excuse for a man didn't want anything to do with his newborn child—or my sister. I showed Ginny the list I'd made, the one I promised to show Pete the next time I saw him: "Things I Could Say to Girls to Get Them to Like Me." I tore it up instead and told her she was lucky. Later in the year, Ginny's divorce from Alvin became final.

* * * * *

Cherry blossoms bloomed in Washington D.C. around the first week of April. It was a wondrous display of nature that also coincided with our sixth grade field trip to the Smithsonian Institution, the Capitol, the Washington Monument, the Jefferson and Lincoln Memorials, and the White House. When the permission forms were given to parents a few weeks before the event, my heart dropped to my gut when I realized the trip wasn't free. Mrs. Jester relieved that sick feeling, saying that funds were available for families like mine. The school provided box lunches, and Mom and Ronnie gave me a little souvenir money. They must have known how much it meant to me.

The Washington trip was unlike anything this country boy had ever experienced. I stood in absolute awe at the sights and sounds of the place. I had seen bits and pieces of cities in my travels, but nothing as grand and awesome as this—my first real tour of a big city, and it just happened to be the capital of the United States of America. Everything looked so beautiful and the trip would have been perfect, except for the presence of three people.

First, there was Renee Brown. Not only had she tried to follow me home from school several times that spring, but I noticed her shadowing me and my group as we walked the streets of D.C. I managed to shake Renee off my tail as we passed the main gate of the long, iron fence in front of the White House. I remember commenting about the nasty mess pigeons were leaving on the benches, and trash cans. I thought they were ruining my perfect portrait of D.C.

I was laughing about this when the second person, young Lee Knotwell, stepped up beside me.

"Hey Dixon," he said, "I hear you like Renee Brown."

"Yeah, I like Renee. She's nice. So, what's it to ya?"

"Well, people are saying she's your girlfriend."

Shocking! How could he make such a foul accusation? At the time I didn't "like" any particular girl. In fact, the revelation surprised me so much that I shouted, "What? You gotta be kiddin'!"

I had barely finished the sentence when the third person, Mrs. Jester, smacked me in the face in front of my classmates. The blow almost dislocated my jaw.

"Young man," she said, "we don't raise our voices like that in my class." Stunned and embarrassed, I rubbed my jaw, trying to restore blood circulation and determine if it was still functional. I tucked my tail, buried my red face in the crowd of students, and continued on with my touring, a much wiser young man. From then on I paid more attention to what I said, how I said it, and who might be within earshot.

In May, *Herman's Hermits* released a hit single, "Mrs. Brown You've Got a Lovely Daughter," but there was a touch of irony in the song as I saw very little of Renee Brown. She, like Shirley Dobbins, had given up on me. She had probably decided to focus attention on someone more receptive.

* * * * *

At age thirteen, in the summer of 1965, I experienced my first true summer romance. The *Beatles* were piling up more hits, including

"Help" and "Yesterday," but for some reason I didn't initially like many of their songs. I couldn't identify with the British accent, the haircut, or the concept of a human Beatle—even with a different spelling. *The Supremes* was my group. They gave me the special itch that only a dance floor can scratch, and if I just wanted to shake my head and tap along with a good beat I'd listen to "I Can't Get No Satisfaction" by the *Rolling Stones*. Petula Clark's "Downtown" and *The Righteous Brothers'* "You've Lost That Lovin' Feelin" stirred up strong emotions, and at just the right time.

As I said, my neighbor Daphnie and I were in a slowly evolving friendship. We started out sneaking about in the dark, rushing through the occasional make-out session. Within two years, or by the time I turned 15, Daphnie and I were well ahead of the curve with the introduction of heavy petting. In between all that, we listened and danced to a lot of music. Edwin Starr's "Your Love Keeps Lifting Me" became a fantastic hit. We practically wore out a pair of shoes dancing to that one.

Daphnie's twelve-year-old cousin Mattie was spending a few days with her that summer and my heart fluttered the first time we met. She looked so pretty. Her silky-smooth blond hair reached well below her waist, complementing her enchanting eyes, as blue as a tropical lagoon. She had a fair and unblemished complexion, a kind and soothing voice, and a friendly demeanor. I'll never forget our marathon, late-night kissing session. Yes, kissing session. And Daphnie did more than approve of this—she actually encouraged her. Maybe Daphnie thought her slightly younger cousin was overdue for some practice. On the last night of her stay, Mattie and I stood under the apartment porch, talking and kissing for nearly an hour. We finally said goodnight long past my bedtime.

After walking Mattie back to Daphnie's house, I snuck into our apartment and crawled into the top bunk, being careful not to step on

Gary below. Once all was calm and my breathing had returned to normal, a strange, spooky pressure rolled across my lips, as though Mattie was still there, kissing me. I fell asleep thinking and dreaming about her ghostly kisses. That kissing experience made up for all my earlier lost opportunities. Clarence, my good buddy and neighbor back in fourth grade at Falls Mills, would have been so proud of me. Wow! I just hoped that he was having as good a time. I saw Mattie again only once or twice, in passing.

* * * * *

Paul was having trouble finding even a menial job. He thought he had landed a good one with a local construction company, but they fired him after two days when they discovered he wasn't "qualified" to drive a dump truck.

In the early 1960s the nation's economy was spiraling downward, with unemployment and social unrest on the rise. In response, President Johnson established the Job Corps in 1964 as part of his "War on Poverty" and "Great Society" initiative. Economically deprived young men (black and white, of course, but predominately black) between the ages of 16 and 21 (mostly dropouts with a ninth grade education) were selected with a noble goal in mind: teaching good work habits and specific vocational skills.

Paul joined the Corps around the first week of August. He spent half the workday designing, constructing, and placing signs; classroom work filled the other half. His letters home indicated that he liked the Corp and was doing well. I, too, began to consider that option, should my education end prematurely, as had happened to my five oldest siblings.

Looking south: the train station, railroad underpass, Dupont employee parking lot and Water St. apartment building by the Christina River (center), c. 1962. (Courtesy of the Delaware Public Archives.)

Looking north: the Newport Bridge, Dupont employee parking lot and Water St. apartment (center). The Krebs/Richie athletic fields are at top left, c. 1966. (Courtesy of the Delaware Public Archives.)

The family received a letter from Wesley in September. He said he had been assigned to temporary duty at Fort Benning, Georgia, a staging area for soldiers being shipped to Vietnam. Soon he'd be fighting a war and nothing about it was to anyone's liking, especially Kay's. She would return to Bluefield, Virginia, to live with her mother during her husband's war stint.

Wesley arrived in Vietnam the first week of October. In November he mailed two more letters home: one for Ginny (dated 20 October) and one for Mom (dated 10 November). Mom had told Wesley in her letter that our cousins, the Miller family, had moved off Jenkinjones Mountain and into a small shack a few houses away from where we had lived on Newhill Road. Wesley replied that he knew about this and had visited them the past summer. They had given up the farm and moved off the mountaintop because of Uncle Burl's failing health and the lack of family or farm workers to maintain the old homestead. Wesley said that even without the farm the Millers were living the same old way.

Wesley had spoken to Dad. Soon after Mom and Ronnie brought the family to Delaware, Dad had moved from Falls Mills and settled into a beat-up house beside Mama's old place on Boissevain Mountain. He still behaved the same way: sittin'-n-spittin', chewin'-n-brewin', and drinkin'-n-drivin'. Between his cussin'-n-fussin', Dad always hoped that Mom would come back to him, but as far as the family was concerned, 440 miles (or 270 as the crow flies) of separation seemed to be working just fine.

Writing from Vietnam, he said they had been "running hills for almost ninety days" without a break, and without sighting a single Viet Cong guerrilla or North Vietnamese soldier. He said they were trying to do too much with fewer and fewer men, and that a lot of people were getting killed. Wesley had lost twenty pounds, but he said he felt good. He told Mom to encourage us kids to do well in school and "unless you have to—do not join the military."

Wesley's October letter urged Ginny to be careful with Charles, a man she had recently begun dating, someone the family had already taken a liking to. Charles just happened to be young Daphnie's uncle. (Remember our cute friend and neighbor?) Wesley had gone to school with Charles and some of his family in the Abbs Valley, Virginia area. He warned Ginny to be smart—"make it last"—and "don't repeat with Charles what you did with Pete in Texas."

Wesley's warning came a little too late. Before Mom had read the letter, Ginny had moved out of the apartment and into Charles's trailer, and by the time Ginny read the letter (late November), she and Charles were married. The family liked Charles; he seemed to care deeply for our sister and he obviously cherished little Pamela, treating her as if she were his own. Ginny seemed happy.

Wesley professed his love and affection for Kay, along with some doubts about her ability to stay faithful with him so far away and for so long. He acknowledged that it might be difficult for someone so young and so high strung.

Mom received another letter from Wesley in December. He had just been released from the hospital, after having acquired a mild case of tonsillitis. He enclosed a few greenbacks, wishing all of us a Merry Christmas and a Happy New Year, all-the-while hoping that he'd be home for the next one. "Only 277 days to go," he noted. Not surprisingly, I sensed that my brother's letters were typical for soldiers so far from home. Wesley turned twenty-four over the Christmas holidays: "An old man," he said.

The following year, Barry Sadler's "The Ballad of the Green Berets" became a #1 hit single. The song brought the war home to many, especially me. Thinking about my big brother trying to stay alive, I bought Barry's 45 single and played it over and over.

Sports and Other Explorations

Dean Peacock and his cousin Derek Peacock were from the Beckley area of West Virginia. Their families had also recently moved to Newport, no doubt seeking a better life and employment that didn't involve digging coal. We became good friends, probably a consequence of shared southern Appalachian roots. Jack Fleetman, John Wyman, Nate Mackowski, and John Caldwell also became good friends, although they had spent most, if not all, their lives in the Newport area. The Peacock cousins and I sometimes prowled the Newport streets until way after dark—that is, until the town police began chasing us for loitering and mischief-making. I gave up the streets first in search of a quieter and safer pastime, one less likely to land me in the reform school.

That September we all began seventh grade gym class at Krebs School. We were issued lockers and purchased spiffy looking gym shorts and t-shirts with numbers and the Krebs Vikings logo. I remember the first night I brought my gym uniform home. After changing in the bathroom, I walked into the hallway near the living room entrance to proudly show off my new outfit.

"What do you think, Mom?"

"Wow!" she said. "Ginny, would you look at those legs."

"Look at those muscles," Ginny added. "My little brother's becoming a man."

Embarrassed, I dashed back to the bathroom to change, feeling sorry I'd even asked their opinion. In a way, this family episode confirmed my suspicions—I was experiencing an adolescent growth spurt.

My athletic abilities in gym class didn't go unnoticed. Our gym teachers, Mr. Davis and Mr. Toliver, and other coaches as well, were pushing me and a handful of "athletes" to sign up for various sports. I decided to go out for the sport I thought I could do best in—wrestling. The wrestling coach seemed pretty cool, so I signed up, and the school nurse scheduled a physical exam. A few days later I stood in line outside the nurse's office with about a dozen other potential athletes, awaiting my examination. Lee Knotwell was there too, leaning against the wall and helping me hold it up; that is, until a teacher spotted us.

"Hey you two, you've got healthy backbones. Now get off that wall and use um!" Lee and I quickly jumped to attention.

As soon as our embarrassment subsided, I said, "You know, I don't think I've ever had a complete physical before. What's it like, Lee?"

"Oh, it's not bad," he said, "except for the part where the doctor grabs your balls and asks you to cough. That sucks."

"He grabs your balls?"

"Sure, he has to do that to check you for a hernia."

"Oh."

"Oh yeah, Dixon," he added, "you'll just love it when he sticks his finger up your butt hole."

"Gross! What's he doing that for?"

"I don't know. Maybe he likes it."

I wasn't exactly sure what a hernia was, but I thought it best not to ask Lee. I would ask someone else later.

I had been attending wrestling practice for a week when the head coach, Mr. Poorman, called me into his office. I was taking to the sport; so well, in fact, that I thought the coach wanted to compliment me on my good work.

"Tommy, I have the results here from your physical. Everything looks great except for your heart."

"My heart? What's wrong with my heart?"

"The doctor says you have a heart murmur."

"What's a heart murmur?"

"It's an irregularity or malfunction of the heart. Until it's checked out by your family doctor and deemed healthy enough, the school can't allow you to participate in any sports. I'm sorry, Tommy."

That night I told Mom what the coach had said about the doctor's report. She stopped ironing my sister's blouse and placed her fists on her hips. "You don't say? Was this the doctor hired by the school?"

"Yeah, I think so."

"Well, we'll see about that," she promised.

For the next week, Mom followed me through several examinations and cardiac stress tests, aimed at pinpointing the severity of my heart condition. The medical results finally showed that I really did have a "functional" heart murmur. Since my heart was functional, the heart specialist gave me a signed medical note to take to my coach. A few days later, after the school nurse received the official copy from my doctor, they allowed me to rejoin the wrestling team.

I wrestled very well my first year. The first (and only) time I got pinned, I walked off the mat stunned, like I didn't know what hit me. My coach said he knew exactly what I needed to do: "Stay off your back!" I found out later that the kid who pinned me had older brothers who were good wrestlers. That made me feel a little better, but I knew I had some catching up to do if I wanted to be top dog.

As if worrying about my heart wasn't enough stress, I also entered junior high suffering from weird dreams, maybe nightmares. I'll bet most junior high students had similar dreams haunting them, with all the changes being heaped upon us—homerooms, lockers, sports, and changing classes and teachers every hour.

Off and on for three months or more, I dreamed of waltzing my way into the main office to request a copy of my first semester class schedule. The first dream had me running late for school, so I reported to the main office and confronted one of the assistants.

She said, "Tommy, we mailed a copy of those to all the parents weeks ago. You mean to tell me you didn't get one?"

"Yes ma'am, I know that, but I lost mine."

She begrudgingly handed me a copy of my schedule and told me my homeroom teacher's name and room number. Before I could enter homeroom, the bell rang and the class was dismissed. I had to stand aside or else be trampled by a horde of nervous students scurrying out the doorway to their first class. I apologized to my homeroom teacher and asked if I had missed anything important. I guess I was worried about creating an unfavorable first impression.

He said, "It's important that you make it to your homeroom class on time, Tommy—every day. Understand?"

"Yes sir," I said nervously, and he handed me another copy of my first semester class schedule.

Please God, tell me this is just a dream. I couldn't understand its meaning. I thought I had already settled into a routine. So why was I stuck in the throes of these crazy, mixed-up hallucinations?

To add insult to injury, I always dreamed that I failed to recall the combination to my locker, even though I had it written down somewhere. Imagine my surprise and frustration when I realized the three most important numbers in my life were scribbled inside my locker, along with my first semester class schedule. Just three two-digit numbers, and I couldn't remember them. Wouldn't that be enough to wake you up?

* * * * *

Near the middle of March 1966, Mom received a letter from Paul. It carried some good news, but also some alarming and unfortunate news about his progress in the Job Corps. The camp director and Paul's supervisor were very impressed with his abilities, attitude, and performance. At eighteen he showed confidence and maturity, qualities the Corps sought in a team leader. Paul had been promoted to dorm captain, in charge of organizing and maintaining order for thirty young men. In the process of carrying out his duties, he had ruffled the feathers of most of the young black Job Corps members. He had insisted they stop huffing glue and drinking alcohol, and threatened to report them if they didn't cease their use.

Following this warning Paul returned to his bunk, where he fell asleep reading his favorite comic book. One of the young men Paul had chastised was named Darrell, and he stood six foot six and weighed nearly three hundred pounds. Darrell's first punch landed on the left side of Paul's sleeping head. A fist to the stomach followed. In spite of all that, Paul managed to spring from his bed to confront his attacker. Through watery eyes and blurred vision, he saw Darrell and about ten of his "brothers" dancing and prancing about, ready for more action. Before Paul could retaliate, the dorm supervisor and another man arrived to smother the flames.

The cowardly act gave Paul a bloodshot eye and a severe headache that lasted several hours. When Paul took his case to Corps management, they tried to cover it up by sending Darrell to Texas to finish his training. The poor handling of the incident was very discouraging for Paul. Two weeks later he completed his eight-month course and graduated on the sixth of April.

Through friendly contacts at the Corps, Paul landed a temporary surveying job at Cape Cod. In his letter he said he was coming home for a two-week visit. When he arrived I detected a change in him—a diminished sense of innocence and trust, replaced by a wary and somewhat bitter disposition. He was definitely more street smart. After two weeks at home he returned to Cape Cod and the surveying job, where one of his Corps instructors, Mr. Roland Verfaille, provided him a room in his home and treated him like family.

President Johnson had stated that the Job Corps' goal was to teach young underprivileged men vocational skills, good work habits, and proper attitudes. Obviously some young men, like Darrell, weren't learning the best of attitudes. Paul also suspected that many corpsmen (including Darrell and others in his dorm) were sent there with criminal records. In fact, years later the Nixon administration described the Job Corps as "a country club for juvenile delinquents." To me, placing criminals in a dorm setting with well-mannered and ambitious young men seemed criminal in itself. Paul's sour experience with the Job Corps prompted me to give stronger consideration to finishing high school and maybe going on to college.

The unprovoked sneak attack on my brother had another consequence—it made me wary of the few black classmates I had at Krebs. People often wonder how and when the first seeds of racial prejudice get planted. Stories like this can (and often do) define that moment.

* * * * *

Wesley, Kay, and their ’65 Mustang at #10 Water Street.

Wesley returned to the states on July 22, 1966. Somehow he had survived nine months in that hellhole, Vietnam, with only minor scars, and not a one of them were the visible kind.

Gary had stood guard for an hour or more at the intersection of Water and James Streets, hoping to be the first to get a glimpse of his big brother and sister-in-law. Except for a slight sunburn, it was a good plan, since he knew Wesley would be arriving about that time, driving another beauty of a car—a 1965 Mustang with a 289 cubic inch V8 engine and a freshly waxed bright red exterior. And it worked; Wesley had barely completed the right turn onto Water Street and Gary was there, waving him down.

"Who are you?" Wesley asked, teasing his brother.

"It's Gary," Gary said with excitement, "and you're Wesley."

"Right!"

"So, where's the apartment, Gary?" Kay asked.

"It's right there," he said pointing. "Mom said you can park under the shade tree beside the building."

Wesley and Kay laughed, seeing Gary hot, shirtless, and all out of breath, sweat dripping from the tip of his nose.

During his first week home, Wesley and Kay had walked into a Bluefield used car lot and bought his latest toy. Boy, could it move! One sunny afternoon I happened to be riding with him on the way to visit our cousins, Reds and Cherry. They had just moved from Richardson Park to Latimer Estates, a mostly Polish neighborhood a few blocks east of the Browntown section of Wilmington. I overheard Wesley bragging to our cousins about the Mustang. "Okay, Wes," Reds said, "take us for a ride and show us what it can do."

Eager to show it off, Wesley loaded up the four of us and picked up I-95 South (newly built) at the Jackson Street entrance ramp, headed for Baltimore. It was my first time on the route and a ride I'll never forget.

As we entered the on-ramp, Wesley pushed the engine to full throttle, rushing through the gears. With the Mustang's four-barrel carburetor burning wide open, it took us two minutes to pass the Newport exit, just three miles down the turnpike. (No need to do the math.) My heart stuttered when I saw the speedometer reach 110 (this was two decades before seatbelts were required). I breathed a sigh of relief when we hit the Newark exit doing 50 miles per hour. We spent the next hour driving around the Maryland countryside, joking and admiring field after field of corn. I had a good time, but was happy to get home unscathed.

It would be several months before the family would see Wesley and Kay again. He was assigned to duty at Fort Ord, California, the major training center in the nation at that time, and another staging area for military units departing for overseas.

On her forty-third birthday in late June, after several valiant but unsuccessful attempts at dumping the nasty habit, Mom essentially smoked her last cigarette. A year earlier, the 1964 Surgeon General's Report had hit the headlines. The adverse health effects of smoking were front-page news and the lead story on every radio and television station in the United States. On the first day of January, 1965, Congress passed a law requiring cigarette packages to carry a health warning, and six months later it banned cigarette advertising on television and radio, to be effective September 1970.

Mom may have snuck a drag or two after that, but I never saw it. After nearly thirty years of smoking she had finally conquered her addiction, providing a strong example for her children. Her non-smoking children, including me, were especially proud of her.

* * * * *

History and English were my weak subjects that year, but I did well enough to be promoted to the eighth grade. June fell upon us and I wondered what type of summer activities (or adventures) awaited me. I still had a restless drive to explore the unknown.

With Paul away, I took his old bed in the corner bedroom, sharing the space with Ronnie. I was initially thrilled to be sharing a room with my big brother instead of sleeping in the top bunk in another room. Soon after I moved in, however, I realized that Ronnie was often sleeping elsewhere. One evening just before bedtime, twelve-year-old Gary strolled into my room and closed the door behind him.

"Gary! Leave it open. I like sleeping with the door *open*."

"Wait, Tommy, I want to show you something."

"What?"

Gary reached under Ronnie's mattress and pulled out a magazine. "This," he whispered. "Ronnie has been hiding this dirty magazine under there." Upon recognizing the cover and the telltale bunny icon, I jumped from my bed and snatched the magazine from Gary's hand. Gary had found Ronnie's secret stash of *Playboy* magazines, and ten seconds of peering had me in a panic state. Shocked and embarrassed, I slammed the magazine closed and stuffed it back under the mattress.

"Gary, don't tell anyone else about this. If I catch you looking at it, I'll tell Ronnie on you. You hear me?"

"Yeah, I hear you, Tommy."

"Now, go to your room—and don't forget to *close* the door on your way out."

Now and then, over the next few days, I'd wrap the magazine in a towel before sneaking it into the bathroom. Secure in my privacy behind a locked door, I set myself to reading the "Playboy Advisor" and other articles.

Also, there were rumors about a new motorcycle club making the rounds for several months in the tri-state (Delaware, Maryland, New Jersey) area, prompting Ronnie, Reds, Cherry, and a few of their friends to develop a sudden interest in bikes. Ronnie decided, rather astutely, that owning a bike would be important if he wanted to become a member of a motorcycle club, so he bought himself a small 250cc BSA "starter" motorcycle. He quickly mastered and outgrew the BSA, then traded it in for a new Triumph, an awesome looking machine. Not only was his Triumph more powerful (650cc with twin carburetors), it was also bigger and sleeker, a huge improvement over the BSA. On the first Saturday after he acquired it, Ronnie and his new friend and Chrysler coworker, John Floyd, took several of us kids for a ride up and down Water Street. He even took Daphnie for a spin, enduring such a tight squeeze from her that he thought he'd cracked a rib.

Later that afternoon, after everyone had gotten a ride, Ronnie parked his cycle on the sidewalk in the shade of the towering sycamore tree standing guard beside our apartment building. How well I remember that notorious tree. Bored to death and in a rare mischievous mood, I climbed it early one morning during rush hour. Midway up the tree, about 18 feet, I began to pepper some of the cars with sycamore seed balls as they rolled down Water Street.

Pling! Plang!

The loud, resonating sound of the balls hitting the roofs and hoods of the cars startled me, putting a halt to my childish prank. Partially hidden by the tree's broad leaves, I froze as a driver stopped his car, stepped out, and inspected the damage. He looked up, noting the seed balls hanging overhead. He must have been amazed that such a tiny object could impact his car with such force. I relaxed a bit when he returned to his car and drove off.

But I wasn't finished yet. The traffic light at James and Water Street had just dumped a new wave of cars my way and I prepared myself for another barrage. This time I retreated higher into the tree after slamming three more cars with balls. Only one car, the last one, stopped. Quick as a monkey, I clawed my way from one branch to another, ascending even higher in pursuit of more cover. But no one stepped out of the car. Instead, it moved on down the street.

At the same time I felt a tingling sensation throughout my body, followed by a buzzing sound. Three seconds later, the current began surging through my body.

"Ahhh! What the hell!"

I released my grip and fell three feet before catching hold of a lower branch. From there, I saw that the limb I grabbed earlier had wrapped itself around a *live* power line.

Safe on the ground, I looked to the top of the tree and the blue sky above, and I thanked God for getting me there. From that day forward I promised myself I'd never again pull a prank like that.

So, Ronnie had parked his bike under that very same sycamore tree after giving us rides.

"Hey Ronnie," I said, "your bike got pretty dirty today."

"Yeah, I reckon it did," he said, looking it over. "Tommy, I'll pay you two dollars if you'll wash it real good."

"Okay," I said enthusiastically.

Thrilled that my brother had entrusted me with the task, I rushed into the house and grabbed a sponge, a bucket of hot soapy water, and another bucket of rinse water. I returned to the cycle and earnestly began washing it, as Ronnie watched my progress and chatted with John. When I started to wash the seat, I reached for the chrome exhaust pipe to support myself.

"Don't touch that!" Ronnie screamed.

Too late. Only a thin film of detergent water separated my skin from an extremely hot exhaust pipe. In an instant, that layer of water sizzled and turned to steam.

"*Owooch!*" I screamed, jerking my hand away, almost certain I had left a chunk of skin behind. As I stared at the palm of my hand, Ronnie ran to my side.

"Tommy, I tried to warn you! You can't touch a hot exhaust pipe like that!"

"Yeah, I know that now," I said.

Through watery eyes and extreme pain, I watched large blisters form on my palm and fingers. For the first time after a serious injury I did not cry. Ronnie and I hurried into the house. Once again, Mom was hit with yet another of Tommy Mack's medical emergencies. It was a very painful lesson, one that Ronnie and I will never forget. Two weeks later my hand had healed and I watched Ronnie move out of our apartment. But not before I washed his Triumph and collected two dollars, my first and last payment for cleaning a motorcycle.

Puppy Love

In the early spring of 1967, Paul returned home. Winters on Cape Cod were too cold for him and he had no desire to endure another New England freeze. He had landed a cleaning job for the railroad that ran by the General Motors plant. After two weeks of sweating in hot, stinking boxcars, he went to work at Capital Airways repairing aircraft interiors. Around this time Paul became engaged to Linda Miller, an attractive young woman and an older sister to Tommy Miller, my young and industrious skateboarding friend from The Park Skateboarding and Bike Club?

Several weeks of steady paychecks helped Paul purchase a used 1957 Chevy, turquoise blue with white side fins and top. If its 283 cubic inch engine, electric power windows, and polished chrome didn't impress his new fiancé, it sure impressed me.

After football in the fall and wrestling in the winter, I took on baseball. My enthusiasm waned, however, after I sprained my ankle sliding into third base. I can vividly recall the injury. I was standing on second base, another runner at first, when a ground ball to the second baseman forced me into a play at third. I could see the third base coach motioning me to slide. The nasty condition of our infield—uneven, hard, and rocky—made me hesitant to do so. Being an obedient serf, however, I did what I was told. My cleats caught the packed clay dirt, forcing my foot and ankle into a position that Mother Nature never intended. As my body came to an abrupt halt six inches shy of the base, the third baseman tagged me as I let out a loud cry.

The coaches and managers rushed to my side. After checking my ankle, a coach and student manager helped me to the locker room. They applied ice and called my neighbor to notify Mom. Paul arrived an hour later and carried me to his Chevy. The hospital took X-rays and a doctor determined that the injury was a severe sprain. It took almost two weeks for my ankle to heal. I missed critical practice and conditioning time and wound up mainly warming the bench.

At this point the country had become excited about an upcoming May wedding: Elvis Presley was about to marry Priscilla in a small, private ceremony at the Aladdin Hotel in Las Vegas. I remember watching the press conference on television as I nursed my injured ankle.

* * * * *

The month of May also presented Mr. Mountain's English classes with an opportunity to brush up on their singing skills. Mr. Mountain brought his own personal tape recorder to class—a new and expensive reel-to-reel type that used separate portable speakers and provided high quality playback sound. He truly liked his new toy and seemed eager to show it to the class. Someone asked, "What's with the tape recorder, Mr. Mountain?"

"I'll be using it as an audio and visual aide to promote greater class participation today," he said. He took a couple of minutes to explain the contraption and then asked for volunteers to have their voices recorded by singing a song. Believe it or not, a few kids actually raised their hands. I was one of them. I'm not sure what caused me to overcome my usual shyness that day. Perhaps it was because I had just memorized the words to two of my favorite songs. Mr.

Mountain called on me first. As I walked to the front of the class, I could hear a few snickers and hushed comments.

"Tom," Mr. Mountain said, handing me the microphone, "what are you going to sing for us today?"

"I'll be singing Elvis Presley's 'Return to Sender,'" released in 1962 and featured in his *Girls! Girls! Girls*! movie that same year.

"Okay," he said, turning on the recorder. "Let's hear it, Tom."

I proceeded to deliver my best rendition, not holding back a bit. Thirty seconds into the song I had several of the boys rolling on the floor, laughing their asses off. I don't know why, but the girls managed to stay in their seats. Maybe their short skirts kept them there. Most were just stunned that I had summoned up the nerve to make such a spectacle of myself, as I most certainly did. I wanted to do my best, eager to hear how I sounded on playback. My strong desire to stay focused and results oriented only increased the entertainment factor—tenfold, I'm sure. When I finished, the boys crawled back into their seats and mildly applauded me.

"Good job, Tom," Mr. Mountain said, taking the microphone, "we all enjoyed your enthusiasm." My face flashed several shades of red as I walked back to my seat. "Anyone else?" he asked. "Curtis! Didn't you have your hand up earlier?"

Curtis was one of our few black students. Older and much larger than the average eighth grader, he was one of our best basketball players, too, and a really nice guy. His hesitancy caused me to wonder: *Is he afraid he'll look bad now that he's heard me sing? Or, is he reluctant to outperform me?* Well, he hadn't lost his nerve. He walked to the front of the class, took the microphone, and announced that he'd be singing "Moon River," a song written by Johnny Mercer in 1961 and made popular by Andy Williams in 1962.

The class grew quiet, anticipating Curtis's delivery. I don't think they had ever heard him sing, and he put on a stellar performance.

The class applauded enthusiastically. I knew right away he'd made me look bad—real bad.

"Well," Mr. Mountain said, "anyone care to follow that?"

No hands went up. No one wanted to follow Curtis or even talk into the recorder.

"Oh, come on," Mr. Mountain said, "I know there are others besides Tom and Curtis." He looked about the room and, seeing no other volunteers, prepared to rewind the tape for a playback.

"Mr. Mountain!" I shouted, raising my hand. "I'll do another one!"

The class booed and moaned, but I didn't care. I was on a mission.

"Okay people!" Mr. Mountain shouted, calming the protest. "Let's show a little respect here. We have time for one more song, and since Tom is the only one willing to sing again…well…Tom, come on up here." I walked to the front and took up the microphone again. "Tom, what's it going to be this time?"

"I'll sing 'All I Have to Do Is Dream,'" a 1958 hit by *The Everly Brothers*."

Mr. Mountain looked me straight in the eye, pointed his finger at me, winked, and made a motion with his thumb as if cocking a pistol. This time I gave my best performance—ever. The song's romantic lyrics stifled most (but not all) of the audience's laughter and antics. Perhaps they'd laughed themselves into exhaustion. I finished and slunk back to my seat, red-faced again.

"Thanks, Tom," Mr. Mountain said, "I think that was your song." He began rewinding the tape, saying, "Now, let's play some of it back. I'm sure you boys are anxious to hear how you *really* sound." He played back portions of the recorded songs, pausing at times to explain the difference between what the speaker (singer) hears and what the audience hears. It had something to do with hearing one's own vocal cords resonating throughout the skull and jawbones in ways that produce a distinctive voice. The listener, however, hears only the sound that is transmitted through the air—a different sound. "To hear your true voice," Mr. Mountain said, "you have to record it and play it back."

Mr. Mountain's class on sound recording and reproduction became a hit with students that year. Before the year ended, he had convinced a few of my more curious and less inhibited female classmates to recite bits of poems and song lyrics into the recorder, all in an effort to hear their true voices. I had heard enough of my singing voice that day and I didn't like it. Oh, I'm sure I had heard much worse, but I knew no future awaited me in the singing department. My hope was that I had not tortured my classmates too cruelly in my quest to discover some latent talent. Looking back, maybe Curtis and I gave them something they'll always remember, and hopefully, when they hear any of those three songs, they'll smile and think fondly of Tommy and Curtis.

* * * * *

A new tenant moved into the #4, first floor apartment with a three-year-old boy. Her name was Valerie, a sweet and strikingly attractive single mother in her early twenties. Since she spoke with a cute French accent, we all enjoyed eavesdropping on her conversations with our mom. We soon observed that an older man, perhaps in his mid-thirties, had visited her apartment several times each week.

One day Valerie cornered me and asked me if I wanted to be her babysitter. I accepted the challenge, after having sat a couple of times for my neighbor in apartment #6 below us. Like Valerie, this mom was also single. Her three young kids were such a handful that I declined a third offer to watch them.

Before leaving that evening, Valerie introduced me to her friend Don, the stranger we had seen ducking in and out of her apartment. He seemed likable and always showed up well dressed and well groomed. He told me he managed a local Babe Ruth team and asked if I had played any baseball. When I told him I played in junior high, he expressed interest in having me join his team.

Valerie's son behaved well enough, at least during the earlier hours of the day. I was chipping away at his bedtime crankiness when Gary, now thirteen, walked into the apartment without knocking.

"Gary! What are you doing here?"

"I came to see how you and the kid's doing."

We played with the little tyke for a while, changed his diaper, and powdered his behind. We noticed him getting tired, too. He began to rub his eyes, fighting to stay awake so he could party-on with his new sitters. Around ten o'clock I began to wonder, *How long can a toddler stay awake*? There were late night movies to be watched on Valerie's TV—Boris Karloff and Lon Chaney reruns. But soon the fight was over. The young man fought a brave battle, but Mr. Sandman won.

"Hey, Tommy, what's this?"

I turned around and saw Gary standing beside the dresser, one drawer open. Two pair of Valerie's underwear were on the floor and another pair in his hand. If that wasn't bad enough, I noticed him holding a plastic battery-operated vibrator.

"Gary! What are you doing?"

"I just wanted to see what kind of stuff she keeps in her drawers."

"Put that back!" I shouted, snatching Valerie's personal items from his hands. "You don't rummage through peoples belongings like that!"

"What do you think it is, Tommy?"

"I think it's called a vibrator. I've heard my buddies talking about these things. She probably uses it to massage her sore muscles."

"Oh."

"Now, where did you get these things?" I asked, looking into the drawer. "We need to put them back exactly where you found them."

"The vibrator was in the back, hidden under her bloomers."

I closed the drawer and grabbed my brother's arm. "Okay Gary," I said, "it's time for you to go home."

"No, I want to stay with you and watch TV."

"No way, Gary!"

"Oh come on, Tommy. Why can't I stay?"

"Because I'm the babysitter and you're not supposed to be here. If Mom knew what you just did, she'd have me cut a switch for you! Besides, I want to watch television by myself."

I had to physically force my pesky, grumbling brother out of Valerie's apartment, locking the door behind him. Valerie never asked me to baby sit again. I wondered if she suspected something.

* * * * *

The summer of 1967 was destined to be one of the busiest and most interesting seasons of my youth. In May, Ginny and Charles presented Mom with her second grandson, Mark, who would become quite a rough-and-tumble kid by his fifth year. He radiated energy and became a real treat for everyone, especially his uncles. A month after Mark's entry into the world, Wesley and Kay welcomed their first child, Ramona Dawn. In August, Wesley and his new family were assigned to a military facility in Fairbanks, Alaska. They would spend two-and-a-half years there, eventually becoming accustomed to the frosty climate.

Once the school term ended, Paul drove Mom, Donna, and me to the Social Security Administration office in Wilmington, where we spent about two hours acquiring our social security cards. We felt so proud and a little bit grown up. A few days later Mom signed us up for a summer job through the city's Youth Opportunity Center (Y.O.C.), a state-funded youth program that provided summer jobs and other activities for low income and welfare families. Donna and I thought, *Oh boy, now we'll have some spending money.*

Early in June we began our summer employment at the New Castle County Engineering Building on Kirkwood Highway. Donna landed a secretarial job inside the administration building and I was assigned a grass cutting job. I felt fortunate to have landed my job in the way I did. While Donna remained inside the administration building waiting for her assignment, I joined a line at the county truck yard in back of the building. The supervisors were screening our papers, checking our physical sizes and personality traits, and who knows what else in an attempt to match each kid to an appropriate job and supervisor. As I watched this activity, I thought I saw a familiar face in the crowd of mostly young black men, and he stared back as if he knew me. I pointed my finger at him. "Lolley?"

"Dixon?" he said, pointing back. We shook hands and began a lively discussion about school and sports. Steve Lolley was a likable guy, one of six black kids from a team of forty Krebs football players. Our friendly conversation didn't go unnoticed by the county supervisors. By ten o'clock, Steve and I were selected to join Francis Norris, a great supervisor who had been working with county programs for several years. Every weekday morning, Francis would load his two helpers, two lawn mowers, and two cans of gasoline into his dump truck, and we would spend the rest of the day cutting the grass around various county sewer pumping stations.

Summer came quickly that year. That meant time for family swimming and picnic outings, mainly at Brandywine Creek State Park, Lums Pond State Park, and Becks Pond County Park. During one of these outings I began to have serious "feelings" for one of my sister's new friends, Jeanie White. She was lean, athletic, attractive, and at least a year older than me. Her walk, talk, and manner demanded attention, and it certainly drew mine. Jeanie also had a summer job, but in the city, and she usually caught the bus at Maryland Avenue, a block from her house in Newport. I would sometimes wait for Jeanie at the bus stop when she finished work, often greeting her with an affectionate peck on the lips. After walking her home, I would spend a few minutes with her and her little brother, waiting for her mother to return from work. She usually had to watch her five-year-old brother Michael, another tough little kid.

I wasn't the only one interested in Jeanie; I'm sure she had more than a handful of guys shadowing her. But I may have been the youngest and the only one without a car. At times I thought she might be a tease. One day she chose not to take the bus home from work and instead sailed past as a passenger in a sharp-looking red Chevrolet convertible with the top down. The car turned around and pulled over beside me.

"Hi Tommy," Jeanie said. "This is Jimmy. Jimmy, this is my friend, Tommy, the one I told you about." Jimmy was a tall, lanky kid, about seventeen. He wore thick black-rimmed glasses and looked a lot like Buddy Holly, except skinnier. I thought, *What's she doing with this guy?*

"Hi," I said. "Nice car. Is it yours?"

"You bet," he said. "I just bought it last month. Want a ride?"

"No thanks, maybe some other time. I'll catch you later, Jeanie."

Jimmy seemed so friendly and on top of the world, and why not? He was driving a shiny new car with a fine looking girl beside him. As I walked away I felt a strange lump rising in my throat, coming out of nowhere, and I found it increasingly difficult to swallow. *Does she still like me, or is it over between us?*

* * * * *

Paul,18, Tommy, 14, and Ronnie, 23, joking around for the camera at the Water St. apartment. (Hey, dig that wild looking shirt, man.)

One day in late June, Valerie's boyfriend Don finally asked me to join his Babe Ruth baseball team. I accepted and he began picking me up after work at our apartment on Water Street. After two practices, he complained about too much traffic at the James and Water Street intersection, what with all the DuPont employees leaving work. To save time, gas, and aggravation, he asked me to wait for him at the Basin Road/I-95 crossover where my mother thought it was a bit dangerous to wait. "Tommy, you be careful over there on that road. There's a lot of traffic and crazy drivers out there."

"Oh, Mom."

"Don't 'Oh, Mom' me. There's perverts out there too, and you could be kidnapped."

"Mom, you worry too much. Nobody's gonna try to kidnap me."

"Well, you just keep your wits about you over there."

Since I wasn't actually waiting on the interstate and no cops tried to arrest me, it must have been okay. How well I remember those days: arriving home around 4:00 p.m. after six or more hours of grass cutting, wolfing down a baloney or peanut butter and jelly sandwich, changing into my baseball gear, walking to Basin Road, waiting in the hot summer sun, riding to Newcastle with Don, and finally practicing or playing baseball. On the ride home I would get a chance to relax, talk, and get to know the coach. My energy level back then was boundless.

When I wasn't playing ball, cutting grass, or trying to court Jeanie, I hung out with my buddy Dean Peacock. We'd decided to build a cabin in the wooded lot between Water Street and the railroad tracks. It took less than two weeks, and by the middle of July our eight by twelve foot shack was complete, mostly composed of building materials purchased from Hollingsworth Lumber Co. and Wroten's Hardware, the town's one-n-only hardware store. Some materials were donated and my friends may have pilfered others. I didn't ask.

Anyone who patronized Wroten's will certainly recall its sweet, pungent odor. Such an attack upon one's olfactory senses stemmed from decades of feed, grain, fertilizer, paint, and solvent storage, coupled with an inadequate amount of fresh air. Today, I suspect OSHA would cite the place for exceeding the recommended exposure limits (RELs) for hazardous workplace substances. It's no wonder Mr. Wroten always insisted on keeping the front door propped open during fair weather.

Looking west: Wroten's Paint & Hardware at the corner of James and Justice St., c. 1956. (Courtesy of the Delaware Public Archives.)

The so-called cabin sat a stone's throw from the apartment, and it became a casual retreat for a few select friends and me. I sometimes stayed there alone late into the night, reading comic books and practicing pencil sketches of various superheroes by candlelight. One night one of my buddies brought his girlfriend and we played games. A few days later his girlfriend brought her girlfriend and another male friend I didn't know, and we played more games. Before long I found evidence of people drinking alcohol and having sex in the cabin. I finally put a padlock on the door and told all my friends to pass the word: no more alcohol or girls allowed.

Around that time Donna asked me if I wanted to go swimming with her, Jeanie, and Jimmy at Becks Pond.

"Really," I said. "Does Jeanie know you're asking me?"

"Sure she knows. It was her idea to have you go with us."

"I don't understand. Isn't Jimmy her boyfriend?"

Donna said, "No, not really. Jeanie wants to go swimming with you and me. Jimmy's another friend who happens to have a nice car."

Just like that, Donna's words had resuscitated my interest in Jeanie. Donna and I walked the three blocks to Jeanie's house that Saturday afternoon and waited for Jimmy. I mustered up the courage to give Jeanie a great big hug. Jimmy arrived on time and we all piled into his convertible. With the top down, I enjoyed seeing the wind whipping the girls' hair as we headed west. Donna and Jeanie joked and teased about this and that. I couldn't help feeling sorry for Jimmy, knowing that the feelings he had for Jeanie were not mutual. The four of us avoided the high noon sun by splashing about in the shade of Becks Pond Bridge. I especially enjoyed the brief moments Jeanie and I shared while Donna was diverting Jimmy's attention. I felt a sudden surge of heat as I pulled her into me, her soft breasts caressing my soul ever so wantonly. Her nervous, silly giggles prompted me to shower her with my most affectionate kisses. The interlude lasted only a few seconds, not nearly long enough. I surmised that she didn't want Jimmy to see us. Was she playing us both? Feelings of inadequacy began to consume me, leaving me discouraged and frustrated.

After two hours of swimming and fun we headed home. We all had fair complexions, and I felt my skin burning in the wind and sun. I knew I'd pay for it that night; it was just a question of how much. But that would be later, much later. At that moment I was in heaven, reclining in the back seat, my head nestled comfortably in the warmth of Jeanie's lap.

"Hey, Tommy," Jimmy shouted, "do you want to drive?"

"Sure," I said. "But I don't have a driver's license."

"That don't matter," he said, pulling the car to the side of the road.

Donna said, "Jimmy, are you sure you want him to drive?"

"Ah, he's a big boy," Jimmy said, "I'm sure he can handle an automatic transmission."

"Yeah, Donna, an automatic's a piece of cake to drive."

Jimmy and I exchanged places. Maybe that was the point of him having me drive. I headed in the direction of home at about 40 mph. I deferred to Donna's directions, since she was the only one who knew how to get us there.

"Now, Donna," I said, "be sure to tell me when to turn."

"I will."

I had been driving for less than five minutes when we arrived at the "notorious" intersection.

"Turn left!" Donna screamed. "Turn here!"

She had waited until the last second and I was traveling way too fast. I jerked the steering wheel sharply to make the turn. The car did a complete 360 in the middle of the intersection, rolled up a bank on the side of the road, and came to a stop. We were now perpendicular to the road we wanted to take. Stunned, we looked at each other, surprised to be alive after my crazy maneuver. Fortunately there had been no traffic and there was no damage to Jimmy's new car.

"Get out! Get out!" Donna screamed hysterically, pummeling my shoulder with her fists.

My heart shifted into a drum roll.

"Get him out of there, Jimmy!" she shouted again. "Get him out!"

I feared my shoulder might break from my sister's fierce pounding and hurried to exchange seats. Jimmy backed the car off the bank and we headed home. I felt so embarrassed and kept apologizing for the near accident. I didn't see Jeanie for a few days. I was afraid she'd never regard me as anything more than a kid.

Skullduggery

Baseball practice and conditioning had ended, and we soon found ourselves in the thick of competition. I began to think I'd started my baseball career about three years too late. Although far from the worst player on the team, I spent a lot of time on the bench. Maybe it was because I had struck out twice and gotten picked off first base. I also got nailed in the groin by a hard ground ball hit to me in center-field. The coaches spent fifteen minutes comforting me and getting me to the bench. And all this occurred in the course of a single game. I thought about quitting the team, but with only two weeks of the season left I decided to tough it out.

One day while warming the bench, I watched an attractive lady in her early thirties stroll over to Don and plant an affectionate kiss on his lips. He gave her a quirky smile and resumed his managing duties. She was his wife, and that's when I realized why Valerie, my pretty French neighbor, never came to any games. When Don would drop me off at my apartment I'd watch him interact with Valerie, and I could see from their behavior they were serious. At that point I felt positive that Valerie had been massaging his aching muscles with her hidden vibrator. I almost quit the team that day, too.

I was putting a lot of energy into late night pencil sketches at the cabin and even more into my grass-cutting job. Steve Lolley and I were becoming good friends, tearing up grass with our county lawn mowers. We would practically run with our mowers side by side. On one job location Francis brought along a hand scythe for cutting tall grass. Little did he know it, but I was quite familiar with the tool, having watched my older brothers use it on several occasions. Mr. Norris was tickled to see me cutting and lifting the tall grass. "Wow," he said to Steve, "look at that kid go! I'll let you and Tom do that. I'm getting too old to be swinging one of those things."

One sweltering day, while cutting weeds around a station near Delaware City, we were practically overcome by sewer gasses and the emissions from nearby refineries. It was a miserable spot. Steve, Francis, and I also blundered into a big patch of poison ivy there. Francis ended up with a bad case of the nasty weed and had to miss an entire week of work. Steve and I were okay, but we had to break in another supervisor. That weekend I walked three miles to Mr. Norris's house in Elsmere to see how he was recovering. On our last day on the job, Mr. Norris thanked us and told us we were the best workers he had ever supervised, and probably ever would.

* * * * *

One day I spotted Jeanie with another man—an older man—and they looked like they were serious. Trying to gauge the situation, I asked Donna that night how Jeanie was doing. She said, "Jeanie's fine, Tommy. She's involved too." Donna gave it to me straight; she said Jeanie wasn't the one for me. She said I should forget about her and start looking for a girlfriend closer to my own age.

Well, I wasn't ready to give up just yet, so I decided to visit Jeanie late one day when her mother was away and only she and her brother were at home. With little Michael occupied in another room, Jeanie and I began to make out on the sofa. I showered her with one flurry of passionate kisses after another, each increasingly intense. It was too much; Jeanie resisted and broke free from our embrace.

"Tommy, you should go home. We can't be doing this anymore."

"Why?"

"It's not right. Besides, I'm seeing someone else."

"Oh, I see."

Seconds passed. Her eyes glistened with moisture and a look of pain rolled across her face. I wasn't exactly surprised to find myself numb and speechless. Yeah, Donna had warned me, but I wouldn't listen. Now my pride had *really* been wounded and I had no desire to linger.

"Okay," I said. "Thanks for being honest, Jeanie."

"Let's just be good friends. Okay, Tommy?"

My eyes began to burn. I opened the door, preparing to leave.

"Sure, Jeanie. No problem. We can be friends."

"Good night, Tommy."

"Good night, Jeanie."

I hurried home, avoiding the gaze of anyone passing near me. That lump had crawled back into my throat again and all the way home I fought to keep it down.

A day or two later, while hanging out with the Peacock cousins, Derek sensed something amiss about me. I must have looked down in the dumps.

"What's the matter, Tommy? You're awful quiet today."

"Well…I guess you could say, I kinda broke up with someone I was never really going with."

"Was it Jeanie?" Dean asked.

"Yeah…it was her."

Derek said, "Hey, Tommy, you know what I do when I break up with a girl?"

"No, what's that?"

"I get another tattoo."

"Ha! Ha!" Dean and I laughed. Derek had at least three tattoos. They weren't professional looking, but they were good enough for me. So I agreed to a tattoo and we made an appointment for the following Saturday afternoon.

That night I realized I could be the first of Mom's children to get a tattoo. I didn't recall seeing them, hidden or otherwise, on any of my brothers. God forbid should one of my sisters show up with one—Mom would kill her. Nevertheless, I did a lot of thinking about what I wanted for a tattoo and about finding a place to do it that would provide some privacy. Since Gary constantly shadowed me, my cabin was out of the question. More and more, I found myself having to sneak away from my younger brother.

Saturday arrived, and Derek and I found a secluded spot under a large willow tree a quarter mile east of Newport, on the marshy southern bank of the Christina River. I was ready for my tattoo, but to reach the spot without being seen I felt forced to do something that has bothered me ever since.

Derek asked, "Tommy, did you really have to punch Gary in the stomach like that?"

"Derek, you saw him. Nothing I said would stop him. He just kept following us. What else could I have done to make him go home and leave us alone?"

"I don't know. We should have thought of something else."

"Yeah, you're right. But it worked, didn't it?"

I hated seeing Gary walking away, hunched over and holding his stomach. His cries of pain were chilling. I felt immediate regret, but I couldn't take it back.

Derek had brought along his tattoo kit, which consisted of a few sewing needles, two small bottles of India ink, cotton balls, gauze, bandages, clean water, and a couple of new sponges. The quality of Derek's kit alleviated most, but not all of my concerns about infection. Yes, at fifteen I was hip to that possibility.

"Didn't you bring something to sterilize things?" I asked.

"I sure did," Derek said, as he reached into a brown paper bag and pulled out a bottle of whiskey. "Jack Daniels works great as a pain killer, too."

"Damn, Derek! Where'd you get that?"

"Oh, I have my sources, but I promised not to tell anyone. That includes you, Tommy. Here, try a swig."

I took a swig from the bottle. It burned my throat a little as it went down, but a second swig burned less and left a warm and fuzzy feeling in my chest. It reminded me of Dad's moonshine whiskey, except smoother and a lot tastier.

"Okay, Tommy. What do you want for a tattoo?"

"I think I've set my mind on a snake or serpent."

"Well, if you want a snake you'll have to draw it yourself. My skills are with lettering. Are you sure something like GIRLS STINK or maybe MOM won't do?"

"No, I want a snake, and I'm pretty sure I can draw one."

I drew a good facsimile of a coiled snake on my right bicep and then watched Derek perform his magic. I didn't think getting a homemade tattoo would be so painful. But after dozens of needle sticks and several swigs of Jack Daniels, I went numb.

I waited several days for the tattoo to scab over and heal before showing it to Mom, figuring she would be less likely to cut a fresh switch. Surprisingly, she didn't seem very angry with me. I'd call it disappointed. "Tommy," she said, "someday you'll regret doing that—just you wait and see." At the time I was pleased with the results, but Mom's words rang true. Within two years I was wishing I hadn't marked up my body like that.

* * * * *

On August 22, a Saturday afternoon, Paul and Linda tied the knot. The church rushed them through the wedding so fast that some of us late arrivals missed the ceremony. By the time we reached the church parking lot, the newlyweds were driving away. Paul and Linda stayed with her parents for several weeks until they were able to find a place of their own.

The Manor Park baseball team won the district championship playoffs that summer, and I received my first and last baseball trophy. My baseball career had come to an end. I saw Don only a couple of times after that. I think he and Valerie broke up. Moreover, our ten-week summer job had ended, and Donna and I began shopping for school clothes. The three hundred dollars we each earned didn't go very far—especially after Mom took her cut.

One Friday night Donna and I were in our rooms trying on new clothes. The house was suddenly shaken by sirens from the Newport Fire Station, just four blocks away. We rarely heard sirens that loud, and they were getting louder and coming closer. When we realized the fire trucks were outside our apartment, the whole family rushed onto the porch balcony to investigate. From there we watched two fire trucks stop at the sewer pumping station across the street, about sixty yards away. We were all relieved to see that our apartment was safe. At first I thought that the pumping station had caught on fire, but before I could get down for a better look I spotted Gary charging up the porch steps.

"Tommy!" he shouted, almost out of breath. "Somebody set your cabin on fire!"

"You're kidding!"

"No, I'm not! The flames are coming from the woods, right where the cabin is."

"Oh no," I cried. "Who would have done that?"

I looked up to see Mom standing above me. "Tommy, did you start that fire?"

"Mom! Why would I burn down my own cabin?"

"Gary," she said, "do you know anything about this?"

"No, Mom, I don't know a thing!"

I said, "Gary, you better not have anything to do with this."

"No, honest Tommy, I didn't do it."

The trucks left about an hour later, but the fire marshal had some questions for Mom and me. I admitted that my friends and I had built the cabin, but insisted that I wasn't the one who set it afire. Early the following morning I dashed to the woods to inspect the damage. What a mess! I spent the entire morning hooking up with some of my buddies and asking them if they had any idea who could have done such a dirty deed. All the evidence pointed to Derek Peacock. *But Derek's a friend! He gave me my tattoo. Why would he have done such a thing?*

Mom also walked to the woods to inspect the fire damage and the fire marshal paid her another visit. He asked her questions for which she had no answers and I wasn't present to help explain the incident. I returned home for lunch that afternoon to find Mom in an agitated mood. She confronted me in the kitchen with a switch in her hand. I argued with her, telling her that I had discovered who set the fire. But she didn't care. In her mind I was due for a beating. It was all my fault because I shouldn't have built the cabin in the first place.

She had the switch raised, but I kept retreating until we were outside on the second floor porch balcony.

"No, Mom, don't do it. I didn't do anything!"

She backed me all the way to the corner of the porch, where I quickly decided that her first swing of the switch would be her last. I caught it with my hand, and in the process of wrestling it from her grip I spun around, causing her to stumble and fall against the railing. Mom stood up and stared at me with a surprised look on her face.

"Mom, you're not whipping me anymore," I said. "It's not fair." I broke the switch into pieces and threw them over the railing.

Without saying a word, she turned her back on me and headed for the kitchen. I followed her. "Why would I burn down my own cabin, Mom? I put a lot of work into it."

I could tell she was emotionally hurt. She ignored me—something she had never done—as I tried to explain. I hurt, too. For some strange reason, it hurt me that I had denied my mother her parental right to discipline me. But I was approaching sixteen, too old and too big for that kind of unjust punishment. I knew that I had to stand up and resist the abuse, no matter how much it hurt both of us.

Seething with anger, I put out the word that I was going to find the person responsible for the fire and kick some ass. My buddies did a good job of also spreading the word, and a short time later I stood in the open field near the cabin ruins facing half the Peacock family. They wanted to kick some ass, too. Why? They were supposed to be my friends. I hadn't done anything to them. I certainly hadn't burned down any of their cabins. This was developing into the biggest showdown of my life. Since the odds might be three or four against one, I had Nate, Jack, and John backing me up.

"What are they doing here?" Derek asked, pointing at my backups.

John said, "We're just here to make sure it's a fair fight—nothing else."

"Derek," I said, "why did you burn down the cabin?"

"You told us we couldn't bring girls, we couldn't smoke, and we couldn't drink. The thing was infested with spiders, too. And it was beginning to stink."

"Maybe so," I said, "but it wasn't your cabin or your decision to make."

I headed directly for Derek, waving my arms. Borrowing from the Thing character in *The Fantastic Four* comic book, I yelled, "It's clobberin' time!"

High on adrenaline, I ducked under Derek's guard and performed a double-leg-pickup, tossing him over my shoulder. I didn't see the landing, but he must have hit the ground hard. When Dean moved in I punched him in the stomach, pushed him aside, and spun around, ready for the next charge. Suddenly, the youngest Peacock began climbing my back like a monkey, trying to choke me. I slung him to the ground and followed up by driving my elbow into his stomach. With the wind knocked out of him he let go and I scrambled back to my feet.

Derek had survived his landing and charged me again. I had no desire to inflict serious harm, so I sidestepped Derek's charge and with an open hand smacked him hard across the jaw, forcing him to the ground. I spun around, trying to protect my back, but there was no more fight left in them. All four opponents were looking at one another, hoping someone else would charge me again. One of their friends hadn't made a single move against me. As I walked toward them, they closed ranks and began backing away toward Water Street. I focused my eyes on Derek and faked a move toward him. He turned and ran, and the rest followed. I turned to thank Nate, Jack, and John.

John said, "Tommy, that was so cool. You whipped them all."

"Thanks for watching my back, fellas."

The following Sunday afternoon, Jack and I were relaxing at Nate's house, shooting pool on a cheap, plywood table in his attic and listening over and over to the Beatles' "Yellow Submarine" song. Around one o'clock the attic started to heat up, so we moved to the air-conditioned family room to watch the Phillies game. A minute or two later, Nate's mother stuck her head in.

"Tommy, there's someone here to see you."

Nate, Jack, and I scrambled to the front door. It was our buddy John Wyman. John said, "Tommy, Derek and his big brother Kenny want to see you outside." I looked across Nate's front yard and saw Kenny and Derek standing on the sidewalk leading up to the Mackowski house. My first thought was, *Oh my God! What am I going to do now?*

I heard Nate's mother say, "Young man, you better get off my property and leave this boy alone, or I'm going to call the police!"

Oh crap. Now I've done it! I've gotten Mrs. Mackowski involved.

Nate, Jack, and I kept our positions on the porch, as I struggled to decide my next move. I didn't want to cause any trouble for Nate's mother. She'd always been so nice to me.

The two brothers moved back into the street and Kenny shouted, "Tommy, all I want is to talk with you!"

I had met Kenny months earlier. He wasn't much bigger than me, maybe two years older, and he seemed rather calm and polite. I decided to leave the porch and risk getting my ass whomped. I approached with caution, keeping about seven feet away from him. Derek gave me even more space.

"Derek tells me you beat up on him and Dean. Is that right?" Kenny asked.

"Yeah, them and two more," I boasted.

"Was it your cabin that burned down?"

"Yeah, why do you want to know?"

"Well, Derek took me to see the cabin a few days ago. Since it was on county property, we agreed that it should be burned down before it became infested. Derek set the fire and I called the fire department. He didn't tell me that you and Dean had built the cabin."

"Oh really," I said, glancing at Derek.

"Well, I'd like to apologize for what we did, Tommy. Friends don't tear down their friend's hard work. Isn't that right, Derek?" Kenny and I looked at Derek, who just nodded his head. "Tommy, Derek wants to apologize, too." Kenny motioned for Derek to move closer to me, saying, "Don't you, Derek?"

"I—I'm sorry, Tommy," Derek muttered. "It won't happen again."

"Apology accepted," I said.

Nate's mother really did call the police. Derek and Kenny were barely two blocks down the street when we saw the Newport sheriff stop and question them. We told the police that it was just a misunderstanding. "Everything's cool, sir."

Jack said, "Well, that sure turned out a lot better than I expected." We watched the police cruiser roll slowly down North Walnut Street. "Tommy, I was worried about-cha, boy."

Kenny won a lot of respect from us that day. With apologies made, the Peacocks and I were on our way back to being friends. But it never was the same after that. We slowly drifted apart. I saw Derek once or twice that year and never again. Years later I ran into Dean and he seemed different, quieter, like a lost and wandering soul.

Ronnie and Paul visited us at the apartment, asking me to show them the remains of the cabin. We stood at the edge of the wooded lot, gazing at the scattered and charred remains. I began to explain to them what the cabin looked like before the fire.

"The fire spread fast," I said. "The cabin was mostly two-by-fours, plywood, and carpet nailed together on a railroad tie foundation. I added a few—"

"Tommy," Paul said, interrupting me, "I hear you broke the switch when Mom tried to whip you."

"Uh…yeah, I did."

"Mom said that you tried to push her over the porch railing, too," Ronnie added.

"What!" I was stunned and hurt by the accusation.

Fighting back tears, I spent the next ten minutes with my big brothers discussing the event and defending my position. I knew Mom had lost her balance when I wrestled the switch away, but I had no idea that she thought I was trying to hurt her. Paul and Ronnie seemed to understand my position. Who knows, they might have already had their own defining moment with Mom. They promised to try to put her at ease, as long as I did the same. It took me a day or two to gather up the nerve, but I pulled Mom aside and apologized. I told her I would never deliberately hurt her and that all I wanted to do was take the switch away.

She seemed calmed by my apology and explanation, but I think it took a few months before she regained her usual trust in me.

* * * * *

A couple of weeks before school started, Nate and I began practicing with the junior high football team. Nate's mother was still feeding us well after each practice and by the middle of September we had little doubt that we'd make the team. Nate had clinched defensive and offensive end, and I had defensive and offensive tackle nailed down. Krebs School played only four games that year. After the third game I thought my strength and athletic skills were being wasted in the tackle position. But since I had minimal knowledge of the sport and we had such a successful season (3-0-1), who am I to complain.

They recorded the Mount Pleasant game on film. Our coach showed the movie to us before practice one afternoon, focusing our attention on one particular play. Steve Lolley, my grass cutting buddy, was carrying the ball downfield. Only one defensive player stood between Steve and a touchdown, and that player was about to tackle him. All of a sudden #62 (me) came to the rescue. I caught up to the defender and blocked him hard with my arm and shoulder, knocking him for a loop. This was my one and only moment of glory for the entire season.

Coach Mazza said, “I want you players to note that play as an example of textbook downfield blocking. Good job, Dix!” Mr. Mazza had given me the nickname and other coaches were also using it. They added a severely cropped photo of that play to our yearbook, along with the team’s record.

Krebs 6, Mt. Pleasant 6
Krebs 20, Alexis I. 6
Krebs 35, Claymont 6
Krebs 32, Mt. Pleasant 18

My ninth grade sports and academic skills were beginning to earn me rewards. My grades were getting better, and when football season ended that year I went on to my third year of wrestling, a sport at which I was beginning to excel. At 138 pounds, I had become the team’s “utility” wrestler. During practice the coach would match me with a few of the lighter wrestlers and most of the heavier ones, and I would outwrestle all comers until exhausted. I also found myself wrestling the coaches. Other than that, Mr. Poorman and Mr. Meys didn’t know what else to do with me. I had flunked third grade and was a year older than most of my teammates, which may have played a big part in my early wrestling success. By the middle of January I had won four out of five matches. The one loss taught me that I needed to wrestle smarter and quicker, and not depend so much on strength.

Just for kicks, a few friends joined me at a boys club that winter. Mr. Bart, the club owner and organizer, had invested a few thousand dollars in pinball machines, pool tables, and jukeboxes, which he had installed in a rented hall behind the Newport Fire Hall. Derek, Dean, John, and I began hanging out at the club, but I limited my visits, thinking I should be concentrating more on homework.

One night Bobby Jones and I stopped by the Newport Teen Club to shoot a game or two of pool. It was about 7:30 and chilly outside. Bobby stood about my height and maybe 70 pounds heavier, a real Humpty Dumpty. I kind of felt sorry for him, and I was annoyed by the way many boys and girls picked on him and teased him. I liked Bobby, but comic books were about the only thing we had in common. At the time I was even beginning to lose interest in those, as they were well on their way to being replaced by *Playboy*.

That night, our new club had attracted two or three unsavory characters. Little Johnny Waters and his friend had been shooting pool for over an hour. In spite of the clearly posted rules, Johnny wouldn't relinquish the table for others to use. So when he pocketed his last ball, Bobby and I quietly took over and started racking up.

"Look out, Tommy!" Bobby shouted.

Too late. The pool stick came down hard across my shoulder and back. I watched wood splinters slide across the linoleum floor. Grimacing in pain, I turned to face my attacker who had the other half of the stick raised. Before I could retaliate, and I definitely would have retaliated, Mr. Bart stepped between us.

"Young man, give me that stick!" he demanded.

Johnny handed him the broken stick, saying, "He started it!"

Bobby and I tried to explain the situation, but Mr. Bart didn't care who had started the fight. Johnny and I were officially kicked out of the club. We had to turn in our membership cards on the spot. I walked home that night in pain, mainly the emotional type.

I can't believe this! I've never been kicked off, or out, of anything. I didn't do anything wrong. It was our turn at the table—not his. Johnny Waters breaks a cue stick across my back and gets away with it. Dammit! How can I get even with the little bastard?

The next day I had a light bruise on my back but only minor pain. I was now sixteen, two years older and at least thirty pounds heavier than Johnny. I decided to leave the young punk alone, although for his sake I also hoped I didn't run into him again. *What a nut! Where do little punks like him get their nerve?*

Speaking of nuts, I encountered more than my fair share during my junior high years. Woody Archer and Harvey Collins were close pals and two of the biggest, nuttiest, wannabe bullies in the school. What they lacked in stature and strength they more than made up for with their nasty mouths. Nobody seemed immune to their name calling, wisecracks, and insults. Yeah, not even me. They had spent years honing their skills, bringing them to a razor sharp edge.

Dean, John, and I ran across the pair and two of their female friends that spring at a small park in West Newport. We were trying to be nice, but they always seemed to inject a nasty insult. They were unusually sharp that day, too, probably because they were trying to put on a show for the girls. Harvey pretty much did the talking.

I grew nervous as we approached the group. I said, "Hey you guys, what's up?"

"Look who it is. It's the Dixie gang. What are you and your goofy friends doing around here, Dixon?"

"Just passing through," Dean replied.

"Well, you can keep on passing for all I care."

"That's not a very neighborly thing to say," John declared, "what you got against us, Harvey?"

"Nothing personal, we just don't want you hanging around here."

I said, "Sounds personal to me."

"Okay," he shouted, pointing. "For you dumbasses who don't know any better, the exit is that-a-way."

Unfortunately for Harvey, he was within striking distance when he let go that comment. I punched him in the stomach and watched him double over in pain.

John said, "Oh, shit! Dixon's pissed."

Yeah, that's it—I was pissed. I couldn't let this loud mouth ruin our peaceful day by shouting insults and telling us what to do. They were showing off and being disrespectful. I thought it was my responsibility to see that they didn't get away with it. I wanted to make their day as miserable as they were trying to make ours, and maybe in the process help them think twice before attacking and demeaning others.

Woody made a move toward me, then stopped dead in his tracks when I showed him my white knuckled fists. "What did you do that for?"

"Yeah, Dixon," Harvey grunted.

"I don't like your smart mouth," I said.

"Kiss my ass—you hick."

I punched him in the stomach again, stepped back, and again watched him double over in pain.

Dean said, "C'mon Tommy, let's go."

"Up yours, Dixon!" Harvey screamed, having regained his breath and nasty tongue.

I almost hit him again but pulled back when the light bulb went off in my head. *Who's the bully now*? I hated to think of it. I wasn't accomplishing anything with these types and never would. I was learning, rather slowly I'll admit, that the smart thing "is" to avoid them whenever possible.

I said, "Yeah, come on fellas, let's leave these idiots alone."

The pair spoke few words to me after that and, when they did, their voices seemed to take on a kinder, gentler, and more respectable tone. They didn't know it, but they could have said anything they wanted and I would have left them alone. I had done enough damage.

III

THE PARK

1968-1969

Ronnie and Charlene, everlasting, newly-wed, at #2 Schoolhouse Ln.

2 Schoolhouse Lane

The 1967-68 Krebs wrestling team had its best record in the school's history (4-2-1). On a cold weekend in January we took first place in the district junior high wrestling tournament. In addition to myself, four other wrestlers won district titles—Butch Colazzo, Ed Janvier, Ryan Deshong, and Ron Janusz. I pinned my final opponent, the only one in the district to have defeated me, and savored the sweet taste of revenge.

The glow of victory had barely subsided when the spotlight turned to my siblings. Ronnie and Charlene were married in January on Donna's eighteenth birthday. Donna's best friend (and my friend as well) was now our second sister-in-law. Donna couldn't imagine a better birthday present. The two young women had partied, danced, gone swimming, harmonized, studied, and read together. They had shared a lot, but one thing they had not shared was a position on the girls' basketball team. That talent belonged to Charlene. Donna wanted nothing to do with athletics.

Socializing issues, graduation worries, and general teenage angst weren't the only things bothering me early that year. I watched Mom deal with apartment issues and a landlord who didn't care. The roaches were a nuisance, but nothing compared to the cold nights we endured. Pipes froze overnight, leaving us without early morning water. Our electric bill doubled one month, the consequence of having to heat the apartment with the kitchen stove. The situation forced every family in the apartment building to use extra blankets at least half the time. I remember seeing more than the usual number of little kids with snotty noses running about the apartments.

In December and January the apartment remained so cold that Mom threatened to take Mr. Metzger to court. He told us a new boiler was a big expense and would require a twenty-five dollar rent increase. Mom said she would take him to court on that, too. That's when Mr. Metzger told Mom (in writing) that we had a week to vacate the apartment. He was evicting us—kicking a family of six out into the cold streets—and seemed totally untroubled by the decision.

How could a human being do that to a young family? How could a landlord collect rent and not provide reliable heat in the middle of a cold winter? Greedy scumbags are what I called them.

These were troublesome times for the young man of the house, yet I was happy to defer weighty decisions to my mother and older brothers. Mom presented the letter to the welfare agency and they reminded Mr. Metzger about tenant laws. A written thirty-day notice must be given before eviction.

Around that time we learned that the state had begun planning the construction of a bypass highway through the area. It just so happened that our apartment building sat directly in the path of this project, construction of which was scheduled to begin in 1971. We believed our landlord was plotting to maximize the final sale price of the property by adding (more like slapping together) a new wing with extra rooms and raising the rents without installing a new boiler. Looking back, however, I can see how he'd misjudged. The state declared eminent domain and swallowed up the property (along with the unfinished addition and old boiler) sooner than expected.

It took us less than two weeks to find another place. By March we started packing our belongings and preparing for the move, one that coincided with my appointment as student manager of the Krebs junior high baseball team. I was sixteen and too old to compete, so I took pride in helping coaches Mazza and Ernst.

Since she was already attending Conrad High, Donna wasn't affected by the move. But David, Debbie, Gary, and I had to be pulled out of our Newport schools and placed in the Richardson Park schools. None of us were pleased with this move. I had only two months left before I graduated from Krebs and joined my sister at Conrad. The situation stressed me out for a few days, but when my coaches and the Krebs administration learned about it, they pulled some strings that allowed me to finish ninth grade at Krebs. There was a problem, however: how would I travel the one and a half miles from Richardson Park to Newport without a school bus?

My coaches, Mr. Mazza and Mr. Ernst, and my Spanish teacher, Miss Sikorsky, all came to the rescue. For eight weeks they took turns picking me up at designated locations and delivering me to and from school. If I didn't have a ride and the weather was bad, I walked four blocks back home and played hooky. Otherwise, I walked the ten blocks or so to Krebs. Only two or three times did they forget me.

I hadn't seen the new apartment at #2 Schoolhouse Lane until the day we moved in. It wouldn't have mattered anyway, as the decision was totally out of my hands. Good thing, too, because most of us would have preferred to stay at Water Street. For some silly reason I would miss the old neighborhood. Other than my friends, maybe it was the cozy town's quaint history, or the neat places and businesses I frequented: I enjoyed fishing and firing shotguns from the banks of the muddy Christina River, sneaking in late and leaving early for Sunday morning services at the St. James Episcopal Church, and I missed playing basketball in the parking lot of the Newport Methodist Church. I had enjoyed my first "professional" haircut at Jack Hanna's Barber Shop (Mom's hand clippers were for kids). If you looked hard enough, you could find almost anything at Wroten's Hardware. Several important family gatherings and celebrations took place at the Hi Ho Liquor Store and pool hall. I'll never forget Justice Brothers Appliances & Repair (where we brought our TV for repairs and eventually bought our first new one), and Richardson's Variety, a Five & Ten where I shoplifted my first (and last) plastic model car—a 1964 Ford Thunderbird. A week after the dirty deed I promised myself I'd never steal again, and didn't. Well, almost.

The new apartment was located in the second of five buildings on a dead-end lane. At first glance it seemed a better bachelor pad than a family dwelling, and that's exactly what it had been. The apartment was the same place Ronnie and my cousins had shared years earlier. It had five rooms: a narrow, elongated living room inside the front porch entrance; a large kitchen connected to the living room via an eighteen-foot hallway; a small full bath that separated the two bedrooms; a large bedroom just off the living room that contained a double bed for Mom and Debbie, and a single bed for Donna; and a small bedroom on the far side of the kitchen that held a set of bunk beds for Gary and me.

Two of my bedroom walls were exterior walls, exposed to the elements; of the other two, one shared a wall with the bathroom and the other adjoined the kitchen. It had to be the coldest room in the apartment. David didn't have it much better—he slept on the living room sofa. Other than the cook stove, the only source of household heat was a medium-sized vented kerosene heater in the kitchen. It might as well have been sitting on the front porch for all the warmth it supplied. Most mornings we awoke to near freezing temperatures, since the small kerosene tank seldom lasted through the night. Other times the heater malfunctioned. Then, just like at Water Street, Mom would have to turn on the cook stove and open the oven door. If it's that cold in March, how cold would it be come next January?

And the cockroaches? The new place had more than an adequate supply.

* * * * *

On April 4, James Earl Ray shot and killed Martin Luther King in Memphis. While the country mourned his death and searched for his assassin, many cities prepared for a violent reaction. The following week all hell broke loose in Wilmington. Minor rioting took place the day before King's funeral, but prominent black leaders, espousing the spirit of King, quickly controlled it. By nightfall, however, Wilmington suffered from vandalism, looting, fire bombings, and shootings. The disorder and unrest intensified, and Mayor John Babiarz finally asked Governor Charles Terry, Jr. to call out the Delaware National Guard.

On April 9, the day of King's memorial services, over 3,500 soldiers flooded Wilmington's streets. Two days later—after forty injuries, more than 150 arrests, and several hundred thousand dollars in damages—the National Guard force was reduced to around 1,000 and the city curfew shifted from 7:30 p.m. to 10:30 p.m. Mayor Babiarz wanted the soldiers removed for the Easter holiday (April 14), but Governor Terry turned down his request, considering it premature and dangerous. We were all back in school by Monday,

April 22. Many hush-hush conversations filled the halls and school grounds that first week, with nearly everyone condemning the senseless violence and destruction.

My younger siblings had begun attending Richardson Park School, just outside the Wilmington city limits, and soon after that the newspapers began reporting beatings, muggings, and extortions at P. S. DuPont High School in Wilmington. The violent black-on-white crime there began to increase tensions in my own school. At the time, Krebs had a very low black student population—about five percent, mainly from the small town of Belvedere. My grass-cutting buddy and teammate, Steve Lolley, lived there, as did Mitch Herbert, another black football teammate.

John Caldwell, John Wyman, Mitch, and I were working as a group in Mr. Erickson's art class, conducted in a large room with plenty of space to spread out. This was near the end of April. Not surprisingly, we began to discuss the Wilmington riots and the violence at P. S. DuPont High.

"The rioters were breaking the law," John W. said, "and they were lucky the police didn't shoot them on the spot."

Mitch responded, "You white people don't get it. They murdered one of our leaders. Something needed to be done about it."

All four of us were becoming agitated and other students were beginning to tune in.

I said, "Mitch, that kind of violence and destruction does nothing for the colored people's cause."

A stab of pain crossed Mitch's face. My innocent, yet clumsy, use of the slightly outdated word had taken him aback.

I continued, "It only makes them look like a bunch of uncivilized …uh…well…to be frank—niggers."

Mitch's eyeballs ballooned. "It's black," he said.

I said, "Huh?"

"We're black, Dixon—we're not colored—and we definitely don't like being called niggers, especially by white boys."

"Mitch, I'm not calling you that. All I'm saying is that from the white perspective, when blacks behave like that, you know, like a pack of wild animals, you shouldn't be surprised to see that name pop up. Heck, even some of your own people are calling each other that."

"Mitch, don't forget...you *are* colored," John C. said, chuckling. "Haven't you seen yourself in a mirror?"

Mitch was neither amused nor mollified by this remark.

John W. said, "Yeah, Herbert, if the shoe fits, wear it!"

"I don't like your attitudes," Mitch responded. "I think you all owe me an apology."

John C. said, "What are you going to do if we don't, Herbert? Beat us up?"

"We're not apologizing for anything," John W. said. "If the shoe fits, wear it."

At that point I wasn't the only one beginning to chuckle. Most of us couldn't help it. John W. was such a clown. He was a natural funny guy, and just the way he said some things made you double over with laughter. Our commotion finally caught Mr. Erickson's attention.

"John, do you and your buddies have something you want to share with the rest of the class?"

All four of us stiffened and remained quiet.

"All right, then. Keep it down over there."

Mitch whispered, "John, you and I can finish this in the men's room between classes."

John W. looked at me with "HELP!" written all over his face. His mouth had formed a big O and his eyes were bulging. He knew he wouldn't have a chance against Mitch in a fight. And it was my big mouth that got him in trouble.

I said, "Herbert, if anybody's going to finish this, it's going to be me and you."

"Okay, Dixon," Mitch said, "if that's the way you want it—me and you in the men's room after class."

Well, Mitch and I met in the men's room just down the hall from our art class. A couple of my buddies wanted to watch, but I said, "This is between Mitch and me." There was no reason for all of us to get into trouble. And the bathroom wasn't big enough for both fighters and spectators.

Once alone, Mitch and I began to spar. We threw jabs here and there and circled this-a-way and that-a-way—you know, testing the water, looking to land the first blow. I had zero thoughts of talking my way out of this. Mitch had asked for a fight and I was there to oblige. I had to defend my buddy and I wasn't going to back down. But I quickly realized that I was in over my head with Mitch. His skill, height, and extremely long arms, together with the bathroom's close quarters and hard, slippery floor, were just too much.

All of a sudden, I didn't want to get into trouble. I wanted both of us to arrive unhurt at our next class. I backed away from Mitch.

"We're not getting anywhere like this," I said, breathing heavily. "Let's finish this on the baseball field after school."

"Okay, Dixon—any time, any place. You name it."

Two hours and two classes later, I joined John C. and John W. and two other boys outside the rear entrance of the gymnasium. Again, my buddies had spread the word that we were going to fight. I was surprised to see Renee Brown, my old secret admirer and occasional shadow, join us for the short walk to the ball field. The pressure was on.

Mitch and I squared off twenty feet behind the batter's box as the crowd formed a circle around us. I think he expected me to continue sparring, but I wasn't about to fight his fight. Instead, I faked a punch to his head, dipped below his guard, and tore into him, performing a near-perfect wrestling maneuver—another double-leg takedown. Mitch was now flat on his back, staring up at me with fear-filled eyes. I straddled his thrashing torso like a cowboy riding bareback and pounded my fist into his face.

But before I could do any damage, I felt a sense of weightlessness. Someone lifted me and then dropped me to the ground beside Mitch's sprawled body. A familiar voice screamed, "What do you boys think you're doing?" It was my English teacher, Mr. Mountain. Gripping my shirt with one hand, he helped Mitch to his feet.

"I want to see both of you boys in the principal's office at 7:45 sharp in the morning. You kids go on home, now. You should all be ashamed."

The crowd scattered.

I took the shortcut home through Bestfield, and along the way I began to feel a little ashamed of my behavior. *Why did I want to fight Mitch? Why didn't I try harder to put him at ease? I like him, and my buddies like him. But he wanted to fight, too.*

On the other hand, we couldn't condone what was happening in Wilmington and in many of the city's schools. But had the ratio of blacks to whites at Krebs been reversed, our fight would not have been one-on-one. Instead, it would have been many-on-one, with grave consequences for me.

I was about to face my first school disciplinary action and I was more than a bit fearful.

The next morning Mitch and I met in the principal's office. While we waited for Mr. Mountain and the principal, we worked out a strategy that we thought might help us avoid serious punishment.

Our principal, Mr. Calm, said, "Why were you boys fighting?"

I said, "It was just a friendly wrestling match."

Raising his voice, Mr. Mountain said, "Do you boys think I was born yesterday? I know fighting when I see it. Now tell me, what were you really fighting about?"

"I was just showing Mitch some wrestling moves, Mr. Mountain—right Mitch?"

"Yeah, that's right, Mr. Mountain. Tommy was just showing me some moves."

"Okay," Mr. Mountain said, "so this is how it's going to be?" Turning to our principal, he said, "Jack, I think these boys have rehearsed a story. What do you think we should do?"

"Tom," Mr. Calm said, "this is your first time in my office. Mitch, I believe you've been here once before. You're two of our best athletes, and I'm ashamed and disappointed in you. I'm putting both of you on in-school probation for the rest of the school year. Now, I don't care what your problem was—or is. I want to see you boys shake hands and apologize." Mitch and I locked eyes, shook hands, apologized, and rushed off to our homerooms.

Later that day, Renee Brown apologized to me and told me that she had informed Mr. Mountain about the fight. Apparently she hadn't wanted to see either of us get hurt or suspended. It wasn't difficult for me to forgive her.

Mitch and I never had any issues after that. He even signed my yearbook: "Good luck in the tenth grade."

A Hometown Review

It was a beautiful Saturday afternoon in mid-May. The governor had just removed the 10:30 p.m. curfew for Wilmington and New Castle County, and Mr. Bart had collared me and a handful of other teens to help spruce up the new teen club on East Newport Pike, near the Newport town limits.

I said, "But Mr. Bart, don't you remember? You kicked me out of the club and took away my membership card."

"Well, you seem like a nice kid, Tommy. I'll bet you've learned a good lesson. You have learned your lesson, haven't you?"

"Oh yeah, you can bet on that."

I thought, *Great! Johnny the troublemaker isn't around, and Mr. Bart has forgiven me for the poolroom brawl, the one I never participated in but got punished for*.

Our job involved painting drywall, shelves, and cabinets, and performing a few other tasks around the brand new building. On my first day I saw two young girls stroll in and begin painting shelves. Curious, I approached the pair. One girl said, "Hi. I'm Deanna, and I already know who you are. You're Tommy Dixon, aren't you?"

I said, "How do you know me?"

"We both go to the same school, silly."

"You go to Krebs?"

"Of course," she said, "I've been going to Krebs for years."

I couldn't believe it. Deanna didn't look familiar to me at all. I must have been walking the halls half asleep to have missed a pretty thing like her.

"You mean you don't remember seeing me there?"

"I'm sorry," I said, "I just don't remember seeing you at school."

Later that afternoon she allowed me the privilege of walking her home. The more I talked with her, and the more I kept staring into her dark brown eyes, the more I felt...well, trapped—like a fish on a hook. She lived three blocks from the club, so we decided to walk around the development and spend more time getting acquainted. I learned she had just turned fifteen a few days earlier. We stood chatting outside her second floor apartment until her younger sister and brother came out and announced that it was dinnertime. We said goodbye and made plans to meet at the club Sunday afternoon for another painting session.

On Monday morning I strained to catch a glimpse of Deanna between classes. Then, a class or two past our lunch period, I spotted her in the hallway. As we approached each other, I found myself enthralled by her sparkling eyes and bright smile. They were fantastic.

"I still can't believe I haven't noticed you before."

"I've always been here, Tommy," she whispered, "you just haven't been paying attention."

* * * * *

The Memorial Day recess was upon us. Paul and Linda had set aside a four-day weekend for a vacation trip back to Tazewell County, Virginia. Wow! It had been four years, almost to the week, since the family had packed up and left that part of the country. I eagerly accepted their offer to join them and visit Falls Mills, Boissevain, Pocahontas, and Jenkinjones. Reconnecting with some of our relatives and Paul's old friends seemed like a good idea and a great adventure.

Traveling with Paul and Linda in their '57 Chevy was like a dream, yet I managed to stay awake the entire trip, unlike the family's journey through that part of Virginia back in 1964. We had an eight-track player under the dash and a bunch of *Beach Boys* songs like "I Get Around," "Good Vibrations," and "Fun, Fun, Fun." When we tired of tapes we blasted other hit songs on the radio, picking up stations here and there, all in an effort to relieve boredom and drown out the traffic sounds. With a 283-cubic inch V8 under the hood, we were passing just about everyone while avoiding a speeding ticket.

We put the Baltimore congestion behind us, and then stopped briefly in Charles Town, West Virginia to gas up, grab a bite to eat, and walk about the historic town. As we drove past Winchester, Harrisonburg, and Lexington by way of U.S. Route 11, I marveled at the beautiful rolling hills, valleys, farmlands, and ranches along Virginia's Shenandoah Valley corridor. After about seven hours of driving, we rolled into the mountainous terrain surrounding Roanoke and Christiansburg. The Chevy's engine began to warm up, so we stopped to add more coolant. We had checked the oil level back in Charles Town and it was good.

I enjoyed the last leg of our journey the most. After passing Roanoke and Christiansburg, we left Route 11 near Wytheville and took U.S. 52 north toward Bluefield, West Virginia—Bluestone River country. At this point we began to notice a few mud and gravel parking lots crammed full of heavy duty construction equipment. Workers and surveyors were everywhere. We were traveling in the shadow of Big Walker Mountain, which was getting a facelift and acquiring a 4,200-foot tunnel. After passing more rolling hills, valleys, and mom-and-pop country stores, we came to the southern base of East River Mountain, 1,400 feet high and nearly 4,400 feet above sea level. It was also slated for a tunnel. Since 1960, the E.R.M.

Overlook, near its top, had served as the state's first Visitor Information Center.

The mountain presented drivers with four miles of steep, narrow, two-lane roads, replete with dangerous switchbacks. Paul and I were in awe of the potentially spine-crushing truck escape ramps located every mile or two on the steep downgrades. God help the trucker who had to veer off onto one of those. Should brakes fail, however, the ramp was a better choice than the terrifying thousand-foot drop.

We passed the last escape ramp and looked down on our destination, the small city of Bluefield, West Virginia, nestled in a valley on the north side of East River Mountain. At 2,655 feet above sea level, Bluefield is West Virginia's most elevated city. The town's moderate summer climate has earned it the title of "Nature's Air Conditioned City." On the few rare days that the temperature exceeds 90 degrees, the Bluefield Chamber of Commerce serves free lemonade, a fun way of drawing attention to the community's mild weather. It felt strange to be returning to the city of my childhood and seeing again such familiar landmarks—the Greyhound bus stop, for example, and the Norfolk & Western Railroad loaded with dozens of coal cars. Traveling west and parallel to the rails, we followed Bluefield Avenue until we crossed the state line into the sister city of Bluefield, Virginia. A mile later we turned north onto Rt. 102 at North College Avenue and followed this highway until it became Falls Mills Road.

As we approached Falls Mills, the sky grew cloudy and dark. Paul crossed over to the opposite side of the road and stopped the Chevy at the bottom of Kevin Lane, where we'd made our home from 1960-1964. A strange feeling came over me as I stared up that rocky road and listened to Paul explain the setting to his new wife. Yes, it had only been four years, but it seemed like ten.

"Look, Linda," Paul said, pointing. "It's still there, just above the tree tops. You can see the roof and dormer windows of the old place."

Old memories, good and bad, raced through my mind as shivers gripped my spine. Each breath of air seemed to grow crisper. It all felt so exciting—electrifying—just being there.

"It looks run down," Linda said, as raindrops began to blur our view through the windshield.

"Let's get a closer look," Paul said, shifting into first gear and starting the steep climb up the lane.

"Paul, I don't think we should go up there," Linda warned, "it doesn't look safe."

Paul only smiled and said, "It's alright," and continued climbing.

A bolt of lightning flashed nearby. Seconds later, thunder rumbled down from the mountaintop, followed by a heavy wall of rain that obscured the road ahead.

"Hey Paul," I said, "do you remember when we went fishing below the dam and got caught in a thunderstorm like this?"

"Yeah, I'll never forget that one, Tommy."

The Chevy's tires were slipping and spinning on the flat, slippery rocks, forcing the car to a stop barely twenty feet up the hill. Paul struggled with the gearshift.

"Damn!" he shouted.

"What's the matter?"

"I can't get it out of first gear."

"I told you not to try it," Linda said.

Five minutes later, with buckets of rain falling, Paul was still unable to release the transmission from first gear.

"Paul, I don't think Mother Nature wants us to go up there today."

"It sure looks that way, Tommy. We'll come back tomorrow when the weather is better. That is, if we ever get off this darn hill."

"Yeah," I said, "we can walk up there and get a better look when it's not raining."

Paul continued his struggle with the transmission, while torrents of rain poured from the sky. Disregarding the river of water gushing down the lane underneath us, Paul crawled under the car to reach the gearbox and see if he could get a fix on the problem. Having no luck, he crawled back into the car, quietly cursing while drying himself off.

"Now what are we going to do, Mr. Smarty?" Linda moaned.

"I'll figure out something," Paul patiently replied.

Pondering our next move, we waited for the rain to subside. So far we'd been lucky. We were blocking Kevin Lane, but no vehicle had needed to get by. I knew nothing about cars and transmissions, but I was sure my big brother would get us off that hill. As the storm clouds rolled away, the sun began to bake Kevin Lane and the flat rock strata around us. Water vapor began rising from the hot rocks, but the air was getting cooler, thanks to the cold front that had rushed through.

We'd been stuck for about an hour when Paul said, "Let's try something." While revving the engine, he held down and then popped the clutch. Then, as easily as it got stuck in first gear, it got unstuck. Paul said, "It took me a while, but I finally remembered that trick. Ronnie showed it to me months ago." We all breathed a sigh of relief as the car retreated down the lane and we headed back toward Bluefield. A clean motel and a cool shower sure sounded inviting.

* * * * *

The following morning we enjoyed a nice breakfast at the popular Graham Pharmacy in Bluefield, Virginia, then drove toward Falls Mills again, stopping along the way in Hales Bottom to visit Mama (Dad's 80-year-old mother) and Aunt Gertrude (Dad's sister).

"Well, look at that…it's little Tommy," Mama said, "all grown up and nigh-on a man. Come on over here and give your granny a kiss. You know…I won't be around much longer."

I hugged Mama's shoulder as she sat in her wheelchair and planted a long-awaited kiss on her cheek. Her shoulders felt soft, like cotton, and her cheek cool and clammy. The aroma of weed, probably chewing tobacco or snuff, teased my nostrils. We chatted, and then they both suggested that we visit Dad, who was now living in the house next to Mama's old place on Boissevain Mountain.

"I don't know about that," Paul said.

Mama said, "Young man, your father isn't holding any grudges agin you boys. He'd be real tickled to see you. It's too bad your mother isn't with you, he'd be happy to see her too."

"Humm," Paul mumbled, "I don't think Mom wants to do that, Granny." I shared that view.

Aunt Gertrude said, "Well…you be sure and tell your mother what we said when you get back to Delaware. Your father loves your mother and he'd like for her to come on back to him."

We visited with Mama and Gertrude for less than an hour before heading on up the road to Falls Mills. This time we walked up Kevin Lane, stopping near our old house. It had been fixed up a little—a new door, some new windows, and gone were the pointy gable sections of the two dormer windows, flattened by the installation of a new tin roof—but it still looked dilapidated. It also looked occupied, so we took two or three quick pictures and retreated back down the hill. Paul had told his new bride about some of our family experiences while living on the hill at Kevin Lane. Now he was more than happy to also show her some of the scenery. Boissevain would be our next destination, but before we headed there, we spent the next two hours marching through the woods and climbing around the cliffs we knew so well.

Although covered with weeds and graffiti, and nearly every window broken, the old Boissevain Company Store and Post Office still stands; echoing nature's lust for reclamation, and man's lack of will and resources to either tear down, maintain, or rebuild.

We turned right off Boissevain Road onto Tankhill Road, and Paul stopped the car at the bottom of Boissevain Mountain. He turned to me: "Well, do you want to see Dad?"

"Sure. It's up to you, Paul. After all, you're the one who had the big fight with him."

"Yeah," he said, looking at Linda, "do you still want to meet our old man?"

"Yes, I do. He's your father, you know, and it's been a few years since you've seen him. Your aunt and grandmother think you should."

"Okay," Paul said, exhaling nervously, "let's do it!"

As a cautionary measure, we drove slowly past the property. We didn't see Dad. However, we did see a skeletal-looking woman walk across the yard and disappear behind a building that resembled a chicken coop.

"Who was that?" I asked.

"That must be Blanch," Paul said with his usual chuckle. "I heard that Dad has a new live-in helper."

The woman reappeared. "Oh my God," Linda said, "She looks old."

"Mom knows Blanch," Paul added, "said she's about her age. It looks like all that drinking, smoking, and chewing has piled on some extra years."

"I don't know about you guys," I said, "but she looks like she's been in the sun too long. She's gotta be at least eighty."

Paul and Linda laughed.

"I doubt that, Tommy," Paul said. "But Mom did say that Blanch can wield a mean axe." Paul slowed the car and came to a stop near the end of the paved road. "Mom said she can cut and stack wood as good as any man," he added, turning the Chevy around.

"I guess someone in your father's position can't be too picky."

"You can bet on that, Linda," Paul said. "Come on, let's get this over with."

I sensed that Paul was doing this as a favor to his wife. She wanted to meet her father-in-law. I just hoped she wouldn't regret the decision. We drove back down the mountain and stopped at Dad's driveway. Paul said, "I'm gonna back this baby into the driveway in case we have to leave in a hurry." With that comment, Paul and I both were feeling a bit on edge. It was getting real hot inside that Chevy and I felt the first trickles of sweat. Paul had to gun the engine to get past the deep ruts in the sloping dirt driveway. The reverse gear made the maneuver more difficult. Our wheels squealed and spun out several times before we reached the crest of the drive, thirty feet from Dad's back porch.

"Well," Linda said, "if your Dad's in there, I'm sure he knows he has company by now."

Linda was right. Paul had just stepped out of the car when I heard the screen door slam. A skinny, weathered old man sauntered to the end of the porch and stared down at us. It was Dad.

Paul stood tall, his hands resting on the roof of the car. "Do you know who I am?" he shouted.

Dad hesitated, then stepped off the porch. "I reckon I know my own son when I see 'em. You're Paul, ain't cha?"

Paul smiled and said, "Yeah. I brought Tommy with me. And my new wife's here, too."

Seeing that Dad meant us no harm, Linda opened the car door and stepped out. I slid out of the back seat right behind her. Dad now had a good view of us both. His eyes grew big as he looked Linda over. He stepped toward us and offered Linda his hand. "Um-um, ain't she a beauty. You did good, Paul. It looks like you have a keeper." Paul smiled and walked around the car.

"We were married last August," he said proudly, shaking Dad's hand.

"Congratulations, boy."

Dad shook my hand, too. "Look at little Tommy," he said, grinning ear-to-ear, "boy, ain't he gettin' big—strong lookin' too. I'll bet all my boys are growin' strong these days."

I said, "Yeah, we're all doing fine, Dad." Paul and Linda smiled, sensing my nervousness.

The four of us chatted for a while, and then Dad called Blanch out to meet us. She seemed very shy and nervous, and had little to say. I watched her rush back into the house, thinking, *Wow, was she rough looking. Even more so than Dad.*

We listened to Dad's complaints for a few minutes before saying farewell. He informed us about his failing health, how black lung and emphysema were wracking his body, how he loved our mother, and how willing he was to take her back. He promised to make it up to her if she'd only come back. He had a nice place there on the hill waiting for her and the rest of us kids. *Yeah, right. Let's all rush over to Dad's place. The outhouse and chicken coops are beckoning.*

On our last day we enjoyed a brief visit with our Aunt Helen, Uncle Burl, and Cousins Bruce and Bessie. It amazed me how little their lives had changed. They were still using an outhouse, like at Dad's place. But they also had some modern conveniences—television and running water plumbed to a heavy-duty, white enamel sink in the kitchen. And the smells of home cooking from my childhood were ever-present—dough, homemade gravy, biscuits, and cornbread.

Linda, city girl that she was, got a good dose of country folk living that day and a good look at the switchbacks on Jenkinjones Mountain. Paul drove the long, winding back roads so fast that Linda almost got sick. To be honest, I felt a little queasy myself. It was sad to see the quaint towns and places of my early childhood—Anawalt, Jenkinjones, Trestle Hollow—decaying from poverty and neglect. Knowing these things were inevitable didn't make it any easier, and viewing the graffiti-covered ruins of the old Company Stores and Post Offices became especially depressing. The next morning we headed back to Delaware.

The dilapidated shells of the Pocahontas Fuel Company Store (left) and Post Office (right), Viewed from the entrance to Newhill Road in Jenkinjones, WV. There is little doubt that these structures will fall someday, but the memory of The Company Store will live on through songs, photos, museums, and books like this.

Trestle Hollow Rd, seen from atop the Trestle in Jenkinjones, WV.

Summer of '68

Two days after arriving home we learned that Senator Robert Kennedy had been shot. He died the next day, on June 6. The stench from Dr. King's assassination, only two months earlier, still lingered in American cities. I couldn't help but wonder: *When will it end*? *Who's going to be next*?

I started my second summer job around the middle of June, again through Wilmington's Youth Opportunity Center. After the Center's management teams interviewed about a dozen poor white kids and eighty or so poor black kids, the agency broke us into work groups and assigned us to various sites. Four white kids and I were placed with a group of twenty black kids, and assigned to work at the Delaware State Hospital for the Mentally Disturbed and Insane (Farnhurst). Our jobs included cutting grass, pruning hedges and shrubs, raking, weeding, sweeping; picking up trash, twigs, and limbs; cleaning floors, and attending to messes in the wards. Pay was about one dollar per hour.

Each weekday morning I walked three blocks to the intersection of Matthes and Maryland Avenues and caught the city bus to Fourth and Market Street in Wilmington. From there I walked about six blocks to 8th and Pine Streets on the east side of Wilmington, where, with the rest of the boys and girls, I boarded a school bus for the twenty-minute ride to Farnhurst.

The first day half of us gathered around the maintenance headquarters (part of the greenhouse) to be greeted by the grounds foreman, a short, stout chap with stubby hands and an impressive beer belly. Mr Ogle was a jolly fellow, too, but my first impression told me he was firm, not the kind of man you'd want to cross. Our new boss also seemed to be well liked and respected, and, as I would soon learn, had considerable pull around the institution.

We were also introduced to Troy and Roman, two Amish conscientious objectors working for the state to earn credits toward their military obligation. At that time there were two types of conscientious objectors: 1) a person who objected to combat duty but not to military service could serve in a noncombatant role, and 2) a person who objected to all types of military service was eligible for "alternative service." Troy and Roman fell into the second group, and they were two of the proudest, most energetic, and skilled workers I ever met. I can still see them leaning against the dump truck as we all waited for our morning work assignments, wearing their Amish hats, overalls, and boots, and sporting proud smiles while chewing on a fresh sprig of something. There was no doubt in my mind that these two were true objectors, operating out of genuine principles.

I spent most of my first week with a small group of kids, trimming, cleaning up hedges, and wondering which of us would be assigned to the two tractor jobs Mr. Ogle had promised. The maintenance section had an old yellow Case tractor that pulled a mowing deck, and a spanking new red Massey Ferguson tractor with a hydraulic, adjustable-lift mower deck. If I had been the least bit vehicle-crazy, I would have fallen in love with that lady-in-red.

By the fourth day, it was my turn. I spent the next two days on a small riding mower, cutting grass around the many buildings and parking lots on the hospital grounds, and I carried out the task without damaging the mower (unlike some of the other boys). That weekend I felt certain I'd earned at least one of the small riding mower jobs, and I enjoyed telling my new girlfriend all about it.

Deanna and I were spending more time together, mostly alone at local parks and at home with family and friends.

Sunday, June 16, was Father's Day. That's probably why Mr. Ogle didn't show up for work on Monday morning. With the big man away, our young college student supervisor decided to perform a little experiment. He yanked me off the mowing job that morning. I wondered: *was it his idea or the home office's idea*? Anyway, someone had decided to send me and three other boys to work in one of the male patient wards.

I had only a small inkling of what was waiting for me at the Biggs building. The four of us spent most of that morning helping the staff clean up messes (mostly bodily fluids) that some of the patients had deposited on the floors, walls, and furniture. One of the adult workers said, "This is one of the better wards. You kids wouldn't be allowed to work in most of the other buildings." Part of our job was also to monitor the patients' behavior and report any potential violence or abuse of other patients or staff, while staying away from the patients as much as possible. I prayed several times that morning: *Please Lord, get me out of this craaazy place.*

The student supervisor stopped by at lunchtime and told me to report to the greenhouse after I'd finished eating. As soon as I entered the building, I knew that some sort of shit had hit the fan. I heard Mr. Ogle making himself perfectly clear. "I won't stand for any of my boys working in the patient wards," he shouted, "not even the Biggs building!"

A big-shot representative from the Y.O.C. said, "We thought it would be good for these young men and women to gain experience, to see what it's like in the hospital wards. Some of them might want to work full-time there when they graduate."

Right after that exchange we were told to wait in the parking lot, while the adults "further discussed" the issue. I don't know exactly what the final outcome was, but I knew that Mr. Ogle had gone to bat for all of us. And although he may not have won the war, he won a battle for some of us that day. He called several of us boys into his office and assigned each of us permanent jobs on the grounds maintenance teams. As long as we performed well, he said, we could keep the jobs. I guess my prayer had been answered. I never again set foot in another psychiatric ward.

The following day Troy took me for a spin on the Case tractor. Light yellow in color, this workhorse would soon reach antique status. He demonstrated the use of its controls and showed me how to safely operate and maintain it. From that point on the Case belonged to me. I was assigned to mow the grass around the large fields on the lower hospital grounds. During those hot summer days I could often be seen wearing a long-sleeved shirt, with a white handkerchief or t-shirt draped over my head and neck, and a wide-brimmed straw hat. Aside from potential sunburn, it wasn't a bad job; no one bothered me, and I cut a lot of grass without getting hurt or damaging the equipment.

* * * * *

On Saturday, June 22, I attended Donna and John's wedding, my very first. Sporadic gusts of wind badgered the wedding party on what otherwise would have been a bright and sunny day, just enough wind to play havoc with the women's new hairdos. I made a brief appearance at the reception that followed at her mother-in-law's house. I say "brief" because someone had to drive me home early to baby sit my younger siblings.

Donna said something that day that scared the dickens out of me. She said, "Tommy, you're next." Yes, all my older siblings (Daisy,

Wesley, Ronnie, Ginny, Paul, and now Donna) had taken the plunge. In spite of my growing affection for Deanna, I saw marriage as a very distant prospect.

Married or not, Donna was determined to continue her education and become the first on this side of the family to complete high school. The newlyweds rented a nice apartment in Newport and Donna, about to join the ranks of the few married Conrad seniors, grew nervous with butterflies as the new school year approached.

Midway through July I had made a positive impression on Troy, Roman, and Mr. Ogle. Being such a responsible and capable young man, they had decided to let me operate the new Massey Ferguson tractor. Evidently, all the other trainees had somehow failed the test. Mr. Ogle understood that the mowers wouldn't be cutting much grass if they were constantly banged up and sitting in the repair shop. I soon began to sense a certain degree of jealousy and envy on the part of a few minority co-workers.

By that time, however, we all were enjoying the company of two other state workers in the maintenance yard. Granville Manlove was a short black man with salt-and-pepper hair, in his early to mid-fifties. Not only was he an employee of the state, he was also a ward of the state. A little "slow" but quite competent, Granville performed all the tasks the Y.O.C. had contracted us to do that summer. He wasn't allowed to operate any vehicles or other motorized heavy equipment, and was often teased, sometimes by me. Some of the adults teased him about the size of his "manliness" and warned us teens to avoid the subject, since Granville would be more than happy to whip it out and give credence to the stories. None of us wanted that to happen, so we kept our mouths shut. One morning the adults' teasing went too far and Granville went for his zipper. Man, you should have seen us boys scatter.

Hardrock Shoun, another state worker, was a thirty-year-old black man with a pleasant disposition and remarkable sense of humor—and an embarrassing prison record. His most distinguishing feature had to be his physique—one glimpse could tell you he'd been a serious bodybuilder, and he was just a little taller than me and about twenty pounds heavier. They coined Hardrock's handle long before he started lifting weights. You could say he'd been educated in the School of Hard Knocks and perhaps Hardknock should have been his nickname. But, Hardrock had been applied—and it stuck.

One late July morning, Troy and Roman gathered up most of the work crew, including Hardrock, and dropped us off at the chicken coops of a small, state-owned farm on the edge of the hospital grounds. Our job was to use hand scythes and sickles to cut the tall weeds and bamboo that were slowly overtaking the farmhouse, chicken coops, and grain silo. By ten that morning we had worked up a good thirst by cutting a thirty-foot swath all around the silo. Before heading over to the coops, we took a water break on a grassy knoll in the shade of a big oak tree.

While reclining there, we enjoyed a show: Hardrock and another young co-worker pretending to fist fight, or slap-box. I thought, *I guess they haven't been working very hard. They seem to have a lot of energy*. I watched them box for a minute or so, then had another thought: *I'm not that tired, either*.

For weeks I'd been wondering how I could break the ice with these young men without being too obvious. The black teens didn't seem to want to get too cozy with the white boys. Then I thought of the mild-mannered Hardrock and how the other kids looked up to him, and saw my chance.

"Hey, Hardrock," I shouted, "you know how to wrestle?"

The two stopped their sparring. All the kids looked at me, then back at Hardrock, no doubt curious as to his reply.

"I've done my share," he said with a smile, walking over to me. "Why? Do you want to wrestle me, Tom?"

"Sure, I'll wrestle almost anyone. I'd box ya too, except I'm afraid that without gloves you might mess up my pretty face." Most of the gang doubled over with laughter, including Hardrock.

"Okay, okay," he says, curbing his laughter, "let's get started."

As I faced this powerful looking man, I remember thinking: *If he's better, I hope he goes easy on me. And if I get the best of him, I hope he doesn't get pissed off.* That happens sometimes.

Starting from the takedown position, we circled each other, looking for an opening. All eyes were probably on me and all bets were on my opponent. I played with him a little by giving him the first opportunity for a takedown. When he finally dove for my legs I flattened out, throwing my weight on his back and shoulders. The burden was too much and he collapsed to the ground, releasing his grip. If I hadn't stunned him with a quick, hard cross-face, he would have pulled me back in for the takedown. But my strong cross-face threw him off balance, and it was relatively easy for me to then spin around behind him for a takedown. I squeezed him hard with a tight waist hold, until he collapsed to the ground again, out of breath. I then used a half nelson to turn him over for the pin.

Our audience looked bewildered. Hardrock looked stunned, but he took what some would call an embarrassing defeat with grace and style.

"You did good, Tom."

"Hardrock, I think I had an advantage. You must have been tired from boxing."

"I don't think so, Tom. You're just better than me. Where did you learn to wrestle like that?"

"Oh, I forgot to tell you. I wrestled for three years in junior high, and I'll be taking it up again in high school this fall."

"That's great," he said, "keep up the good work."

"Thanks."

"Okay, boys," Hardrock shouted, "grab your tools and let's clear out around this chicken coop!"

Troy and Roman stopped by with the truck around lunchtime to take those of us who didn't brown-bag it to the cafeteria. Before we piled into the truck, I heard a loud scream from behind. I turned around, and Hardrock almost knocked me over as he raced past and sprinted away. We all wondered where the heck he was going. I looked back toward the coops and saw Roman holding up a seven-foot-long blacksnake. Roman and Troy laughed uncontrollably as Hardrock disappeared in the distance, running until he hit the asphalt.

"Alright, men," Roman shouted, "get in the truck! Let's see if we can find Hardrock."

Most of us continued chuckling as we piled into the truck, but some of the boys took the long way around Roman and the snake. Roman let the snake go and it slithered away into the brush. The poor snake. It had been minding its own business until we came along, smacking the weeds and bamboo.

We caught up to Hardrock later that afternoon. He said, "I can't stand snakes. They scare the crap outa me!"

"We believe ya, Hardrock," I said, "you proved that when ya flew the coop."

Several days passed before Mr. Ogle could find enough volunteers brave enough to finish the job around the farmhouse and chicken coops. Hardrock said, "It'll be winter before I go back to that place. They say that's when snakes hibernate, ya know."

What a man, that Hardrock.

* * * * *

In between working all day in the hot sun and sleeping through the night, I found time to see Deanna. She had a summer job, too, and we had fun sharing our work stories. I usually walked to her house after dinner and sometimes stayed until her mother said, "Goodnight, Tommy." I think I was pushing my luck on weekends, lingering until around midnight. In spite of being tired from working all day, I enjoyed my solitary, late night walks home. My mind worked overtime forming promises, and my heart pounded with the emotions of young love.

Early August arrived and with it some blistering heat. I inhaled my lunch one day and returned to my grass cutting duties, using the new Massey Ferguson tractor. One cottage, only two blocks from the greenhouse, had a healthy patch of tomato and green pepper plants growing near the sunny side of its foundation. I took care not to mutilate them with the mower deck as I glided past. After several passes, I noticed that a resident had stepped outside to inspect the plants. *Is he checking to make sure I haven't damaged them*? I swung the mower back around for another approach. The man stood his ground and motioned me to stop.

Oh crap, don't tell me I've damaged something. I'm sure I didn't touch his vegetables.

He was tall and broad-shouldered. As I pulled to a stop and he placed his hand on the fender of the tractor, I immediately noticed his powerful tanned forearms.

"Morning," he said in a loud voice, making sure to be heard above the hum of the idling engine. "Is it hot enough out here for ya?"

"Yes sir," I said. "It sure is, but I've gotten used to sweatin' in the hot sun. Is everything okay? I didn't damage any of your vegetables, did I?"

"Oh no, not at all! Everything's fine. The main reason I stopped you is to let you know what a great job you're doing and to offer you a cold drink. Maybe a nice, ice-cold beer?"

Damn, I thought, *that sounds good.* I had developed an appreciation for cold beer during the previous year or so, after stealing a can or two from my brother and brother-in-law. But in an instant, my Spidey (Spider Man) senses began to tingle. *Is this a set-up? Does he want to get me fired for drinking on the job?* My imagination was working overtime.

"Wow! That really sounds great. But I'm not allowed to drink alcohol on the job, you know. Thanks anyway."

"My name's Bud," he said, offering me his hand.

"I'm Tom," I said, applying a firm shake.

"It's nice to meet you, Tom. My offer is good anytime. I'll be staying here with my friend for the next week or so. So feel free to stop by for a cold one."

"That sounds good," I said, reengaging the mower blades. "See ya later!"

I whisked the tractor around the yard once or twice, and then saw Bud walking toward me again. I slowed down and he handed me a can of ice-cold Coca Cola. "Thanks!" I said. "Maybe I'll swing by for that beer sometime this week when I'm on my lunch break." He waved in acknowledgement and returned to the cottage. I pulled the metal tab on the can, dropped it into the cola, took a refreshing sip and finished another hot day, sweating hard in the cruel sun.

I ran into Bud again a few days later, and he invited me to have lunch with him and his friend at the cottage. Bud was a bachelor and the foreman of a sixty-acre estate in Massachusetts. He wasn't trying to get me fired by offering me a beer—he actually thought I was older. His friend Bob, also a bachelor, was a resident doctor working at the hospital. They were very friendly and seemed to take a keen interest in me, asking questions about how I got my job, the Y.O.C., my birthplace, my parents, my brothers and sisters, and on and on. Both men gave me their work and home phone numbers, and told me to give them a call if I ever needed anything or if I just needed to talk to an adult. Except for a couple of my football coaches, no adult had ever taken such an interest in me.

I wrapped up the job in late August and Mr. Ogle said he was counting on seeing me again next summer: "The tractor jobs will be wait'n for ya." I talked with my newfound friend, Dr. Bob, about my high school curriculum; he said I had made a good decision by taking some of the more challenging college preparatory courses. Bud was back at the estate in Massachusetts. I called him collect from a pay phone, and he, too, encouraged me to study hard and to keep wrestling.

* * * * *

Deanna and I celebrated Labor Day by joining most of my family for a picnic at the Sand Pit, an old rock quarry across the Delaware-Pennsylvania state line that had been converted into a popular swimming hole with a sandy beach. Unlike Delaware's popular Becks Pond and Lums Pond, the Sand Pit drew few swimmers, which suited us just fine. The deep, dark, cold water, and the fact that there were no designated lifeguards, paid or otherwise on duty, only added to the excitement of picnicking and swimming there.

So, two ponds and a pit were the closest things to a beach for miles around, unless you wanted to drive about 50 miles east to the crowded New Jersey shore or 100 miles to the just-as-crowded southern Delaware beaches. I liked the beach, but not the crowds or the hot sun. I envied people like Deanna and my brother Paul, who tanned so easily and could enjoy the beach without an overwhelming fear of burning. I would eventually learn to appreciate quiet evening walks along deserted beaches, preferring the sound of calm, gentle waves and the feel of cool wet sand squishing between my toes.

Paul (with Linda at shotgun) and John (with Donna) provided the transportation to the Pit for Mom, Deanna, me, and my three younger siblings. Ronnie paired with Charlene on his motorcycle. My two cousins rode their motorcycles, each accompanied by a significant other. The smaller kids enjoyed the late morning hours, splashing around in the shallow water near the sandy beach area. Only adults and savvy teenage swimmers strayed far from shore into the black water. Awareness of The Pit's steep drop-off and cold, dark water was a requirement for any safe swimming. Cramps were considered a constant and potentially deadly threat.

After an hour of swimming and roasting in the sun, many of us donned hats, pants, and long-sleeved shirts before joining in on the real fun—the picnic. Mom and other women had packed several coolers full of meat and cheese sandwiches, tomatoes, lettuce, and several other fruits and vegetables. Plenty of Kool-Aid and soda were available, and older family members and strangers could be seen drinking beer.

Around two in the afternoon we were back in the water, several of us playing an aquatic version of King of the Hill, called Last Man Standing. Ronnie, Paul, John and I stood in a circle facing each other, belly button deep in the water, with our female partners astride our shoulders. The women would then try to dislodge each other without dunking or drowning the men. Linda and Paul usually won the competitions.

That day, however, ended badly. A stranger had been drinking heavily for a number of hours, and someone noticed the man having difficulty staying afloat just before he disappeared. We were ordered out of the water. A few good swimmers began searching near the area where he had gone down, but they found no trace of the man. Most of us were packed and ready to leave when the rescue teams arrived. We watched for a few minutes as responders began dragging the area using ropes and hooks. We left about that time, as Mom didn't think it would be good for the little ones to see a lifeless body. That was the second and last time I visited the Sand Pit. Not long after, authorities barricaded the spot and posted signs all around: DANGER—DO NOT ENTER.

Henry C. Conrad, home of the Redskins, Woodcrest, DE. (Nov.2013)

High School

I began my sophomore year and Donna her senior year at Henry C. Conrad High School. Those first few weeks were so stressful. In addition to all the new students, classes, and teachers, I strained to cope with more personal issues. First of all, I couldn't read the blackboard from the back of the classroom. I liked it back there, where I could see everyone and everything, but all my teachers eventually allowed me to move closer to the front. A couple of them even asked if I'd seen an eye doctor. "No," I replied, "I haven't had a problem until now."

My spirits took a deeper dip when, two days after moving closer, I still couldn't read the board adequately. For the first time in my life, I wondered how I would look in glasses. *Like a nerd, probably.*

Mr. Williams, my English teacher, said, "Tom, I want you to stop by the nurse's office and get your eyes tested." And so I did. The nurse said it was definite. I needed corrective lenses and wouldn't be able to get through school without them.

I really liked Doctor Goldberg. It didn't matter to him that my family lived on welfare; he worked with Mom and the agency to fit me with a good pair of affordable glasses. In the selection process I deferred to Mom and Donna's opinion. Otherwise, I probably wouldn't have picked the Clark Kent style. I think Deanna was being nice, too, when she said I looked fine in them.

The second issue was dermatological in nature, a slowly emerging acne problem that had begun to rock my self-esteem. I was fighting a two-front battle—glasses and zits—that no high school kid wanted. But, again, Deanna was so sweet; she didn't seem to mind.

Looking back, I consider myself lucky to have worked that summer with such a good group of minority teenagers. Some city schools were hit hard that fall with serious racial incidents, including Wilmington High, and several schools began to see an exodus of white students. Racial tension had also increased the number of gangs, with gang activity spreading to the suburbs. Richardson Park had at least one gang and I knew a few teens who were forming another.

On a cool night, about an hour before dark, I encountered two wanna-be gang members while hanging out by the playground in Canby Park East, just within the Wilmington city limits. I made the mistake of trying to have a civil conversation with them while their girlfriends looked on.

One young punk (I'll call him Mark) said, "Tom, I think you'd be a good addition to our gang. Those Elsmere creeps need to have their heads bashed in. We could use someone like you."

I had heard about some of the gang fights. Rumor was, they were using clubs and baseball bats to settle their differences. I also suspected that knives would eventually be used, if not already.

"I don't like fighting unless I have to," I said, "and I don't like fighting other people's battles for them."

Mark let go of his girlfriend's hand and turned to me. "Are you sure you aren't just scared?" Then he emitted an annoying giggle. "Maybe we should call you Puddin'."

"I don't like gangs either," I said, "and I prefer fair fights. Is there anything fair about fightin' in your gang?"

Mark glanced over at his buddy and winked. "I think he's yellow," he chuckled, "don't you, Harry?" He looked back at me with a mischievous grin.

Mark's comments and attitude were making my blood boil. *Is he picking a fight, or is he just another loud-mouthed bully showing off for his friends?* I should have walked away. Instead, I totally lost it when he called me puddin' again and flashed me another cocky grin.

"I'll show you Puddin'," I said, and tackled him low at his hips. In one fluid motion I arched my back and straightened my legs. Using my shoulders and arms, I tossed him over my head, a move I had darn-near perfected. I did a quick about-face to see Mark clawing at the air, looking like a cat tossed to the wind. He landed with a thud and grunt, sitting Indian style, his mouth open in shock, and a dizzy, stunned look in his eyes.

Harry shouted, "Why'd you do that, Dixon?" and ran to help. Mark was okay, but needed a little help getting to his feet.

Composing himself, he said, "Yeah, Puddin'...why'd you do that?"

I stood waiting for them to retaliate, thinking: *They can't catch me. If they pull a weapon, I'm outta here.* But they just continued to run their foul mouths, repeatedly insulting me. I couldn't believe it; they had no idea why I would lose my temper and react the way I did. Having been through this many times, I said, "You guys are pathetic." I then turned and hurried home.

They bothered me only once thereafter, a few weeks later when they tried again to recruit me. I told them I wasn't interested.

* * * * *

Although weakened from a heart attack in October, Governor Terry continued his campaign for reelection against Russell Peterson, and even after losing the election to Peterson that fall, stubbornly continued to maintain the National Guard's presence in Wilmington.

The swearing-in of the new governor in late January finally put an end to what had been the longest occupation of an American city since the Civil War. Many people despised Terry's stubbornness. I'm sure a few saw him as a racist. But many others, like me, were proud of the man. The issue wasn't race, it was criminality and delinquency. After all, what would Martin Luther King have really wanted from his people? He definitely wouldn't have approved what happened in Wilmington and other cities. A near disaster had occurred on the governor's watch, and he wanted to make sure the seeds of such rebellion and lawlessness did not continue to germinate. I gave the man points for sticking to principle.

In October we got some good news from Fairbanks, Alaska: Wesley and Kay's second daughter, Melissa, had come into the world. The family tree was growing, one leaf from each branch in due time.

I started my first year of high school wrestling in November, dealing with a good case of nerves. Having a few of my old Krebs teammates come along with me helped smooth my transition jitters. After a week or two of practices I began to feel like part of the team. Coach Baker and the assistant coach, Mr. Maurer, had earned the respect of all the returning junior and senior wrestlers. I suspected that all the sophomore wrestlers would feel the same before long. Coach Baker was also my math teacher and an excellent one at that. At first I worried that the combination would negatively affect both my wrestling activity and math studies. Looking back, this dual role may have provided an overall positive benefit—that is, until my senior year.

Some of my friends were doing well in their various sports. It had been months since I had hooked up with Nate Mackowski and Jack Fleetman, so I walked the two miles to Nate's house, dribbling a new basketball all the way. I had been thinking of buying a nice football, too, but decided I might have to wait until next summer's employment, when I could better afford it. My basketball was top-shelf and my very first. Nate liked it, too, and we decided to take it to our favorite hoop in his neighbor's driveway. Moments later, we picked up Jack Fleetman and John Wyman for a little two-on-two.

Nate and Jack were taller and much better basketball players than John and I. In fact, they were promising candidates for next year's varsity team. Knowing they were better didn't matter to them, they insisted on pairing up anyway. We told them it wouldn't be fair.

"Well," said Nate, "it's my neighbor's hoop. If you don't like it, you can take your ball and the two of you can play somewhere else."

I was surprised that my longtime friend would cop such an immature attitude. Until that day, my two buddies had always treated me with respect, the same way I treated them. To maintain peace and friendship, John and I tried our best to give them a good game. But it wasn't to be. The two of them ran away with the game, giggling and laughing at our performance like some *oh-so-funny* joke.

"Give me the ball!" I shouted, disgusted with their behavior.

"Why?" Nate asked, holding on to it tightly.

"Why? Because I'm leaving—that's why!"

"Here, Jack," Nate said, tossing the ball to him, "give him his ball."

I turned and walked toward Jack to retrieve it.

"No, Nate," Jack said, tossing it back to Nate, "you give it to him."

"Hey Dixon, let's play keep-away. You can have the ball if you and John can take it from us."

John said, "No way, I'm not playing that game. Besides, I should have been home a while ago. I'll see you guys around." He left, leaving me alone to face my tormentors.

Nate and Jack had me running back and forth between them in a futile attempt to recover my ball. A minute of that and I'd had enough of my so-called buddies.

"Nate, give me the damn ball. Now!"

Nate giggled and tossed it back to Jack.

I turned to Jack. "Give me the ball, Jack."

Jack, grinning, tossed the ball to Nate.

"Oookaay," I sighed, "you guys asked for it."

I walked over to Nate. When he tossed the ball back to Jack, I grabbed him and threw him to the ground. Then, with my knee punching a hole in the small of his back, I twisted Nate's arm so far up his back that he was moaning through his tears. By now he knew I meant business.

Jack said, "What do you think you're doing, Dixon?"

"Breaking his arm, and maybe yours too, if you don't give me back my ball." I applied extra twist to Nate's arm until he screamed in pain. "Well, what's it going to be, Nate?"

"Jaaack! Give him the damn ball—will ya—before he breaks my freakin' arm!"

Jack rolled the ball across the lawn and it stopped right at my knee. I pushed down hard once more on Nate's arm, and he emitted a muffled grunt as I released my grip. I picked up the ball, jumped to my feet, and headed home.

"Some friend you are!" Nate shouted after me.

"The same to both of you!"

As you might expect, that was the last time we played ball together. I couldn't help but feel a loss; we had been good friends for more than three years and shared many good times. It was, however, less of a loss than I expected. Nonetheless, I was angry at my friends' behavior for days and saddened that I had to resort to arm twisting to get my ball back. I guess it's a fact of life: sometimes certain people just bring out the worst in us. I left Newport that day with my pride intact and not a victim. I didn't see any other options at the time.

* * * * *

Winter and Christmas were upon us. Unable to nail down a varsity position (the two senior wrestlers in the 145 lb. and 154 lb. weight classes were just too experienced and too good), I easily eliminated the rest of the competition to earn a junior varsity position.

Pretty soon I was feeling the special team spirit that goes with participating in a great high school sport. Like many Conradians, I marched beside the band during homecoming parades, and enjoyed getting psyched-up during pep rallies and cheerleading in the gym and on the football field. Once upon a time, I had attained the status of a spirited Viking at Krebs Junior High; now I was even more proud to join the ranks of the noble and highly competitive Conrad Redskins. All this teamwork, spirit, and competitiveness had a profound effect on me. It anchored me. I didn't feel it necessary to join a gang. I already belonged to one of the biggest, coolest, and toughest "gangs" in the county—Conrad High School.

The cold weather, together with school studies and wrestling practices, made it difficult to spend time with my older siblings. They had jobs, too, and if they hadn't already started their own families, I figured they were surely about to. Deanna was also busy. I saw her about half as much as I wanted to. I enjoyed the days when Deanna, Donna, and I shared the same lunch period and could sit together in the school cafeteria.

The apartment at #2 Schoolhouse Lane was packed with family members that Christmas morning; it would be the last time so many extended family members gathered to open presents. Ronnie and his wife Charlene, Paul and his wife Linda, and Donna and her new husband John all stopped by. And, although my sibling-in-laws had their own families, they came with presents for each other and especially for Mom, Gary, Debbie, David, and me. We received several articles of clothing to wear to school in the coming months.

Mid-January blew in some of the coldest nights I had ever experienced, colder than any night I can remember in Appalachia. Back then we at least had the potbelly stove and the cook stove to keep us warm and toasty. I had honestly believed that our move to Delaware would be an upgrade in living conditions; now I was beginning to wonder if that would ever happen.

I don't know what Ronnie and my cousins were thinking when they helped Mom secure the place. I suspect quality, affordable, low rent housing was just as difficult to secure then as it is now. The family had moved from one slumlord and frozen abode to another. Our new landlord was but a shadow, since we hardly ever saw him. No wonder I can't remember his name. Even when we managed to keep the kerosene stove burning throughout the night, we suffered. Mom's day-to-day chores tired and frustrated her, and she hated the thought of arguing and fighting with another lazy and selfish landlord. So she kept putting it off, hoping we could get by.

Gary and I slept in the back "bedroom," which was essentially the back porch or mudroom. It had two poorly insulated walls with two cheap windows exposed to the wind, rain, and snow. At bedtime we'd don socks, underwear, sweatpants, a t-shirt, and a long sleeved shirt. Gary would climb into the top bunk; I would slide into the bottom one. A sheet, two blankets, and a quilt covered each of us. Sometimes I removed my shoes and crawled into bed wearing the clothes I'd worn that day. Of course, in the morning I'd change into fresh clothes before leaving for school.

I heard Debbie ask Mom, "Why don't we close the door to the porch so it won't be so cold in the house?" I almost screamed at my sister when she said that, but Mom beat me to it.

"Deborah, it's bad enough the boys are sleeping out on the cold porch. The least we can do is keep the door open so some heat can get to them."

"Yeah, Debbie," Gary said, "maybe you'd like to sleep out there?"

Debbie mumbled, "No thanks," and walked back to her bedroom.

Waking up and getting dressed in the morning was the worst part. Just like at Water Street, the pipes froze, rendering our bathroom temporarily useless. So, we all went to school without washing up. I began packing my toothbrush and toothpaste in a plastic sandwich bag, taking care of my morning needs in the boys' locker-room. One of the top benefits of competing in sports was the nice hot showers I enjoyed after practices and meets.

When I'd get home after practice I'd find that the strong morning sun had thawed the pipes inside the walls, a cycle I witnessed far too often. On what had to be the coldest night of the winter, I awoke around two in the morning and couldn't get back to sleep. I tossed and turned and eventually peeked out from under the covers to see that the porch door was closed. *Who the hell closed the door?* I forced myself to get up and open it. Sleep eluded me most of that night, and when Gary and I were awakened by Mom's call we were in for a surprise. It had snowed several inches and ice coated the inside of the porch windows. Seeing very little ice on the other windows, it occurred to me that our breath caused the ice formation. And since no one confessed to closing the porch door, I surmised that a draft was to blame. Looking back, I think Gary and I would have been just as cold camped on Mount McKinley.

After that freezing cold night, Mom knew she had to make a change. So, when they canceled school that day because of the snow, we took advantage of the time off to dismantle the bunk beds and reassemble them in a corner of the oversized kitchen. It was a little crowded for a few weeks, until the weather warmed and we could move our beds back to the porch.

Not long after we started sleeping in the kitchen, I came down with a nasty stomach virus accompanied by a high fever and vomiting. Over a twelve-hour period my condition deteriorated. My fever grew worse, I couldn't hold down food, and I was stricken with dry heaves. I was so weak I couldn't stand up, let alone walk.

Back in June 1964, while the family lived with our Aunt Katherine, Mom had established a doctor-patient relationship with Doctors Leonard A. Hershon and Roger B. Thomas. They had a well-established family practice at the intersection of Eureka Street and Matthes Avenue in Richardson Park. The office was only six blocks away. When Mom called and explained my condition, the assistant said that one of the doctors would be right over. Imagine my surprise and relief when Doctor Thomas strolled into our kitchen, black bag in hand. The solemn occasion reminded me of Dr. Murray back in 1959, when he visited Ronnie at our home on Jenkinjones Mountain.

Doctor Thomas said, "Hello, young man," and stooped down beside the bed to look at me. "I hear you're not feeling well."

"Ummmhuh," I muttered.

The doctor checked my vital signs and prepared a syringe and needle for an injection. I wasn't too happy about where he stuck me. It hurt like hell, but the next day I felt much better. Two days after the injection I had enough strength for a follow-up visit to his office. Damn—wouldn't you know it—he gave me another shot in the ass. This time I almost collapsed when I tried to walk out of his office. I have recorded that second shot as the most painful—ever. I missed at least three days of school because of that illness. My wrestling suffered, too. The season was almost over by the time I regained my strength and stamina.

Like so many times before, when the kerosene heater would flame-out, Mom would turn the cook stove oven on and leave the door half open. We went through two heating elements that winter. Fortunately, my new brother-in-law John was pretty good at repairing electrical devices. He advised my mother to keep the oven temperature setting below 220 degrees to keep from burning up another element. The tip worked.

Mom and I agreed: come hell or high water, we were going to find a decent place to rent that spring. We weren't going to spend another winter at #2 Schoolhouse Lane.

Punks and Delinquency

As far back as I could remember, and a little further than that, from about 1940 through 1964, our family had always been dependent on one state social welfare agency or another. Virginia and West Virginia had usually performed their duties. In June 1964, the Delaware Department of Welfare assumed the burden. But change was a-comin'.

From the early to mid-1960s, states had added social service programs and work incentives to the Aid to Families with Dependent Children (AFDC) program. The measures were designed to address increasing rates of illegitimacy, juvenile delinquency, desertion, and unemployment. Eligibility was restricted to poor families—basically, single women with children in school and under the age of eighteen. People like us. Congress was also evaluating the prospects (as well as the ethics) of putting AFDC mothers to work instead of allowing them to stay at home with their children—a view that conflicted with the widely-held belief that mothers should stay at home and attend to the well-being of their children, a belief that I shared.

Four years earlier, soon after we moved to Newport and about the time David entered first grade, Mom had successfully battled the authorities for the right to remain on the AFDC rolls and to stay at home with her children. But now, in February, the system as we knew it had changed. Since she was in good health and had only four dependent school age children, she couldn't make a good enough case for staying home and serving as a homemaker. The state now declared that, except for the summer months, Mom would have to work in order to earn benefits, and the state had a job lined up for her.

So, in February, at the ripe age of forty-six, Mom reported to her very first job—outside the house, that is. Her work hours were from 8:00 a.m. to 1:00 or 4:00 p.m., and the days varied. The workers' chartered school bus usually picked her up at 7:00 a.m. and sometimes didn't drop her off until five or six o'clock in the evening, when she'd walk the four blocks to our house. She was awful tired, but she didn't complain. After all, her workplace had air conditioning and was totally climate controlled. She and a group of mostly black women spent the hours picking mushrooms in the darkened mushroom houses scattered about Hockessin, Delaware and Avondale, Pennsylvania.

Mom didn't seem to mind. She went about her "assignment" with a rare grace and dignity. She said she had collected from the state long enough, and it was time to pay back (through taxes) a small part of what she had collected for so many years. She did this despite having serious reservations about leaving her children alone after school without responsible adult supervision. I hated arriving home from school and wrestling practice and not seeing Mom there doing all the usual chores children so often take for granted—cooking our dinner, dusting and cleaning the house, ironing, mending, and washing our clothes and linens. I didn't think that was fair, especially since some of that work and responsibility shifted to me (a cocky teenage athlete—in love) and to the weekends, along with most of the grocery shopping.

Late February marked the end of the regular wrestling season, and I had won over eighty percent of my junior varsity matches. That made it a good year, although I don't recall wrestling any varsity matches. During the first week of March, Coach Baker hosted several wrestlers from other district high schools for four days of practice.

Most of those invited had earned the right to attend the Delaware State Wrestling Tournament. They were "going to the States," as we put it. Several other junior varsity wrestlers and I were asked to attend this series of after-school practice sessions. The coach thought it would be good experience for his grapplers to work out with some fresh meat, so to speak.

During our round-robin practice sessions I sparred with Blake, a heavier wrestler from another school. I had not seen him wrestle. Although Blake was twenty pounds heavier than me, his coach had determined that he needed more practice against a speedier opponent. That would be an understatement; I repeatedly outmaneuvered Blake and could sense his growing frustration.

Around the fifteen-minute mark he began cursing. Another minute or two of riding time and I had aggravated him enough. He really lost his temper. I had never seen a practice partner get so angry. He shouted, cursed, and thrashed about. Just when I was about to let him up, he slammed his elbow into my jaw—a foul, nasty move, and strictly forbidden. I saw a tiny white object fly onto the mat. *What the heck was that?* Blake stood up, looked down at me, and said, "I told you to let me up."

With my next breath I felt a sharp, piercing pain. When I inhaled deeply through my mouth, the air touched the exposed nerve of my broken tooth. I grimaced in pain, placing my hand over my mouth. When the coach saw me retrieve the other half of my front tooth, he finally realized the two of us were having an issue.

"What's the matter, Tom," he asked, "did you lose something?"

I had to be careful how I talked, or else feel the pain. "It'th my toof, coach. Blake chippth my toof with hith elbow."

Blake said, "I'm sorry, coach. It was an accident. I told him to let me up, but he wouldn't listen."

Accident! That was a revelation to me. Maybe he did tell me to let him up, but I couldn't understand him with all his grunting and cursing. The coach looked disgusted when he saw my chipped tooth; he knew school insurance would have to pay for it. "For crying out loud, Blake," he said, "you should be apologizing to Tom, not me."

"I'm sorry, Tom."

"Yeah. Sure."

I took a quick shower and Mr. Baker drove me to a dentist in the Richardson Park area. Dr. Bloomquist immediately went to work and glued a temporary cap over the stub. That would have to suffice, at least for a few months until my jawbones stopped growing. I made an appointment for December 12 to begin preparations for the permanent crown. That was 10.5 months of jawbone growth and 10.5 months of wearing the temporary cap. I began to worry about losing the cap, or worse, swallowing it.

Mom said, "That's an awful spiteful thing for that young man to do." But we were comforted knowing that school insurance would pay for most of the dental work. Welfare would pay the rest. Until that day, my teeth had been near perfect.

I did not return for the remainder of Baker's practice sessions. Even with Blake's sorry-ass apology, I remained disgusted by his behavior. In four years of wrestling I had never seen such callousness from a fellow wrestler.

When my teammates heard about my chipped tooth, the smart ones rushed to sporting goods stores to be fitted with mouth guards. But mouth guards remained optional and less than a third of the wrestlers opted to wear them. I always wore mine—lesson learned.

* * * * *

Debbie and Gary were spending way too much time at their friend's houses and running about the streets of Richardson Park, when they should have been at home eating dinner and studying. Their grades were suffering too, forcing Mom to start restricting their movements. By April, David and I had begun reporting Debbie's activities to Mom. At age thirteen, my little sister wanted all the privileges of an eighteen-year-old. Mom said, "Tommy, I want you to look after your brothers and sister while I'm at work. Make sure they stay near the house. I don't want them running around the neighborhood after they get home from school."

"But Mom, they won't listen to me."

"They'd better. If they don't, take your belt to them."

My mother couldn't help herself. She had been born and raised in an era and a region (southern Appalachia) where spanking was all too common. When someone grew too big for their britches (or a hand spanking), a switch or belt would do. Her way of using pain to foster discipline had worked for decades. Why shouldn't it work now?

Well, times were a-changin'. More and more people saw corporal punishment as counterproductive, and that it did more harm than good. However, many, if not the majority of parents, still approved of limited physical punishment of children in the home and paddling in the schools. High school assistant principals, like our Mr. Hinnersheetz at Conrad, were notorious for paddling boys, and I'd seen him do it at least once.

At 17 I didn't like being responsible for my siblings, and I cringed at the thought of having to use a belt on them. But I also knew that someone had to be head of the household when Mom was away and working. She had heard about the punks, the street gangs, and the drug use, and she wanted to protect her youngest three, especially her budding young daughter. Clearly, she placed a great deal of trust in me.

Mom didn't normally harvest mushrooms on weekends, but one Saturday in April she did. The four of us spent the entire morning watching cartoons. By noon we were all feeling a bit cooped up.

"I'm bored," Debbie said, "I'm going over to Nyla's house."

I said, "No you're not."

Debbie and Gary, to a lesser extent, were beginning to behave strangely, acting as if they had only one thing on their minds, as if a force was pulling them into the streets and parks, draining any trace of obedience from them.

"Tommy, you can't watch me all day. Sooner or later I'm leaving this house. I'm going crazy staying here."

"Debbie, I don't like this any more than you. If you try to leave, you'll get a taste of my belt."

"Tommy," Gary shouted, "you're not our father! If you hit us, we'll call the police!"

"Until you're both eighteen you'll do what Mom says, or you won't be living here anymore. You'll be sent to the reform school."

David had been sitting quietly in the corner sofa chair. "Would you guys stop arguing? I can't hear the TV."

"Okay," I said, opening the front door, "you can go as far as the driveway and yard—and no farther."

From the front porch, I looked over the neighborhood and noticed a couple of small kids playing ball in a yard. Gary and Debbie stepped onto the porch beside me. "See," Debbie said, as she stepped down into the driveway, "there's nothing to do."

"Hey," I said, "we can play catch with my ball and gloves."

"Nah—that's boring," she says.

"Okay, then how about we all go down to the church and shoot some hoops?"

Debbie said, "Why can't I do something I want to do?"

"Like what?" Gary asks.

I looked on as she nonchalantly baby-stepped her way down the driveway. *How much rope should I give her? Will she run, or is she playing a game?*

Gary kept his eye on her, too. "She's gonna run, Tommy," he said. "How much ya wanna bet, she's gonna run?"

Debbie had just morphed into a little girl. She twirled around in circles, humming some childish tune as she crossed "the line" onto Schoolhouse Lane. I took off after her. Gary thought it was funny when Debbie started running, too. I heard him laughing. "I told ya she was gonna run!"

I caught up to her four blocks away. We were both surprised; she didn't think I would be able to catch her with such a head start, and I didn't think she could run so fast. I dragged her back to the house kicking and screaming. I pulled off my belt and smacked her two or three times on the behind. Debbie screamed and cursed at me. Guilt quickly set in. *Dammit! This parenting thing is tough!*

I felt so bad about what I had done that I said, "If you want to leave, go on. I'm not chasing you anymore. If you want to ruin your life, go ahead. Mom will deal with you when she gets home."

I was oh-so-angry my sister had forced my hand. I walked into the bathroom and washed off the sweat. When I returned to the living room, David said, "Debbie's gone. I saw her jump the fence and run around the block."

"That's alright. Mom will fix her when she gets home."

Debbie walked through the front door right at sunset. Mom was there waiting for her. Maybe Debbie thought that as long as she returned home before dark Mom wouldn't mind. But she did mind. She gave Debbie a nasty belting and warned her to never do it again.

Monday morning, before school, Mom gave us the same standing orders: "Stay near the house when you get home from school. No roaming the neighborhood." She put me in charge of the belt and told the children they were to do as I said. David and Gary ate their Cheerios and milk, and I wolfed down a big bowl of Raisin Bran, one of my favorites. Debbie said she wasn't hungry, which only irritated me. I thought she wasn't eating enough and looked too skinny. Then she started complaining that her clothes were hurting her. They were too tight and rubbing against the raised welts on her skin, a result of Mom's belting.

"I don't want to go to school," she said. "I don't like these clothes, they're uncomfortable."

"That's no excuse. You have to go to school," I said. "You can't stay at home by yourself."

Gary and David were already on their way to school when Debbie started her crying game. She just sat there on the sofa. I couldn't get her to leave the house.

"Let's go!" I demanded, dropping her books into her lap. "You're gonna make both of us late."

"No! I don't feel good, and you can't make me go."

I wondered: *Is she really sick or is she playing a game? Does she want to stay home and roam the streets with one of her friends? Maybe she is sick. Yeah, sick like a fox.*

"Debbie, if you don't get up and get your ass to school, I'm gonna take my belt to your behind again."

Debbie puffed up her chest, looked me square in the eye, and said, "Yeah, and it'll be child abuse, too. They'll lock you up in jail—like our dad."

Frustrated and not knowing what else to do, I unbuckled and pulled out my belt, folded it, and proceeded to smack her three or four times about her behind and upper legs—hard. She settled back onto the sofa cursing me and crying her eyeballs out.

"Let's go," I said, pointing toward the front door, "or I'll do it again."

Debbie rose from the sofa, gathered her books, and walked out the door. I followed her, relieved that I didn't have to belt her again. We hardly spoke a word all the way to Richardson Park School. I watched from across the street as she disappeared inside. Then I continued on, making a right on Boxwood Road and walking the quarter-mile to Conrad.

Mom looked haggard when she got home that evening, and it certainly didn't take any weight off when I told her what Debbie forced me to do. Even worse, Debbie hadn't come home yet. "I don't know what to do with that girl," she sighed.

Debbie made a series of decisions that day that put her and the family on an emotional and nerve-wracking course, one that would affect all of us in a big way.

I joined Mom in the kitchen and took a seat at the table near her. It was a little before dark. We were discussing the merits of giving Debbie another whipping. "Oh, Mom," I said, "please don't whip her again. It won't do any good. And don't even think about asking me to do it anymore, because I won't. If I thought it would help, maybe I would. It's just not worth it, Mom."

Looking up, I saw the frustration in her eyes: like a dam ready to burst. Yet somehow she held the tears at bay. The pain I had felt, I know she had felt a hundred fold.

"Hey Mom," David shouted from the living room, "there's a police car in the driveway!"

Mom and I rushed to the front door. We didn't give the officer time to knock. We opened the door and Mom greeted him as he walked up the porch steps.

"Is everything okay, officer?"

"Are you Mrs. Dixon?"

"Yes."

"Are you the mother of a thirteen-year-old…ah…Deborah Sue Dixon?"

"Yes. She hasn't come home yet. Is she alright?"

"As well as can be expected, ma'am. She's in the hands of Social Services now. They'll be looking after her for a while." The officer looked my way. "Is this your son, Tommy?"

"Yes."

"Did he hit your daughter with a belt this morning?"

"Yes he did. I gave him permission to punish her if she didn't behave."

The officer handed Mom an envelope. "Mrs. Dixon, this is a summons for you to appear before the judge in Family Court next week. All you need to know is stated in the papers." The officer turned and looked me directly in the eye. "Young man, you're lucky I'm not taking you with me." My blood pressure surged and my face turned red. I swallowed hard and turned away from his penetrating stare. Tipping his hat, he said, "Good day, ma'am," and returned to his car.

As we walked back into the house, I said, "See Mom, I just knew hitting Debbie was gonna cause trouble."

The following week, Debbie and Mom went before the judge in Juvenile Court in Wilmington. Debbie told the judge that she didn't want to live with Mom anymore. Mom told the judge that Debbie was uncontrollable and wouldn't mind her. She said, "Whippings don't work, so what else can I do? I just can't control her anymore. The girl has a mind of her own."

"How long have you been having problems with your daughter, Mrs. Dixon?"

"For several months now, your honor. Since she started school last fall, and especially since I started working two months ago."

"Have you tried sitting down with her and having a good talk?"

"Of course I've tried talking to her. Talking doesn't do any good. That's why I use a belt or switch. She's too big for hand spanking."

"Mrs. Dixon, although the law says you can physically punish your child, I'm letting you know this court does not approve of it."

"Then you take her, your honor. You can have her."

"Now, now hold on there, Mrs. Dixon. Let's not let our emotions cause us to do or say something we'll feel sorry for down the road." The judge hesitated, trying to gather his thoughts. "Would you be open to some type of in-home counseling by the state, or maybe counseling at her school?"

"No, that won't do. She won't even go to school. Debbie has made it clear she doesn't want to live with me and abide by my rules, so I'm giving her up. I'm washing my hands of her."

Debbie's mental outlook had compelled the court to take control of her that day. Mom's disposition also affected the decision. She had already raised six children. None of them had been so disrespectful at such a young age. Mom was very hurt and embarrassed by all the trouble her daughter had caused. Debbie had dragged her mother into family court and almost had me arrested. There would have to be a big change in her behavior and attitude before Mom would allow her to come home. Mom also thought Debbie's reckless behavior would eventually result in an unplanned pregnancy, like what happened to her sister nearly five years earlier. Our mother never wanted to be trapped on welfare, and she most certainly didn't want her young daughter to fall into the same trap.

No one should assume that the family didn't care or wasn't upset. We all cared. We were all upset. The family loved Debbie and wanted the best for her. At the same time, we felt sorry for her. We just couldn't understand such irate disobedience. She was only thirteen, too young to play hooky, to run about the neighborhood at will, and to do as she pleased.

Indeed, it seemed to me that my mother had made the correct decision. Debbie had been given many chances to cease her rebellious behavior. Everyone, from me on up to the oldest, knew that without proper obedience there would be no order in the family, only chaos. Mom gave life and thirteen years of comfort to my sister; now she was sucking the life out of her mother. That's what hurt me (and many of my siblings) the most.

What about apologies? Was there any remorse? At least I apologized to my mother for taking the switch from her and breaking it into pieces. But Debbie offered no apologies and expressed no regret for her behavior. Until she reached that point, there was little chance Mom would forgive her.

As it was, Debbie had not gone to school the morning I struck her with the belt. After I watched her enter the school, she went to her classroom, dropped her books onto her desk, and immediately left the building. For nearly three hours she wandered through Banning Park, swinging on the swing sets, trying to decide what to do. When she came to the pond by the railroad, she crossed the tracks and followed the dirt access road that led to Water Street in Newport. There she waited until she met her girlfriend and previous neighbor, Janet Freeman, walking home for lunch. Seeing the belt marks Mom and I had left on Debbie's arms and legs, compelled Janet's mother to call Social Services. The police arrived and escorted Debbie to the Bridge House, a home in Wilmington for troubled boys and girls. She remained there until the end of the school year and then transferred to the Woods Haven School for girls with serious behavioral problems. In August she was reevaluated and moved to the less restrictive

Governor Bacon Center in Delaware City, where staff members would focus on discipline issues and her education.

Sometimes it's a long road to understanding. I know that now. But Debbie would be on that road longer than most. Going to school, studying, obeying the rules, and living a calm and respectful life at home with her family would have been the better road. Debbie didn't see that then, but she knows it now.

* * * * *

For almost a year I had managed to avoid and ignore certain punks from the neighborhood gangs. That streak was about to end.

Two or three times each week, after I came home from school, Mom would ask me to search the neighborhood for Gary. Pretty soon his times away from home grew longer and longer, and his absence was also beginning to have a negative effect on the family. He knew his mother wanted him home before dinner, around five o'clock. When Mom would ask where he'd been all day, he would always have a canned answer ready: "I was over at Eddie's house" or "I was playing ball at the park with Cecil and some other boys." Mom didn't have an issue with young David; he stayed close to home, and so did I. That is, when I wasn't four blocks down the street shooting hoops in the church parking lot or down the road in Newport visiting Deanna. But now Gary, like Debbie, was causing concern. Were it not for my younger brother's poor grades, I'm sure Mom would have been more lenient.

One day, while combing the streets looking for Gary, I came across two young girls and asked them if they'd seen him. They said they'd seen him and another boy walking into a wooded area of the park, each carrying a crumpled brown paper bag in his hand.

Oh no! He's drinking. He's becoming an alcoholic.

I didn't find Gary that day, but a day or two later I found him and his secret hiding place. He had broken free from Mom while she was attempting to give him a whipping for not returning home in time for dinner. Knowing it would be dark soon, I went searching for him with a flashlight in hand. I found the cabin, a small wooden shack no bigger than a large truck bed, only 200 feet inside the park. Hearing voices from within, I banged on the plywood siding with a stick. "Hey, it's Dixon," I shouted, "is my brother Gary in there?"

A peculiar voice said, "Yeah, he's here. Come on in."

I lifted the small flap of carpet that constituted a door and peeked into the dimly lit space. I could barely make out the faces of two young girls huddled together in one corner. I thought about turning on my light, but reconsidered when I recognized a familiar face from the past. "Hey," I said, crawling through the small opening, "what's going on?"

One girl said, "We're having a party."

I took a seat inside the door and waited for my eyes to adjust to the poor light. I smelled something and recognized it right away. On the way over I had a vision of underage punks drinking alcohol, but this was totally unexpected. I smelled the odor of plastic model glue.

My eyes had adjusted to the dim light, and I didn't have to turn on my flashlight to see my brother huddled against the back corner of the shack. Across from him sat Larry, a punk from my earlier days at Krebs Junior High. Imagine my surprise.

"Hey, Dixon," he said, "whut-chu been up to? I haven't seen you for over a year."

"I'm going to Conrad."

He said he was attending one of the local trade schools. Then he grabbed the wrinkled paper bag they were passing around and, burying his face in it, started huffing and puffing. I had heard rumors that kids in the neighborhood were huffing glue like that to get high. Now I had a front row seat. *Disgusting!* Then, flaunting his orneriness, Gary took the bag from Larry and began to inhale the toxic vapors himself—right in front of me. *The glue has gone to Gary's brain. He's daring me to say or do something. Wait a minute, I think I'm starting to get a buzz myself.* One girl said, "Don't forget us," and held out her hand for the bag, which Gary delivered with a dreamy smile.

Shining my light at Gary, I said, "I think it's time for us to go home, Gary." He didn't answer me. So I repeated myself. Then I reached out and grabbed his arm.

"Easy there, Dixon," Larry said, poking a hard object into my rib cage. I heard a clicking sound and froze. Looking down I saw an object, something shiny. Larry had just opened a switchblade. "Gary, are you ready to go home with your brother?" he asked. Gary and I looked at Larry and the five-inch knife blade poised near my ribs. "Yeah, you can put it away, Larry," Gary said, "I'm going home. It's almost dark anyway." I backed slowly away from Larry.

Gary joined me outside and we started walking home. I was furious about what had just happened. We stumbled out of the woods into the faint light of the streets. "Huffing glue!" I shouted. "Don't you know that stuff will rot your brain?" Gary wasn't talking. "Gary, do you have any idea what you're doing?"

"Whatever I want to," he said, "and you and Mom can't do anything about it."

"Well, we'll see about that."

That night I told Mom all about my brief sojourn into the woods. She became very emotional. "Gary, do you want to be put into the reform school, like Debbie? Is that what you want?"

"If you do, I'll run away."

I knew Mom felt helpless. For years, whippings and threats had worked pretty well with her older children, but they weren't working with Gary any more than they did with his sister. I, too, remained confused about my younger siblings' attitude and behavior. This disrespectful and delinquent behavior was unlike anything the family had ever experienced. Mom had tried talking to Gary, but he had perfected the art of tuning out.

That night, for the first time, I heard one of my siblings threaten their mother. Gary said, "Mom, if you hit me again, I'm going to call the police and have you locked up for child abuse." Fear gnawed at my mother: Gary, two years older, was beginning to hum along with Debbie's tune. She had tried to discipline Gary once that day, so she decided to wait and hope that it wouldn't happen again.

Could the glue be affecting Gary's behavior? Or was huffing glue a result of Gary's behavior? I was stumped.

This wasn't the first time that punk Larry and I had banged heads. A year earlier, a bunch of us were walking the Krebs outdoor breezeway, having left Mr. Humphrey's music class, when Larry and Mike, another punk, shoved me hard from behind. Why? I didn't know then and I still don't know for sure. Maybe they saw me as king of the hill or something, and wanted to dethrone me. I'd compare it to the anonymous gunfighter riding into Dodge City, seeking fame by gunning down the reigning fast draw.

The palms of my hands took the full force of my weight as I fell to the asphalt, almost ramming my head into a brick wall. Before I could get to my feet both of them were on top of me, threatening to beat me up. Then, just as quickly, they turned me loose and stood up.

Larry said, "Come on, Dixon!"

I jumped to my feet, thinking of tearing into him, until I saw Mr. Humphrey approaching. "What are you boys doing?" he shouted.

Mike said, "Nothing."

Gary, 15, and Debbie, 13, by the driveway of #2 Schoolhouse Lane.

Larry said, "We didn't do a thing, Teach."

Mr. Humphrey said, "Tom, what happened here?"

"It's nothing, Mr. Humphrey. I just tripped and fell."

Mr. Humphrey was aware of Mike and Larry's reputation as troublemakers. My favorite music teacher had had several run-ins himself with these two characters. He told the three of us to hurry along before we were late for our next class. "I'm keeping an eye on you boys," he added, "and if I catch you screwing up—even once—I'll do my best to see to it that you don't graduate." I assumed he meant them and not me. Again, I wanted to retaliate, but the flames from my fight with Mitch had barely died, so I let the incident slide. I didn't want to get into trouble and maybe not graduate.

However, Larry's pulling a knife on me had really ticked me off. So much so that I told Gary to tell Larry I was "looking for him." It didn't take long. The next day, a Saturday, Gary said, "Tommy, Larry's down at the cabin, swinging. He told me to tell you to come on down."

Gary and I marched down to the cabin, where I confronted Larry. As we approached each other, I scanned his hands and pockets for knives. Seeing none, I said, "You're a punk, and you deserve to get your ass kicked."

"Show me what you got, Dixon."

Larry and I circled each other, looking for an opening. I threw a jab at his face and ducked under his guard, going for my usual wrestling takedown. Larry fell backward, pulling me down on top of him. We rolled around on the ground until I had him pinned against the trunk of a large beech tree. *He's quicker and stronger than I thought.* But just as I was about to pummel him, I saw the knife in his hand, resting near my throat. I froze.

Where the hell did the knife come from? Did someone hand him one?

"It's over, Dixon," he said. "Are you going to leave me alone, or do I have to stick you?"

"I guess I'll leave you alone," I said, releasing my grip from his neck and standing up.

Larry climbed to his feet and faced me, his knife still drawn. Brushing the dirt from my clothes, I backed farther away.

"Larry, you're about the biggest chicken I know. You can't do anything unless you have a knife, and you know I'd kick your ass without it."

Larry just smiled.

"That knife is going to get you into real trouble one of these days. When you're ready to grow up and fight like a man and not a coward, let me know." I turned slowly and walked away, looking back every few seconds to guard my back.

Walking into the house, I said, "Hey, Mom, what's for lunch?"

"We have some bananas over there, Tommy. You can have a peanut butter and banana sandwich. Or you can have peanut butter and jelly. Help yourself—you're not helpless."

I didn't have much time to think about what just happened. I had barely consumed my peanut butter and jelly sandwich when Gary barged into the house. "Hey, Tommy," he whispered, so that Mom wouldn't hear, "all of us guys down at the swing were ribbing Larry about what you said. You know, about him being a coward and always pulling knives on people."

"Yeah? So?"

"Well, Larry wants to fight you again, and he said he don't need no knife to kick your ass. Look!" he said, pointing through the window to the driveway. "See. He's out there now, waitin' for ya."

"Shit, Gary," I said, jumping from the sofa. Peeking out the window, I said, "Why did you bring him here?"

"I didn't bring him. He followed me."

I flew out the door onto the front porch ahead of my brother, and approached Larry and one of his buddies standing in the dirt and gravel driveway. My hope now was to dispatch this ball of scum real quick, before Mom got wind of it. Larry and I went at it. In less than fifteen seconds I had him down again, pounding my fists into his face, trying to finish what I'd started earlier. My heart beat so fast, and my adrenaline surging so high that I barely felt his buddy's fists pounding on the back of my head. I managed a glance at Gary, standing less than eight feet away doing nothing. *Who the hell is he rooting for, anyway?*

"Gary," I screamed, "get him off!"

Ten seconds and three or four punches later, Gary yelled, "Tommy, look out!"

I stood up and turned my head in time to see a large chunk of brick headed for my face. Instinctively I turned away, tucked my chin into my chest, and deflected the brick. It glanced off my shoulder instead of my head, but boy did it hurt! I didn't have much time to think about the pain. Mom stood on the porch yelling at us, and Larry's buddy was preparing to throw another brick.

"You better put that thing down, young man! I called the police and they're gonna be here any minute!"

I stepped farther away from Larry as he staggered to his feet. Gary and I squared off in the middle of the driveway. Mom standing on the porch steps to our left and the punks on our right.

Mom had lied. I knew the cops weren't coming because we didn't have a telephone. But the punks didn't know that.

His friend dropped the brick and they both retreated down the lane, Larry nursing a busted lip and wiping a bloody nose. *I hope he has a black eye tomorrow. He's sooo deserving.*

Mom said, "You boys get in the house and clean up. Tommy, I want to know what all that fightin' was about." As Gary and I climbed the porch steps, I said, "Some brother you are. You're supposed to be watching my back."

"I pulled him off your back when you told me to. That's when he picked up the brick. And I warned you about that too, didn't I?"

Yeah, considering it may have been Gary's first fight, I guess he did okay at protecting his older brother. I gained great satisfaction by finally getting even with Larry for all his threats and bullying, and I didn't have to worry about getting suspended from school. I never saw or heard from Larry after that. Chances are his knife really did get him into trouble. Street fighting is one thing; but when you bring a knife or gun to a fight, nobody wins. Sooner or later, just brandishing a weapon won't be enough.

Whatever his reasoning that day, I'm glad—and lucky—Larry was man enough not to brandish his knife again. Otherwise, the fight could have had a tragic ending.

Mom scolded both her sons that night. She really didn't approve of us fighting, no matter who started it. She said, "Tommy, you've got to learn how to walk away from those kinds of people."

"You're right, Mom. I'll try harder next time, I promise."

"You'd better."

* * * * *

Not only did Gary refuse to stay home, as Mom had demanded, he had also been playing hooky. He thought it was cool to bag school, and hang out in the parks and woods with his little group of punks. The school administration, having reported Gary as truant multiple times that spring, called Mom into the principal's office, causing her to miss a day of work. She threw up her hands. "Gary's worse than his sister. I can't deal with this anymore."

The principal said, "Well then, what do you want us to do?"

"Turn him over to the state. Maybe then he'll learn to behave."

Social Services located Gary and escorted him to the Bridgehouse, a detention center for runaways. He escaped before the sun set that night. The police collared him again the following day and signed him into the Ferris School for wayward boys. After three days there he walked off the premises, becoming a "wanted" young man. Gary returned to the house and confronted his mother. "Mom, I'm not staying at those places. They can't make me. I'll run away every time."

"Gary, you can sleep here tonight, but tomorrow you gotta go back. I can't allow you to stay here if you're not going to behave and go to school."

Gary was tired from being on the lam and slept well that night. Maybe too well. Early the following morning two policemen came knocking, and before Gary knew what was happening Mom let them in. Wearing only his underwear, he made a mad dash for the open kitchen window. Yes, my little brother boldly wanted to dive through the kitchen window, near naked, to make his escape. But escape to where?

Gary didn't know it, but the police had plenty of practice hunting down and capturing juveniles. The second officer, waiting in the kitchen, tackled Gary before he could pull off another daring escape. Collared once again, the police drove him to the station wearing only his underwear. All the cops laughed at him, near naked and handcuffed to a bench. Gary had never experienced such humiliation.

"This ain't fair," Gary cried, "you could've let me get dressed!"

One cop chuckled, saying, "Maybe this'll teach you a lesson."

They booked Gary and placed him into a maximum security home for boys in Claymont, Delaware. He would remain there until his hearing.

The family wasn't surprised at all by Gary's predicament. It did, however, cause considerable consternation. Mom couldn't deal with it anymore. One daughter out of control was bad enough; having a son become utterly uncontrollable finally cracked her velvety smooth veneer.

At first we were all baffled as to why Debbie and Gary were so rebellious and unmanageable. With time, we began to suspect the environment as the problem—the desire to fit in and be part of something greater than one's self. Gangs, punks, friends, and cliques were hip and fun. Family and school required work and commitment.

At his sentencing, Gary found himself sitting in court with Mom, Ronnie, Paul, Ginny, and her husband Charles. Up front were the judge and maybe a prosecutor. Mom told the judge all about Gary—disobedient, failing in school, hanging out with unsavory characters, and doing drugs. She made it clear that she had two well-behaved boys at home who were studying hard and making "decent" grades. David and I were trusted to be at home alone, and that was important, considering Mom's job and work schedule. Mom was becoming afraid of Gary, too. She couldn't trust him, or keep him at home and out of mischief. She also considered him a bad influence on David.

The judge seemed to understand. "What about the boy's father," he asked. "Would he be interested in taking custody of his son?" Believe it or not, Mom didn't think that to be much of an option.

"Young man, you now have a choice," the judge said. "Go and stay with your father in Virginia, or I'm going to put you in a jail cell made of concrete and steel where you can't escape until you're 18 years old."

The family took a few minutes to huddle and discuss the options. During these discussions, Gary's mind wandered back to all the crap he had heard about his father: the drunken rages, the beating of his mother, the shootings, and the attacks upon many of his siblings—all valid reasons for leaving our father back in the spring of 1964. Ronnie, Ginny, and Charles encouraged Gary to stay with his father. They reasoned that after a year with "that" man, he would be begging Mom to take him back. Only Paul disagreed. He said, "Gary, you might be better off in jail."

Three days later, and with Dad's approval, Ginny and Charles drove Gary to Boissevain, Virginia, and placed him in the hands of his father. That was near the end of May. By Labor Day, Gary had registered to begin the ninth grade at Pocahontas High School in Pocahontas, Virginia. Family members were placing bets on how long Gary would last with his father. I didn't bet, but I didn't think it would be too long before something messy hit the fan.

* * * * *

Bud flew in from Massachusetts. He and Bob, from the State Hospital, had stopped by our house to see me and meet the family. Mom was aware of the two men and the keen interest they had taken in me, and she also knew that I had been keeping in touch with them by phone. They wanted to take me to a Broadway show or play in New York City—my first. Just when many kids my age and a little older were turning away from cultural activities and becoming part of the Hippie Generation, these two men wanted to expose me to some worthy culture. Mom left it up to me. I was seventeen, and she couldn't see any reason for hindering my opportunities for refinement. She probably thought it was something long overdue in the family.

That spring launched the beginning of my mini-cultural evolution, a time when I found myself spending less time with my school buddies. For the most part, I enjoyed what little time I had with my scattering of friends. Yet, I was finding our bull-shitting sessions less and less stimulating. Cars, girls, and sex were still interesting subjects, but a steady diet of dirty jokes and degrading wisecracks was getting old. I had too much respect for women to continue wallowing in that stuff.

Instead, I began focusing on my homework, studying for my finals, shooting hoops with the guys down the street, and enjoying one or two visits with Deanna each week. Studying, homework, and the lack of cash and wheels limited our time together. Walks through the parks and local housing developments, and sharing television time and an occasional dinner with her family, became a pleasurable routine. So did our passionate late night make-out sessions. Deanna and I even shared a double date with Paul and Linda at the Pleasant Hills Drive-In. *Planet of the Apes*, with Charlton Heston, was playing. By that time Deanna had accepted my ring and we were officially going steady.

Before the summer ended, I had experienced: 1) the hustle and bustle of New York City, its subways, and taxis, 2) my first opera, 3) my first Broadway play, 4) the Philadelphia Art Museum, and 5) another show in Philadelphia. And there were at least two more movies in there somewhere, *Dr. Zhivago* and *The Graduate*.

* * * * *

Bob pulled his Chevy Corvair into the driveway around midnight to drop me off. We had just enjoyed one of those special performances and I was a bit tired from it all. As an athlete, and wrestler, I had always been an energetic and on-the-go young man, thinking I could handle anything. However, I never could have imagined that sitting near motionless through a two-hour performance while being suffocated by a coat and tie, and then having to sit still for another hour on the drive home, could be so exhausting. Anxious to hit the sack, I thanked my friend, said goodnight, and was about to exit the car. "Oh Tom," he said, handing me a brown paper bag, "don't forget your treatment."

With a puzzled look, I reached into the bag and retrieved a box. "What's this?" I asked. Bob smiled, waiting for my reaction. Looking closer, I saw a box of soap. Written on it were the words "Fostex, cake" and "acne skin cleanser." Bob had noticed my acne getting worse and was concerned it might be affecting my self-esteem. "Where did you get it?"

"The drugstore."

"Thanks. Did you need a prescription?"

"No, no. It's over-the-counter stuff and it's not expensive. It worked for me once. I think you should try it for a while and see if it helps. If it doesn't, you might want to consider a dermatologist."

I began washing my face with Fostex that night. It became a ritual: once in the morning, once at night, and once around noon on the weekends, whenever possible. I had high hopes for Fostex (and my complexion).

* * * * *

It was official: Donna had become the first of nine siblings to graduate from high school. She had completed two years at Krebs Junior High along with the three years at Conrad High. In spite of all this education and city schooling, she had retained her southern accent. But I had a theory about accents, and I wanted to try it out on my big sister.

The family threw a little party at her home and I approached her in the basement family room, where several lively conversations were taking place and some alcoholic spirits were flowing.

"Donna, how come you still have an accent? The rest of us don't."

"I don't know. Tommy, if you didn't remind me—as you so often do—I wouldn't even know I had one."

"That's right. Donna, if you're ever going to lose your accent, you'll have to want to lose it."

"I don't care, Tommy!" she shouted. "It doesn't bother me that I have an accent!"

"See," I answered, "that's called stubbornness! That's why you talk the way you do, Donna." To ease her agitation, I reached out to her. "Congratulations sis." While giving her a big hug, I said, "That's why I love you like I do."

Donna smiled. "Sure," she said, pushing me away, "now leave me alone."

Summer of '69

Mom and I rode the bus to Wilmington, where she (again) signed me up for the nine-week summer youth job. This time I would be working for about $1.10 per hour. Apparently Mr. Ogle had put in a request for me and he seemed pleased to have me back for more grass cutting. Unfortunately, except for Mr. Ogle, there had been a complete turnover of adult employees in the grounds maintenance section. Gone were Troy, Roman, Hardrock, and Granville. I can't recall the two or three men who had replaced them—no strong personalities, to say the least.

Furthermore, I noticed only one or two familiar faces from the previous summer's Y.O.C. workers. I had an eerie premonition that this summer was going to be anything but boring. I would soon find out that the automatic assignment to My Baby, the Massey Ferguson tractor, wasn't going to pull in many friends either. Yeah, I soon began to detect more than a bit of jealousy and resentment coming from my peers. The group of about twelve black teens seemed to be separating themselves from me and the two other white kids. None of them made an effort to initiate a conversation, and when I'd ask a question or make a comment they'd give me the briefest of responses or no response at all. I assumed they were treating the other white kids the same way.

Are they wondering why the white kid got the cool tractor job? Have they ever socialized with white people? Are they still bitter about the King assassination?

Whatever the reason for their standoffish behavior, I was determined to make the best of the situation by being friendly and taking every opportunity to make a friend or two.

Dr. Bob had moved to another job and a new apartment several miles away. There weren't going to be any more free lunches at the cottage with him or Bud. But it didn't really matter. I still saw Bob twice a month and Bud every couple of months, and I had phone conversations with both of them every other week or so. They were great guys and I felt fortunate to have met them. Flickers of doubt, however, were beginning to permeate my thoughts. *What's the true basis for our friendship? Was it a genuine fatherly or big brother interest they harbored? Or was there more to it?*

I thought back to my junior high gym classes and one student in particular, Persie Mondell. He certainly was different. Everything about Persie—from the way he talked, walked, and balked, to the way he screamed, seemed, and leaned—painted the picture of a young woman trapped inside a young man's body. Persie wasn't hiding anything; he seemed quite comfortable in his own skin. Nevertheless, a few students teased him endlessly. One or two students often brutalized him during gym class—to the point of tears. But not me. Oh, I chuckled at some of his antics, but I didn't poke fun at him. I showed him the respect he deserved.

Yet now, in some strange way, I knew Bob and Bud were also different. Whatever it was, it wasn't so obvious as with Persie. Instead, something unique, something just under the surface, was crying out, trying to break free. I couldn't quite understand it. They were grown men, average looking, and they behaved in a normal enough manner. They were educated, successful, and seemingly comfortable with themselves and the path they had taken.

Whatever their withholdings, I liked them and would continue to see them. Until I found a good reason to think otherwise, I was going to respect them.

* * * * *

On Sunday, July 13, the family received some sad news: our Uncle Burl had died the previous day. Ginny and Charles offered to drive Mom to her brother-in-law's funeral the following week, but Mom wasn't interested. She feared Dad would be there and cause trouble.

Mr. Ogle had a special assignment for me when I arrived at work Monday morning. He told me to gas up the Massey Ferguson tractor and meet him down at the chicken coops by the old farmhouse. I drove down and found him waiting for me in back of the coops. He took a sip of his coffee and, being careful not to spill it, stepped slowly from the truck to the ground. "Tom, shut off the tractor and come take a walk with me. I want to show you your job for the next few days."

I followed him around the perimeter of the chicken coops, the farmhouse, the grain silo, and back to his truck, where he put away his empty coffee cup. He said I should cut all the grass in those areas, but not the grass immediately surrounding the farmhouse. Evidently, a family lived there and they were responsible for that portion. My boss then climbed into the seat of My Baby and started it up. "Come on," he said, "climb up here beside me, and I'll show you what else I want you to do."

I stepped onto the tractor's running board, holding onto the back of the driver's seat and whatever else was available. After revving-up the engine and engaging the mower blades, my boss plunged the tractor into the edge of the thick forest of bamboo that covered nearly eight acres of the lower farmland. Suddenly, grasshoppers were jumping and flying everywhere. Dozens of them landed on the tractor, on me, and on my boss. I began to fidget. "Don't worry about the grasshoppers," he yelled, "they won't hurt you any—unless you accidentally swallow too many and choke to death, ha ha." I found myself tongue-tied, afraid to open my mouth and laugh at his joke.

Since most of the bamboo had grown to more than six feet tall, he positioned the mower deck at the three-foot level. Any lower and the cutting blades would start to stall. Then, after cutting down a small section to three feet, we went back over it again, leaving only four-inch stalks. "So, that's the way you do it, Tom. This will be your job for the next few days. Any questions?"

"No, I don't think so."

"Do you have enough water to last the morning?"

"Sure do."

Mr. Ogle then left, and I soon realized what I'd gotten myself into. The deeper My Baby and I penetrated into the bamboo, the thicker it became, and the dozens of grasshoppers seemed to turn into a plague. Suddenly my skin started to crawl. "Yuk!" I was having weird, itchy sensations in odd places. "Yipes!" In a panic, I cut an exit swath from the field.

"Oh no! Oh no! Oh no!" I yelled before slamming on the brakes and parking the tractor. I jumped to the ground, smacking myself, pulling at my clothes, and examining my pockets and personal spaces for hitchhiking grasshoppers. Once rid of the insect infestation, I decided to spend the rest of the day cutting the grass in other areas. Those grasshoppers had given me the creeps. But I wasn't going to give up on cutting the bamboo. That would be childish and I would disappoint Mr. Ogle. I was determined to return the next day, better equipped for the grasshopper plague.

It was now 11:45, lunchtime by the cheap Timex handed down by one of my brothers. My water jug sat empty and my stomach growled. I cut the power to the mower deck, lifted it two feet off the ground, and headed for The Canteen, a small luncheonette near the main hospital entrance. The gravel road leading from the farm to the hospital grounds ran straight, narrow, and flat. About a half-mile long, it provided the perfect opportunity to run through the tractor's gears and open up the throttle a bit. I saw it as a good way to blow out loose carbon deposits, something I'd often heard my buddies and older brothers talk about. Minutes later, as I approached the three-way intersection near the garage, chapel, and greenhouse, my thoughts drifted away from my driving.

It's nice to have someone like Mr. Ogle trusting me and finding me so responsible. At least up to the grasshopper part. After all, he had left me alone that morning with a full-sized tractor, buried in a large field of bamboo, in the hot sun, and a pretty good distance away from help. If something bad happened to me, I could have crawled to the farmhouse to use the phone. That is, if I were to find someone at home.

My mind snapped back to my driving and I skidded to a halt at the intersection. *Whoa! That was close!* I waved on the car I had almost hit. Once the intersection had cleared, I eased off the brake and released the clutch—a bit too quickly. The tractor screamed as if having a fit, then reared up like a wild stallion and charged into the intersection, its nose high in the air, its rear wheels churning.

White-knuckled, I held onto the steering wheel for life. The only thing that kept the tractor and me from flipping backwards was the mower deck in the rear. I quickly released the throttle at the steering column, something I should have done before stopping. I had just pulled a wheelie, my first, and it had been an accident.

Once I had the tractor under control, I scanned the area for potential witnesses who might report me to Mr. Ogle. Continuing past the greenhouse, I made a right and parked the tractor on the lawn near the canteen. I bought a cold root beer and consumed my brown-bagged lunch inside, where it was cool. After lunch I returned to the job and finished cutting the grass around the farmhouse yard, all the while expecting my boss to tell me that I had forever lost the privilege of operating the Case and Massey Ferguson tractors.

But the next day no one said a word about the young, reckless tractor driver apparently practicing wheelies. I knew I'd been lucky and I'd learned my lesson.

I spent the first hour that morning watching the mechanic remove the mower blades, lubricate the deck, and sharpen and reinstall the blades. Driving down to the farmhouse to finish the job, I wore my cheap Mexican sombrero, a t-shirt under a light colored long-sleeved shirt, and I carried an extra t-shirt, several lengths of string, and a partial roll of toilet paper (for blowing my nose). To keep out the grasshoppers I tied the string around my socks and pant legs, and pulled the extra t-shirt over my head, leaving only my eyes exposed. With the rest of the t-shirt draped over my head, neck, and shoulders, I put on my long-sleeved shirt, making sure all the buttons were buttoned. I tied another piece of string around the shirt at my waist and put on my hat. I started the tractor and engaged the mower blades. Mr. Ogle had said that the bamboo field ran flat and hazard free, so I plunged in and quickly found myself covered with grasshoppers and tiny shards of bamboo. The grasshoppers seemed to be pretty good at dodging the mower blades; I didn't notice any pieces of them lying around. It wasn't a comfortable day, but my preparations helped.

* * * * *

I'm 17, clowning with a friend at #2 Schoolhouse Lane, The Park.

The news that week was all about the upcoming Apollo 11 mission. NASA had planned a Wednesday morning lift-off, followed by a weekend landing on the moon and a return to earth the following week. I watched as much of that event as possible.

A light rain started to drizzle down on Thursday afternoon, shortly after I had finished cutting the entire field of bamboo. With a few minor adjustments to my uniform, I had managed to successfully lock out the pesky grasshoppers. Driving back toward the greenhouse, I noticed that the rest of the gang had quit working and were hanging out near the shrubs in front of the main administration buildings. I could hear them laughing and clowning around as usual. I parked the tractor and walked into the greenhouse.

Proudly I said, “Mr. Ogle, I’m all finished cutting the bamboo at the farmhouse.”

“You are? Well, that was quick. Have you developed a taste for grasshoppers yet?” he asked with a chuckle.

“I didn’t have to,” I said, wrinkling up my nose. “The way I dressed, they weren’t a problem. But I did make sure to keep my mouth shut. You can bet on that.”

“That’s good. Good job, Tom.”

“Thanks.”

“It’s 2:15 now. I was about to come and get you. Those clouds up there tell me we’re not getting any more work done today. You can put the tractor away and join your buddies. They’re out there now, waiting on the bus. It might be here early because of the rain.”

I dashed to the tractor and drove it to the garage, and then hurried over to the administration building and joined the rest of the gang. The rain continued, but only as a light drizzle. I took a seat on one of the open steps, stretched out my legs, and began to watch my inner-city co-workers interact. Two white co-workers, Randy and Jason, joined us and took a seat near me. We immediately started a lively conversation, and I told them about the bamboo, the grasshoppers, and how I had dressed for the part. I noticed some of the crew eavesdropping. They said nothing, but I recall thinking they found my animated presentation just as amusing as the white boys did.

A car pulled up and Randy and Jason climbed in. Watching them drive away, I thought: *That's right; it's been a while since I saw them riding the school bus from Wilmington. Family or friends must be giving them a ride to and from the job.*

The car disappeared and I turned my attention back to my co-workers. Some of them were picking small red berries from one of the shrubs nearby and tossing them at one another. Most were laughing and enjoying the game, but I noticed that one of them, Clarence, wasn't participating. He hadn't picked a single berry, much less tossed one. And, not one person at the table made an effort to include Clarence by tossing a berry his way, in spite of him being the centerpiece.

I saw an opening. This could be my best chance yet to be social. I couldn't let it slip away. On impulse, I pulled a handful of berries from a bush and tossed one, then two, then three Clarence's way. One of the berries bounced off his chest and another caught his shoulder. When he and a few others realized that I was tossing berries, too, everyone stopped and glared at me.

"Don't do that," Clarence mumbled, wrinkling his brow and coldly staring at me. Everyone fell silent. Throwing my hands up, I said, "Oh, okay. I'm sorry. No problem." And I tossed the remaining berries on the ground.

Now my suspicions were confirmed. These co-workers, unlike my co-workers the previous summer, did not want to socialize at all with the white boys. Frankly, I was somewhat shocked by their blatant unfriendliness and snobbery. I turned away from them and proceeded to mind my own business.

The bus arrived ten minutes later and I rode with the crew into Wilmington. No one spoke to me, and I didn't speak to anyone. I walked to Fourth and Market Streets, where I caught the 3:20 Newport bus to Richardson Park.

The next morning was Friday, July 18, and the weatherman had promised rain for most of the afternoon. I told Mom about my co-worker issues and that I might be the only white kid left riding the Y.O.C. bus to work. She said, "We'll check the city bus schedule this weekend and see if there's one that will take you to the hospital."

That morning I again rode the school bus with my antisocial coworkers, headed for the hospital grounds and another day of work. On the way, I began to realize the full extent of my co-workers' attitude. If there happened to be an empty seat next to me, no one would sit in it, and whenever I took a seat beside someone, that person would move. Not right away, but eventually they would move to another seat. I rarely reached my destination with someone sitting beside me.

I had laid the berry incident to rest so I could savor the good news that Mom had given me the night before. Aunt Katherine had driven from Alabama to Virginia and had attended Uncle Burl's funeral that week. She and Cousin Marlene were stopping by to visit us at Schoolhouse Lane, and they were expected to be there by the end of my workday. *Wow!*

A steady drizzle had saturated the ground by the time our bus reached the hospital. I saw one of the Y.O.C. supervisors huddled under his umbrella as the bus pulled up beside him. The driver opened the door, and the supervisor closed the umbrella and stepped into the bus. He told us to stay on the bus; Mr. Ogle was waiting for a call from the main office, and they would let us know if we were working or going home.

The bus, over three-quarters full, waited. With high humidity and little air circulation, many of us were dripping with sweat and feeling most uncomfortable. After a twenty-minute wait, the supervisor took attendance and dismissed us—with pay—for the rest of the day. He said, "Have a good weekend, and I'll see you all Monday morning." Almost everyone cheered when they heard the good news. I just smiled.

When we filed off the bus in Wilmington near Seventh and Pine Streets, I started walking west on Seventh Street, the most direct route to Market Street. The rain fell steadily and I worried about the brown paper bag holding my lunch. *If it gets any wetter, my baloney and cheese sandwich is gonna fall out.* I tucked the bag and sandwich under my left arm and increased my pace. I ran my fingers across the eight-foot chain link fence to my left, noting the parking lot on the other side full of city workers' cars. *There's a bus to Newport every twenty to thirty minutes this time of the day. I should be able to make the 10:30 one headed to Newport. Heck, I might be able to enjoy an extra hour or two of Cousin Marlene's company. Maybe I'll even find time to introduce Deanna to my favorite…*

A sudden darkness came out of nowhere and surrounded me. The sky, the clouds, and the rain—everything—gone. I was alone, in total silence, like a deep sleep, minus the dreams. But wait. The light. It had returned, almost as quickly as it had left. The sounds of the city were returning, too, and a distant voice called out, "Are you alright?" Closer still, "Young man! Are you alright? Can you hear me?"

I opened my eyes ever so slowly, blinking repeatedly to clear my blurred vision. I struggled like a newborn to push myself to a sitting position. My arm and shoulder muscles twitched and convulsed, trying to perform basic moves. I felt nauseous and a numb, tingling sensation scratched at the back of my skull. But then I could see a slightly blurred face, a white, middle-aged man holding me by my shoulders as I sat on the wet sidewalk. I grabbed the chain link fence for more support.

What happened? How'd I get here? Did I stumble or trip over something?

"Can you make it to your feet?" the man asked.

I struggled to stand, trying to maintain my balance. Less than a minute had passed since the sudden darkness. The man shouted toward someone across the street: "Why'd you hit this boy!" I turned my head in the direction of the man's voice. There, in the street, I saw a gang of six or more black teenagers huddled together. They were thirty feet away, cheering the one out in front. I blinked several times, trying to see more clearly. *No!* There was no denying it; the one out in front was Clarence. He shuffled about, dancing, jumping up and down, throwing jabs, hooks, and uppercuts. "Come on! Come on!" he shouted. Finally I knew the reason for the sudden darkness and the sick feeling in my gut. I had been attacked from behind and knocked unconscious.

The Samaritan said to me, "Do you know that boy?"

"Yeah."

"Do you want to go with me to the police station and press charges?"

I couldn't make up my mind. The blow to the back of my head had affected my ability to think. It definitely had taken all the fight out of me. I was dead wood in the ocean. For a fleeting second I considered tackling him, but I knew it would be useless. I looked back at Clarence, then waved the punk away, essentially letting him know that I wasn't going to fight him—not then or there, at least. I thought about the man's offer of pressing charges, and strained my brain in the process: "No sir, I jus…just want to go home."

The man stayed with me as I leaned down and retrieved my lunch. Cursing out loud, I threw my squashed baloney and government surplus cheese sandwich over the chain-link fence and watched it come to rest against a car tire.

"Thanks Mister," I said and offered him a handshake.

"Are you sure you're okay?"

"Yeah, I think so. Good enough to get home."

Clarence and the gang had disappeared into the city. I turned away from the stranger, and headed for Fourth and Market and my bus home. Suddenly wary, I glanced back at the man and the mean streets that surrounded us. He studied me close, evaluating my stability as I hurried out of sight. He truly was a Good Samaritan.

By 2:00 that afternoon the rain had stopped. Sunlight brightened the sky and I sat alone at home on the sofa. Because I had missed the 10:30 bus, it had taken me over an hour to get home. The muscles near the base of my right ear throbbed and my head felt like it had been split open. Since my right jaw ached too, I figured Clarence must have landed two punches before I hit the sidewalk. The two aspirin I'd swallowed an hour earlier weren't helping. I took two more, loaded a plastic bag with ice, wrapped it in a wash cloth, placed it against the back of my head, and lay down on the sofa waiting for Mom.

Around 4:00, Donna pulled into the driveway with Mom, David, and Marlene. My Aunt Katherine wasn't with them. Marlene whisked across the room and gave me a hug. I apologized for my lack of enthusiasm and told her I had a bad headache. With David outside and Mom preparing dinner, the rest of us sat in the living room, catching up on news from the home front and watching the latest Apollo 11 broadcast. After dinner I broke the news about being knocked out. Everyone was shocked. Mom looked bewildered. At first she wanted me to quit the job and stay home. I said, "No, I'm not quitting. That would be exactly what those punks would like me to do." We finished our dinner, and Donna drove Marlene back to where she and her mother were staying. Donna told her husband about my incident, and she called Paul and Ronnie that night, giving them the news.

On Saturday we all got together and John offered to take me to the hospital emergency room for some tests. He said I might have a concussion. It seemed unnecessary and I refused to go. Eventually we decided that John would drive me to the Y.O.C. office on Monday morning and the two of us would lodge a formal complaint. Paul and Ronnie had to work, and they were also afraid that they'd lose their tempers anyway and do something stupid, or even illegal. That kind of violent behavior was all too familiar to Paul.

We also examined the bus schedule and realized, a little too late, that a bus stopped in the median of DuPont Highway across from the hospital. A city bus arrived at and departed from the hospital every thirty minutes during morning and afternoon rush-hours.

So everything was set. I wasn't looking forward to lodging a complaint, but I relished the chance to confront my attacker come Monday morning.

Marlene spent most of Sunday with us, the last day before she and her mother would drive back to Alabama. She was so attentive. My headaches persisted, but they became shorter in duration and less severe. We spent much of the day lounging around the house, watching the Apollo 11 news and waiting to see man's first moon landing. At one point when my headache returned, Marlene insisted on applying cold compresses and massaging my sore neck. I said, "Marlene, you'd make a great nurse."

As it turned out, Marlene's visit had perfect timing. I couldn't think of anyone more sympathetic, except my mother and maybe Deanna. If only she were there, but unfortunately she and her family were away that weekend and I wouldn't see her until days later.

Marlene left that night, right after dinner. At least we got to share the moon landing, if not the walking part. It was sad watching her leave. Her family lived so far away, and no one knew when, or if, we'd ever see each other again. She left us a small class picture of herself, with a note to Mom on the back. It read: "Aunt Myrtle—The cutest, coolest, most wonderful and heartwarming aunt I know. May God always bless ya. Remember me always. Luv, Marlene."

* * * * *

John and I peered through the glass window of the Y.O.C. headquarters on Market Street. The place bustled with people coming and going. We were both surprised at the number of people carrying papers and notebooks from one office or desk to another. *Monday morning must be their busiest day*, I thought. I had never seen it so busy. In fact, the place looked so intimidating that I thought about canceling the idea of a complaint.

"John," I said, "do we really want to do this?"

"We shouldn't run away from this, Tommy," he replied. "The people in charge need to know what's going on behind their backs."

"Yeah, I guess you're right. And punks like Clarence need to know they can't get away with sneaking around and decking people for no reason."

We stood outside the office watching people come and go. John said, "They're awful busy in there. Let's walk down the street and grab a cup of coffee or something, and wait for the place to calm down."

We spent the next forty minutes or so at the coffee shop down the street and returned to the office around nine. John asked the first person he saw about where to file a complaint. The worker gave us an odd look and directed us to a Mr. Wilson in one of the offices at the far end of the room. We entered the office and hovered above a middle-aged black man's desk, waiting for him to finish talking to a young co-worker.

"Good morning," John said. "Mr. Wilson?"

"Yes, I'm Henry Wilson. What can I help you with this morning?"

"Are you the man taking complaints?"

"Uh…yes. I guess so," he said, the whites of his eyes growing bigger. "What seems to be the problem?"

"This young man here, my brother-in-law, was attacked and knocked unconscious by one of his co-workers last Friday morning."

The man looked at me. "What's your name, son?"

"Dixon. Tom Dixon."

"Where did this attack happen, Tom?"

"A few blocks down the street after I got off the school bus. We were sent home early from the state hospital on account of the rain."

"Tom, if this happened on city property, I'm not sure there's anything I can do about—"

"What's that got to do with the behavior of one of your employees?" John said. "Don't you care that these young men are attacking their co-workers—unprovoked?"

Mr. Wilson stared at me again. "Do you know who hit you?"

"Yeah, it was Clarence. I don't know his last name."

"Why did he hit you?"

I told the man there was no reason for what he did, other than perhaps the berry-tossing incident at the hospital the day before the attack.

"I thought we were all having fun," I added.

"Well then, young man, you shouldn't have tossed the berries at him."

"What!" I shouted.

"You can't be serious?" John said.

"Well…uh…I'll have to call the men in charge at the hospital about what you've told me. I suggest that you meet with them over there this morning and work this out. Hopefully it will be to everyone's satisfaction."

We ended our conversation and drove to the hospital.

My work group's student supervisor, a young black college student, arranged a meeting with Clarence and me. John was still with me, and Mr. Ogle joined us as we stood on the sidewalk outside the greenhouse parking lot. I noticed John giving Clarence the once-over from a distance. "So that's the kid who knocked you out, huh?"

"Yep, that's him."

"He's a scrawny looking thing."

"Yeah," I said, "I guess it don't take much when you sneak up behind somebody."

I recounted the attack to Mr. Ogle and the student supervisor, giving them the same story I had given Mr. Wilson back at the office. Looking at Clarence, the supervisor said, "Did you hit Tom?"

"Yeah."

"Why? What'd he do to you?"

"He threw berries at me."

"Tom, tell me again why you were throwing berries at him?"

"I was just trying to be friendly. That's all."

"Well, it may sound silly to you, Tom, but you shouldn't have been doing that."

A painful frown tore at my face, and I glanced at John and Mr. Ogle. They had similar looks of disgust. I was about to explode. Four seconds later—I did. I turned to Clarence and shouted, "You're a stinking coward!"

The supervisor said, “Now calm down, Tom,” and stepped between us. I ignored him and continued my tongue lashing, as John and Mr. Ogle looked on, nervous but amused.

“Come on,” I said, pointing my finger at Clarence and pounding my chest with my fist. “Try me now! Try me now!”

Clarence’s cold stare and demeanor finally cracked; he smiled.

“Yeah, go ahead and laugh,” I said.

“Okay, Tom—that’s enough!”

I stood firm, ready and waiting for him, but the punk wasn’t biting. “Where’s all that karate and boxing when my back’s not turned, Clarence?”

“Tom! That’s enough! One more word and you’re out of here.” I stepped farther away from the supervisor, careful not to turn my back on the coward.

“Clarence, I want you to apologize to Tom for hitting him.”

“I’m sorry,” he said, with a smirk.

“Tom, I want you to apologize for tossing the berries.”

“You gotta be kidding!”

“Nooo, I mean it. You’ll apologize, or be fired.”

I couldn’t believe it. Didn’t they understand the seriousness of what this punk had done? He had attacked me from behind and knocked me unconscious—over a couple of berries. I had already told Clarence I was sorry, seconds after I tossed the berries. I thought the issue had been settled. Now, the very idea of me apologizing—again—after Clarence’s nasty deed…well, it was a hard pill to swallow.

John pulled me aside. “Tom, it’s not worth losing your job over this.”

I took a deep breath. *He’s right, I don’t want to lose my job. That would be a double knockout for Clarence—and his buddies. I’m lucky the man hasn’t fired me already for my angry outbursts.*

I looked at my supervisor, barely two years my senior. I looked at John and Mr. Ogle, and I looked at Clarence.

"Clarence," I said, "I'm sorry I ever picked up those berries."

"Good job, Tom," Mr. Ogle said.

The supervisor said, "Okay, that's good enough. Now, I don't want to have any more trouble from you two. Tom, Mr. Ogle has your work schedule for today."

He turned to Clarence, and I watched the two of them walk away together, quietly discussing something. It must have been worthwhile because I never had another issue with Clarence. I saw him a few times after that, mostly at roll call. I made it a point never to turn my back on him or speak to the punk again.

Until that day I had never desired to do serious bodily harm to anyone. Serving some punk a well-deserved busted nose, bloody lip, or black eye always seemed to be enough to quench my anger. On the other hand, it's a good thing for both of us that I never had the chance to be alone with Clarence, because all that would have changed back then. Yes, one way or another, my life would have changed drastically.

Mr. Ogle gave me my work assignment. Walking John to his car, I thanked him for standing by me. At the end of the day I walked to the bus stop outside the hospital grounds, keeping an eye out for Clarence and his punk friends. I felt excited and relieved when the bus arrived on time. It took me directly to Fourth and Market, where I used a transfer to catch the Newport bus to Richardson Park. The schedule worked well and I followed it for the rest of the summer, avoiding any further incidents. Mom was happy, too, knowing her son didn't have to ride the school bus with the black kids anymore.

Tommy and Ronnie at #2 Schoolhouse Lane, Richardson Park, DE.

IV

ELSMERE

1969-1971

Little has changed at #5 Rodman Road in Elsmere (Nov. 2013).

5 Rodman Road

Having perused the classified section of Wilmington's *Morning News and Evening Journal*, for weeks with no luck, a family member found us a new place to live—the tenth move of my life (at least). And I had yet to graduate from high school. The word "gypsy" could accurately describe how I felt.

I had been standing in front of #5 Rodman Road for only a minute when Paul noticed we were blocking traffic on the narrow one-way street. He circled around the development while I walked up and down the sidewalk, checking out the neighboring townhouses. Our new residence: a well-constructed brick duplex located at the northwestern edge of the Canby Park Estates development.

Wow! This might be the nicest place we've ever lived in. We would have the left half of the duplex, adjacent to an empty lot, so we won't be totally closed in by the city. As Paul and I discussed the new residence on the way home, a shocking question arose. "Paul," I said, "isn't Canby Park Estates outside the Conrad School District?"

"Gee, Tommy, don't ask me. Mom didn't mention school districts."

I posed the same question to Mom, who informed us that David would be transferring to the Oak Grove School while I would have to ride the bus to Conrad. Although elated that I could stay at my school, I felt sad knowing that my little brother had to ride the bus to and from school also, and for the first time.

In early August, Mom, David, and I moved in. Ronnie, Donna, and Paul helped us get set up. But an unpleasant surprise awaited me. I quickly realized we were not renting the left half of the building, but only the top left quarter. Yeah, we got the entire second floor of the left half of the duplex—all four rooms.

The landlord had been renting out the bottom left quarter of the building to a young single man. Thus, the front door was almost always left unlocked. Inside the front door were two other doors: one on the left for the bottom apartment and another at the bottom of the stairway leading up to our apartment. Mom and David shared a small bedroom straight ahead at the top of the stairs.

Investigating the layout, I made a left turn at the top of the stairs, walked past a small full bath on the right, and entered a large kitchen area. Past the kitchen table I could see the living room at the front of the building, with two windows facing the street. This is where I would sleep, on a foldout sofa. With very little closet space available, we had to fold most of our clothes and place them in drawers. But at this point it was just Mom and two dependents.

* * * * *

Gary was hard at work while living with his father, cutting grass, splitting wood, stoking the fires, slopping hogs, shoveling snow and coal, and tending to Dad's chicken coop. Not quite the life he'd imagined when he first started skipping school. It's really all about perseverance, he thought—at least until he graduated. But soon the old Sleepy Dixon began to reveal himself. Dad was still a heavy drinker and he began picking away at his son.

One night, as Gary was doing homework and studying for an upcoming test, he could see Dad sitting on his bed watching *The Porter Waggoner Show*, sucking on a rolled cigarette, and taking swigs from a quart bottle of Miller High Life.

"You know, the wood you cut ain't gonna last the winter, Gary. You need to start stackin' some more."

"I'll start on it this weekend, Dad."

Thirty seconds elapsed.

"Gary, I don't think you're feedin' the hogs enough apples from the orchard."

"I'll give them more next time."

About a minute elapsed.

"Gary, them hogs and chickens ain't been fed yet."

"I'll get to it as soon as I finish my homework, Dad."

"No, you'll get out there and do it now, not later. And don't forget to bring in the eggs."

"Dad, I have schoolwork to do and there's a test tomorrow."

"Boy, them books ain't gonna feed the hogs and chickens! Get your ass out there now and do-it!"

"I'll do it soon as I'm through here, Dad!"

"Would you listen to this? I bet you think you're big enough to kick my ass now, don't cha? Just like your brother Paul, huh?"

At this point, Gary wasn't intimidated. He looked up from his homework and glanced at his father. Dad still sat on the bed, but now he had stopped smoking and drinking, and his breathing had become rapid and shallow. Recent eyelid surgery had given him a creepy look, like he was squinting. Gary noticed those beady eyes staring at the loaded .22 rifle leaning against the bedside nightstand.

Dad said, "I won't give you a chance!" and went for the rifle. Gary scrambled from the table and flew out the kitchen door before Dad could even touch the gun. "Gary! You better come back here! I'll bust a cap in your ass, boy!"

Once Gary reached Tankhill Road he knew he'd be safe. Suffering from emphysema and black lung disease, Dad couldn't make it to the outhouse—70 feet away—without sitting down and resting. Pursuit was out of the question for the old man.

This incident and others before it had destroyed all sense of trust for Gary. Now he could no longer live with his father. He quit school and moved in with his buddy, Fred Andrews, farther up Boissevain Mountain. The Andrews' were a nice family and they welcomed Gary into their home, treating him like a son. Gary pitched in, helping around the farm as much as possible. At this point he'd found an island of happiness.

Sixteen inches of snow blanketed Boissevain Mountain that second Tuesday in November, with more accumulation expected. At home alone, and most likely bored, Fred entered his parents' bedroom and grabbed his father's .32 pistol from the nightstand. "Hey, Gary!" he yelled. "Come here and look at this!" As Gary entered, Fred tossed the gun onto the bed, saying, "Check out the pearl handles on that baby."

Gary and Fred inspected the pistol. Somehow it accidentally discharged.

Gary barged out of the house through the thick snow, fell twice, then slipped again while running up his neighbor's front porch steps.

It seemed like he pounded a hundred times on the door before someone opened it.

"Call an ambulance!" he screamed. "Fred's been shot! Call an ambulance!"

"Oh God! Gary, we can't call anyone. We don't have a phone."

Gary practically rolled down Tank Hill Road, slipping and sliding, crying and cursing, the sight and sounds of what happened in that bedroom flooding his mind. Not far from Dad's place, he met Fred's father driving his oil truck up the mountain. Somehow he was able to communicate the gist of what had happened. The rest has been a blur for more than 44 years.

Hearing the news, our family felt helpless and indecisive. Gary felt completely alone; wandering through a deep, dark tunnel. He couldn't (or wouldn't) talk about the deadly accident and had apparently assumed a huge burden of guilt. They held Gary for a week in the Tazewell County jail until his court hearing in mid-November, when he turned 16. The charge: excusable homicide (or something like that). Following the hearing, the court assigned Aunt Christine temporary custody.

The Virginia social services people soon sold Gary on the benefits of joining the Job Corps, and reasonably so, since he also felt the need to get away from Boissevain. While awaiting his Job Corps report date in February, he moved in with Wesley's wife Kay and her mother in Bluefield, Virginia. But he still couldn't talk about the shooting. He would simply say, "It was an accident" or "I did a stupid thing."

Not long after arriving at his Job Corps site in Texas, Gary wrote Mom that things were going pretty well for him. He lied, a little. Most importantly, he didn't want to worry his mother by telling her he stood out as one of only four white teens in a sea of nearly three thousand black teens preparing for their course studies. And, of course he didn't tell her about the fistfight he had with one of the black students, barely three weeks into his training. He then related a funny story: while learning carpentry skills, he had struck up a conversation with Cory, a rather large young black teammate from somewhere out west.

Cory said, "You talk funny, man. Where you from?"

"Delaware."

"What state is Delaware in?"

"Delaware *is* the state," Gary said, a bit surprised.

"That's not a state. I've never heard of a state called Delaware."

"Well, there is. It's on the East Coast, right next to Pennsylvania, Maryland, and…I think, New Jersey."

"You're bull-shittin' me, man."

"No, I'm not. I'll betcha a dollar."

"Okay, you're on!"

Gary and Cory walked the three blocks to the camp library, where they gathered up the biggest and most colorful U.S. atlas they could find. Gary located Delaware and placed his finger on the tiny state, saying, "See, there it is." The young man studied the map—and studied it and studied it. He had to be sure; after all, he had a whole dollar riding on the outcome. Satisfied that Delaware did indeed exist as a state, he shouted, "Damn, I guess you're right!"

"I told you, man."

And with that, Cory and Gary became buddies.

Compounding Issues

I started eleventh grade in the highest of spirits, sporting a new and less nerdy pair of eyeglasses. My acne seemed to be in remission, too, thanks to Fostex, and I was still going steady with Deanna, one of the cutest girls at Conrad. Who could have asked for more?

In January, however, midway through the wrestling season, things began to change. No matter how hard I tried, I could not defeat the two senior wrestlers in the 145 and 155-pound (varsity) weight classes. I came close during one wrestle-off, but I couldn't quite pull out a win. Unable to wrestle varsity, I accepted my destiny and wrestled the first five matches on the junior varsity (JV) team, scoring four wins.

Then, as if seeking revenge for the Fostex treatments, my acne flared up anew. Bob blamed it on my contact with sweaty mats during wrestling. He told me to keep using the soap and to give it more time. "And for heaven's sake," he advised, "stop popping your zits!" I tried refraining, but I wasn't about to let those Cyclops win every staring contest. "The bigger they got, the faster they pop," the saying goes.

On Saturday, January 31, I wrestled my first varsity match against Brandywine. It was Conrad's sixth meet of the season and I managed to score a 3-3 tie, the first and only tie of my wrestling career. I wrestled the next three matches at JV and scored two wins. The last two meets, against Wilmington and Dickinson, were held on successive Saturdays. I wrestled up one weight class for varsity and won a 6-0 decision at 167 pounds. I had to lose two pounds to make weight for the 145-pound varsity match and won that in a 7-3 decision. A picture of my match appeared on the sports page of *The Evening Journal* the following day. I finished my junior year of high school wrestling with a 6-2-0 record at JV and a 2-0-1 record at varsity. Considering the fierce intra-team competition, I was pleased with my combined record of 8-2-1 for the season.

* * * * *

In March, 1970, Ronnie and Charlene became proud parents of a baby boy, R. J., my third nephew. April and May were busy months, loaded with appointments and other concerns. With Bob's help I mailed applications to one in-state college, two out-of-state colleges, and several out-of-state universities. Also, I had just received my SAT results. While the scores weren't great, they were good enough to get me into any of the in-state institutions and many outside Delaware. I hated taking those tests. They were so damn stressful.

Sometime around the beginning of May, college, the military, and the Vietnam War all combined to form one big hot-button issue. In little more than a year (1972), the Military's Selective Service System (Draft) would be conducting another national draft lottery, this time for young men born in 1952. Men like me. Although I felt a certain patriotic duty to (at some point) serve my country, I could not muster much enthusiasm when it came to fighting in Vietnam, a war that I and many other young men didn't understand or want any part of. The words from my big brother's 1965 letter to Mom came back to caution me: "Unless you have to—do not join the military." For me—a current high school student under 20 years old with a "1S" (Student) draft deferment—the option of voluntary enlistment in the Reserves or Guard was out of the question, too, it being only a footstep away from the war. Acquiring a "3A" (Married with Children) deferment, was another outlandish notion at the time—for obvious reasons. I thought my pursuit of a college education, or a "2S" (College Student) deferment, would provide the best rewards and the best excuse for ducking active military service.

(As it turned out, I received a very high lottery number a year later, and the Nixon administration's pulling back of the draft had to be plain-old icing on the cake.)

Then, on May 4, the shit hit the fan when four students were shot and killed by National Guard Troops during anti-war demonstrations at Kent State University in Kent, Ohio. Nine other students were wounded. *What in the world is this country coming to*?

Adding to my stress at this time, the Fostex soap had stopped working completely and my blemishes had evolved into an acute stage. They had spread from the area around my jawbones to my neck and hairline. Mom and Bob were also concerned, so Bob made an appointment for me to see a dermatologist at 4:00 on a school day.

Mom was still at work and, since no one was available to drive me to the doctor's office, I had to catch the bus into Wilmington. I ran the three blocks to the bus stop. At 4:00 I had waited 20 minutes without seeing a single bus. I waited until around 4:30 and then walked home. Why were there no buses? Frustrated and angry, I felt destined to suffer through a hopeless acne condition. Guilt plagued me for days because I thought I had let Bob and Mom down by missing the appointment. Yet I refused to make another appointment, stubbornly hoping for the best.

* * * * *

Deanna and I made plans to attend the Conrad High School Prom in May. I thought it would be cool if I drove us there. With that goal in mind and my learner's permit tucked away in my wallet, I began taking driving lessons from Paul in his stick shift Chevy. I was a fast learner; heck, I'd been driving tractors for the past two summers. I spent several Sundays learning to parallel park and navigating around orange traffic cones in the deserted parking lot of the Delaware Department of Motor Vehicles on Airport Road. Although a little nervous, I felt confident about passing my driver's test.

The testing official seemed impressed with my driving and parking skills, especially considering that I was using a stick shift. While driving through a nearby development, he said, "Tom, what do you do when you come to a stop sign?" I thought he was giving me a pop-quiz.

"Stop," I said proudly, "and proceed with caution after looking both ways."

"Well, Tom, there was a stop sign back there and you just drove right through it."

"Oh no," I said, looking back for the sign I'd missed.

"Now hold on there!" he shouted. "Keep your eyes on the road!"

After bringing the car to an abrupt stop, I turned to face the official. "I'm afraid you've failed the test," he said. "I'm sorry, Tom. And you were doing so well, too."

We headed directly back to the DMV parking lot, where I gave Paul the bad news. He couldn't believe I had run a stop sign. "Damn, Tommy," he said, "what the hell were you thinking?"

Now I would have to wait thirty days before trying it again. Deanna took it well when I told her why I wouldn't be driving us to the prom. On Saturday, May 9, I bought my first corsage and presented it to her in the living room of her apartment. Her mother, sister, and brother got a kick out of all the formalities, and after some clothing adjustments and having our picture taken, her mother drove us to the prom.

Deanna and I were nervous at first. Her clothing seemed to be a major concern and she fussed with it obsessively, trying to get it to hang right and caress her body in just the right way. I thought she looked fantastic and told her so. I had bought a new tie to match my best jacket and wasn't too concerned about my clothes. I knew most of the guys were avoiding the tuxedo route.

My acne flare up caused me some initial embarrassment—why did it have to occur at prom time?—but as the night progressed Deanna and I relaxed and danced to classic sixties hits: "Cherish" by *The Association*, "I'm a Believer" by *The Monkees*, "Summer in the City" by *The Lovin' Spoonful*, "I Heard It Through the Grapevine" by *Gladys Night & the Pips*, and "Dizzy" by Tommy Roe. These were indeed some of the best. Many still are. Thankfully, nothing out of the ordinary happened that night; we just had a great time.

Sometime in mid-May I took the driving test again. Paul was unavailable on this try, but my wrestling buddy Steve loaned me his car and accompanied me to the test. This time I passed and obtained my license.

My Summer of Discontent

Near the end of the school term, Mr. Baker encouraged us to attend a summer wrestling camp where we would run through the basics and learn some advanced moves. The focus was on conditioning, which included wind sprints, round robins, and weightlifting. Because of my busy schedule and lack of access to equipment, I'd never stuck with weightlifting for more than a few days. Knowing that seniors were not allowed to wrestle JV, I also knew the camp would go a long way in helping me make the varsity team my senior year. Unfortunately, it cost a bit more than Mom or I could afford.

I felt torn. A wrestling camp seemed very important, but also frivolous considering how badly David and I were going to need new clothes and other back-to-school necessities. My mother's chief concern was a summer job with me bringing in extra money.

So to the Y.O.C. we once again went, where seven black teenagers and I were assigned to a work crew under the supervision of the Delaware State Highway Department. We were tasked with removing dirt, sand, sticks, limbs, road kill, and other litter from roads and highways around Wilmington. It was a dirty, hot, and sweaty job, but I was young, energetic, and eager to earn a paycheck. This time I worked for $1.25 an hour, approximately, the usual modest increase from the previous year.

The Kiamensi Transportation Yard in Stanton, Delaware, near the intersection of Kiamensi Road and Stanton Road became our base of operations. I still didn't have access to an automobile, but luck was with me: I had a brother who lived a half-mile from the yard. Paul and Linda, who were expecting their first child by the way, happily allowed me to live with them over the summer months, but I still managed to spend weekends at home on Rodman Road.

I didn't have the pleasure of Deanna's company for most of that summer. Her mother thought it would be a maturing experience for Deanna to spend the summer with her aunt in Texas. If not for her steady string of letters, I think I may have gone mad. Her perfume-laced communications were intoxicating, and some days I could hardly wait for the mail to arrive. Linda and Paul had detected the perfume on my letters. "Look at him Paul," Linda would say, "he can't stop sniffing his mail."

By mid-summer I was walking through life in a mild stupor, passing the time until I could see her again. That yearning began to subside one day when I received a curious letter. Deanna said she had met a young Texas "cowboy" named Gabe, but told me not to worry: "He's just a friend. He's too old for me." The tone of her letter seemed sincere, so I tried not to think about it. In my return letter, however, I did ask, "Just how old is Gabe?"

* * * * *

The family received other news from Texas that summer. Officials at Gary Job Corps Center were sending out announcements about my brother's achievements.

"NEWS – for immediate release:

ELSMERE YOUTH WINS HIGHEST JOB CORPS HONOR

San Marcos, Texas—Job Corpsman Gary Lee Dixon, 16, son of Mrs. Myrtle Dixon of 5 Rodman Road, was named by academic and vocational instructors Tuesday as "Corpsman of the Month," the highest single award a Gary Center student can achieve....To be chosen for this award from an enrollment of 3,000 is an honor that merits special recognition by the entire center. Conduct, appearance, attitude, and leadership are all criteria for selection. Dixon is a student in carpentry and has been at the Gary Center for four months. He plans to graduate in October and seek employment in Delaware."

That was encouraging news for the family. We were all proud of Gary, yet as a cocky older brother I couldn't help thinking: *Maybe now he'll get his act together*.

The notice came with an invitation for parents to attend the ceremonies. Mom had to decline the offer, as traveling to faraway Texas was not only too expensive, but totally out of the question.

I consider my 1970 summer job about the worst ever. The day started early with a short walk to the Kiamensi Yard. After the Wilmington school bus dropped off the rest of the gang, we piled into the back of a large orange dump truck, some sitting and some standing. The cool morning air, whipping and tearing at our clothing and skin, often raised goose bumps, but as the day wore on and the sun rose higher, sweat took control and our energy declined.

You could say I obtained some weight training that summer, but not the kind I needed to improve my wrestling. We toiled away with shovels and push brooms in near record-breaking heat, filling five-gallon buckets with dirt, sand, and other debris. Once filled, we emptied them into the dump truck and then repeated the process. As we worked the streets and highways, there seemed to be no end to the dirt, buckets, and heat.

I saw a gradual decline in the frequency of Deanna's letters in August, and their tone had changed. I had a lot of questions for her, when or even if she returned.

And she did. On a Saturday morning late in August, I awoke feeling extra cheerful. Deanna was back from Texas. After wolfing down breakfast, I headed out by foot to her apartment. I had crossed the Elsmere Bridge and turned left, heading south on DuPont Road, when I heard a loud crash followed by the blaring of a horn. I spun around to see a smashed car, its hood wrapped around a utility pole—one I had just walked past.

"Oh my God!"

Within seconds, several people were attending the driver. When the police and ambulance arrived, I continued on my journey. I met Deanna at her apartment and we decided to take a walk through Banning Park, our usual spot for holding hands, picnicking, and you know. I told her about the car crash, the lucky driver, and how close I had come to getting hit. We spent an hour or two, or maybe three—time goes fast when you're in love—catching up on summer events.

To hear her tell it, her Texas summer at age seventeen seemed a lot more interesting than my similar experience at age twelve. What was it about Texas? Was it the air? Was it the sun? I knew the Cowboy State had changed me back in 1964, and I sensed that Texas, or someone in Texas, had changed her, too, and it was making me a little uncomfortable. She looked better than ever, too—tanned and gorgeous—and yet something else seemed different. We walked through a wooded area of the park and stopped on the sidewalk along Maryland Avenue.

"Deanna, how old did you say Gabe is?"

"Twenty-one."

"What's the drinking age in Texas?"

"I think Gabe said twenty-one. Why?"

"Did he take you into a bar and buy you drinks?"

Deanna looked surprised by the question, like she'd been caught lying or hiding something.

"Well…once or twice," she said. "I was afraid we'd get caught if we kept doing it, so we stopped."

"I see. Deanna, I'm surprised you'd take a chance like that."

"Well, then, maybe I'm not the shy, naive little girl that you thought I was."

"What do you mean by that?"

"Whatever you want it to mean," she said in a sassy tone of voice, the first time she had ever spoken to me that way. "Gabe's a real nice guy," she went on, sounding even more defensive. "He has a good job. He also has a car and knows how to treat a girl. That's more than I can say for you."

Her words smacked me. My response? Pure reflex. I lashed out, smacking her, a reaction that would haunt me for days. I staggered backwards and held out my hands, as though saying, "What the hell have I done?"

"Deanna, I'm sorry!"

She stared back at me, rubbing her jaw in shock. Then, like a bantam-hen, she flew into me, pounding at my face and chest with her fists.

"I'm sorry—I'm sorry!" I shouted, using my forearms to block her assault. "I—I shouldn't have done that! Deanna, please! I'm so sorry!"

"I can't believe you did that!" she cried, halting her assault. "Who do you think you are?"

I knew that I had hurt her. But she had hurt me, too, and in my pain and insecurity I had lashed out.

"I thought I was your boyfriend, but now I'm beginning to wonder. So, what else did you and this big Texas cowboy do?"

"That's none of your business."

"Really. Why wouldn't it be? We are going steady, you know."

"Oh yeah, I need to talk to you about that," she said, pulling our ring from her finger.

"What are you doing? Deanna, it's just a silly argument. I'm sorry. Please, let's talk about it. You don't have to do that."

"We're moving next week," she said, placing the ring into my open hand, "and since I'll be going to another school, I think it would be best if we were free to see other people."

I felt like I'd been hit by a sledgehammer. *This is too much. This is all happening way too fast.* The only thing I could say was, "Well…will I still be able to see you now and then?"

"I don't know," she said, turning and walking away. Without a glance, she waved her arm. "Bye, Tommy."

"Bye, Deanna."

Wow! I was stunned; it really did happen that fast. My heart sank as I watched her walk away. It was strange, though. This time I shed no tears and had no lump in my throat. I returned home and spent the next several days in a haze, devastated that I had lost my temper, smacked my sweetheart in the face, and maybe lost her for good.

Just before she moved away, I called her from the phone booth at McDonald's in Elsmere, the family's usual way of communicating. I tried apologizing again. She seemed courteous enough, but our conversation still felt strained. Other, more troubling thoughts began running through my mind. *Did Deanna's mother send her to Texas to separate us? Did she think we were becoming too serious? Did Deanna say those hurtful things to pick a fight with me? If I hadn't smacked her, would she have broken up with me anyway, especially knowing we'd be attending different schools? How big a role did her mother play in this?*

There were so many questions I wanted answered.

Bob and Bud noticed my pathetic, broken-hearted demeanor, so I had to tell them what happened.

Bob said, "You did what!"

"Yeah, I smacked her."

"You boob! You might as well kiss that fish goodbye. You'll be lucky if she decides to talk to you again."

"You might be right, Bob."

That's when they told me I needed a vacation. My two friends suggested I spend a few days with Bud and his sister's family in Andover, Massachusetts. It would be my first "real" vacation away from home since Killeen, Texas, six years earlier. Bob and I dashed over to the Wilmington airport (in New Castle, Delaware), where he bought me a roundtrip ticket to Boston's Logan Airport. My nerves were a bit shaky as the plane rolled down the runway and I grew even more edgy through lift-off. All understandable, I thought, since it was my first flight on any airplane. I learned later that the era of the jumbo jet had arrived that summer, when Pan Am initiated daily Boeing 747 flights from Boston's Logan to London's Heathrow.

Bud met me at Logan and drove us through the crazy Boston traffic, bouncing from one lane to another. Bud's sister Nicole was a very attractive woman in her late twenties or early thirties. She and husband Jim and son Jacob (and a Labrador by the name of Samantha) were enjoying the usual comforts of a middle-class family lifestyle: proud owners of a truck, two cars, and a large three-story Victorian sitting on two well-landscaped acres off Main Street, outside the quaint and prosperous town of Andover.

Bud's family welcomed me in and treated me like kin. During the stay we toured the historic town of Salem and walked some of the rocky beaches on Cape Cod. Most important, Bud took me on a quick tour of his workplace: the R.C. Crown Estate. I quickly fell in love with its sixty acres of woodlands, cottages, driveways, ponds, and gardens. As I prepared to depart, Nicole and Jim told me they had enjoyed my company and invited me to visit them any time, and

I thanked them for their hospitality. While waiting to board my return flight to Delaware, Bud surprised me with a big question: "How would you like to work at the estate next summer, as soon as you graduate?"

"Sure," I said, without hesitation.

"Good!"

I paused. "Bud, where will I stay, and how will I get to the job?"

"Don't worry," he said, "there's plenty of time to figure all that out. You just keep your nose clean. And don't forget to study hard, make good grades, and be ready for college next fall." We said our goodbyes, knowing we would be seeing each other in a month or two.

My vacation had been a great distraction, but three weeks into my senior year I still hadn't made sense of my breakup with Deanna. When it came to dating I was free as a bird, yet as fearful as a mole in a fox den. I didn't know how to go about it or even if I should. With two feet for transportation and only four or five bucks in my wallet each week, I couldn't help feeling rejected and unfit. Deanna's biting comment still gnawed at me, bringing on a load of negative feelings. Yet somehow I mustered up the will and determination to resist, not letting such thoughts undermine my social and academic well-being. I decided to bide my time and see what the year would bring.

I'm 18, spending weekdays at Paul's place in Stanton, Delaware.

Senior and Other Graduations

Gary graduated at the top of his Job Corps class in late September, and in early October returned to Delaware and took up residence with an old buddy and his family. My thoughts were with my brother. Heaven knows he'd been through so much—reform school, locked behind bars, living with his dad, and the accidental shooting death of his best friend. He'd been forced to make many adjustments in the year since Mom, David, and I had last seen him. Outwardly he seemed funny and gregarious, eager to carry on a conversation. The accident seemed to be the only topic he refused to discuss. It must have burned inside him, like a festering wound; not a healthy state of mind.

Mom had reservations about seeing her son. All the bad decisions Gary had made reminded her too much of the bad decisions our father had made throughout his life. Since she was the one responsible for sending him away, she feared that Gary still blamed her for his misfortunes. Nevertheless, she welcomed Gary into the apartment when he and a friend stopped by to see us, and to visit a school buddy, Johnny, who lived next door.

Bob and Bud stopped by later that afternoon to pick me up, and the three of us headed out for a bite to eat and a movie or show. Bob and Bud were familiar with Gary's troubled past but had never met him. I introduced my friends to my brother and we all enjoyed a few minutes of conversation. When I returned later that night, I noticed Gary and another friend lurking in the dark outside the house.

"What are you guys doing out here?" I asked.

"We're catch'n up on lost time, brother."

"Gary, you've been drinking—I can smell it."

"Yeah, want some?" he said, laughing. "We got plenty for ya, big brother."

"No thanks," I said, walking to the front door.

I reached for the door and there was Mom, standing in the dark, waiting for me to return.

She said, "Hurry up and get in here."

"Mom, Gary's outside. I think he's drunk."

"I know, Tommy. He and his friend left a couple of times, but they keep coming back. I told him he couldn't come in. That boy is never going to change. If I had a phone, I'd call the police."

From inside our apartment stairway I could hear Gary and his buddy talking and laughing, but I couldn't make out what they were saying. They were getting louder by the minute. "Mom, do you want me to go to the phone booth and call the police?"

"No! Don't call the police!" David shouted from the top of the stairs.

"No. Not yet, anyway." Mom said. "Hopefully they'll leave in a few minutes now that you're here."

I locked the door and turned to join Mom and David at the top of the stairs. Halfway up the stairs, I heard a loud banging on the door. It was Gary. "Hey Tommy, did you have a good time tonight with your faggot friends?"

"What?" I shouted, stunned by my brother's insinuation.

"Come on, Tommy," Mom said, motioning to me, "get on up here."

"Gary," I said, "you better shut up and get outta here before I lose my temper!"

"Whoowee! Come on out, queer-lover! Show me what you got!"

"Don't pay any attention to him," Mom said, "he's drunk."

Having gone through a significant growth spurt, my drunken brother now decided he was big enough and tough enough to finally best his older brother. And he may have wanted to pay me back for the time or two I picked on him as a child.

"Come on, Tommy! I'm not your little brother anymore! I can take care of myself, and I can take care of you!"

I started down the steps, but hesitated. The image of my brother and me going at it flashed through my mind. I didn't want to deal with that for the rest of my life. Mom must have had a similar vision.

"Tommy, don't you dare go out there and fight your brother!" she shouted. The sound of Mom's voice stopped me dead in my tracks. I looked up to see her staring at me, her face contorted in fear. Again she shouted, "You hear me, Tommy?"

I couldn't do it. I climbed the stairs and walked into the living room. I paced the floor as Gary continued to shout insults in a drunken effort to egg me on. In the past I had usually settled these situations with my fists. Now I didn't know what to do. Gary's behavior disturbed me. After all he'd been through, he had apparently learned so little. Just like his father, the alcohol had taken control, and Mom was scared to death of him.

The hounding and laughter went on-and-off and on-and-off for twenty minutes, and then abruptly stopped. Gary either grew tired, passed out, or someone called the police.

I had trouble sleeping that night, trying to imagine what I should say to Gary the next time we met. What do you say to your brother when he makes such accusations and insinuations? Would he remember the things he'd said? Or had he really been too drunk?

Indeed, that's exactly what he said a week or two later when I met up with him.

"Shit, Tommy, I did all that? I'm sorry, man. You know, sometimes when I get to drinking hard, I can't remember a goddamn thing."

Why did Gary say those things about Bob and Bud? Had he picked up on something about them, that quick?

I had suspected early on that my two best friends could be gay, but I'd never had the courage to ask them. I thought they would tell me when they were ready. On the other hand, the seventies had barely arrived; gay men were mostly relegated to the closet because society had so rudely condemned them. Maybe they were afraid of how I would handle such a revelation.

These two men had traveled the world. They had done and seen many things. They had given me new perspectives and had posed challenging questions. They had made me think. Our conversations went far beyond what I usually talked about with my peers—girls, sex, booze, and cars.

I first thought Bob and Bud might be gay because they weren't married and never mentioned girlfriends. I recalled a conversation we had while traveling to New York City. They were teasing me about still being a virgin at seventeen. I told them that Deanna and I wanted to wait until we were married; we wanted to be working at good jobs and be well settled before having sex. They agreed that this was the best plan. I admitted that I would have succumbed to temptation more than once had not Deanna been stronger and able to redirect my energy. I was thankful for that and proud of her.

Bob said, "Yeah, you would do well, Tom, to resist the temptations of the Black Spider."

I said, "What's that mean?"

Without answering, Bob smiled, looked at Bud, and wiggled his eyebrows, a goofy, annoying habit of his.

Bud chuckled. "Yeah, watch out for those Black Spiders, Tom. They'll bite you, drag you into their deep dark lair, and consume you." Bob laughed along with him.

Their warnings reminded me of Shelob, the giant spider that attacks and stings Frodo in the third book of J.R.R. Tolkien's *The Lord of the Rings*. Ellen Haden, a classmate way back in junior high, had introduced me to *The Hobbit* (prelude to *The Lord of the Rings*), and I fell in love with the concept of Middle Earth. I had read all four books twice by then. (Thank you so much, Ellen.)

"Oh," I said, "now I know what you're talking about. That's real funny you guys. Ha! Ha! That's real funny."

Their comparison of women to black spiders gave me more reason for continued caution. I didn't want to be a father before I had a steady job.

Bud and Bob always treated me like their little brother and never made any sexual advances. At that point, I put aside any negative suspicions.

* * * * *

Wesley and Kay drove their new family from Alaska to Delaware for a visit in October, and I saw little Mona and Missy for the first time. They were so cute. For the next three years (1970-73), Wesley would be stationed at Fort Dix, New Jersey, only 65 miles away, so we expected to see more of them. Not only was Donna several weeks pregnant, but Paul and Linda were well on their way to being parents, too. Linda was about seven months pregnant in November—a bad time for an encounter with one of the local gangs.

Paul and Linda were on their way to visit us at Rodman Road one afternoon when five or six young men in a car, most of whom Linda knew, threatened them. Revenge was on their minds. Having grown up near Linda in The Park, they had apparently decided to pay her back for the times she had bullied them in their younger years. Yep, that's right. Growing up, Linda wasn't just pretty or cute, she was a spitfire too. The punks—led by their biggest asshole, Bunky—forced Paul and the Chevy off the road. Paul wanted to chase them down and retaliate, but he feared for the safety and health of his wife and unborn child. He decided to drop Linda off at her parents' house.

"They've picked on the wrong guy at the wrong time," he said, before heading out to look for the gang.

After an hour of fruitless searching, Paul returned to his in-laws' house, picked up his wife, and headed to our place. On the way, the gang (now reduced to three in number) again forced them off the road. Both cars stopped, and Paul and his adversaries poured out. The troublemakers headed directly for Paul, but he was ready and decked the nearest one. Using a tire iron, Paul clipped the elbow of another gang member, causing him to withdraw in pain. His second swing hit the third victim on the back of his head, opening up a nasty wound. At that point, they all had had enough; they scrambled into their vehicle and fled the scene.

Paul and I thought alike: don't show weakness to an adversary. He had stood his ground, using any means necessary to protect himself and his family. To "turn the other cheek" would have made him a victim again and invited more of the same. Bunky's head wound was treated at the hospital and the assault reported to the police. Paul drove to the police barracks on Kirkwood Highway, where he told his side of the story. Eventually all charges were dropped and no one had to go to court. The three punks may have drawn a lesson from the encounter; they never bothered Paul or Linda again. Two months later, in late January, Paul Jr. was born.

Wrestling season began in November with a conditioning program loaded with wrestling drills, a regimen that made us question the sanity of putting our bodies through such ungodly torture. We endured cycle after cycle of wind sprints, sit-ups, neck bridging, and grueling round-robin sparring. For me, the worst had to be those hellish wall-hugging handstand pushups. Then came Christmas break and everything slid downhill. I started losing momentum, and the teammates that I had bested for years were now squeaking by me. My edge seemed to be gone. No matter how hard I tried, I couldn't quite get it back. On top of all this, I was suffering from serious headaches during practices.

Several weeks had passed since I apologized to Deanna. I'd been thinking about her, and she must have been thinking of me, too. She had called Donna, providing her family's new address and phone number so we all could keep in touch. I had spoken to her only once over the phone. I decided to pay her a visit and get right to the point.

"Deanna, have you forgiven me for smacking you?"

"Yes," she said, "as long as you promise to never do it again."

"I promise, Deanna. I'll never strike you again."

Keeping my calls to a minimum was difficult, but I didn't want to annoy her or seem desperate. I thought we might be growing apart.

I did, however, invite Deanna to our family New Year's Eve party at Donna and John's, and she accepted. *Wow! She must not be seeing anyone*. Or maybe she just didn't have a better offer. She always seemed to enjoy our wild and wacky family get-togethers and, with Deanna by my side, I knew this New Year's gathering would be a memorable one.

Late on a snowy Thursday afternoon, Paul drove Linda and me to pick up Deanna. By the time we arrived back at the party almost two inches had accumulated and the National Weather Service was predicting four to ten more. Light snow continued to fall throughout the night, and some of us were concerned about driving conditions when the party ended.

Spirits flowed freely throughout the evening, and at midnight, New Year's Day, 1971, Deanna and I were allowed a four-ounce glass of champagne—our first. We danced to several hit tunes, including "Judy in Disguise" by *John Fred and His Playboy Band*, Marvin Gaye's "I Heard It Through the Grapevine," and "Build Me Up Buttercup" by *The Foundations*. The fantastic Johnny Adams song "Reconsider Me" came next. This hit evoked pure emotion, driving home a powerful message: that letting go of your first true love can be the hardest separation of all. While putting all my heart and soul into that slow dance, Johnny just kept on singing, "Oh, baby…baby…baby…reconsider me."

But that song wasn't the last. Our family D.J. added insult to injury by playing *Diana Ross & The Supremes'* "Someday We'll Be Together." Oh, the pain, the pain.

The party ended and we shuffled through four inches of snow to reach the vehicles. As Paul headed for Christiana with Linda beside him, making slow progress, Deanna and I attempted to recreate our make-out sessions in the back seat, trying to enjoy what little time we had together. But Linda kept talking to us and wouldn't shut up. Paul finally said, "Linda, leave them alone. Can't you see they're busy?"

* * * * *

Conrad's first scheduled match of the season was against Newark, on Saturday, January 9. Most wrestlers were in terrific shape; not so much with me. I felt like I was running on fumes. For the first time I failed to beat out my teammate, Paul Lockerfield, for the 154-pound spot, a loss that wounded me. I swallowed my pride and walked away thinking that he must have wanted it more. Conrad defeated Newark 24-19 that Saturday, but Lockerfield lost his 154-pound bout in a close (6-5) decision. The following Wednesday night Conrad outwrestled Mount Pleasant, winning 43-8. Again, Lockerfield lost a close decision (2-1) at 154 pounds.

During the following Friday's practice, Coach Baker decided to take another look at his two 154-pounders, perhaps disappointed by Lockerfield's two losses. He owed me another chance to make the team for the upcoming Saturday meet. Competition for the 145, 154, and 167-pound slots was dog-eat-dog. Five tough, hungry wrestlers, including me, butted heads during wrestle-offs every week or two. Nerves were always shaky, and a lot of pride hung in the balance. But at the end of the day (practice), I pulled off a tough win at that week's elimination match. Either I got lucky, or I wanted it more this time. Anyway, I walked home Friday night knowing I would be wrestling my first varsity match as a senior. What a feeling!

Conrad defeated McKean 35-14 on Saturday, January 16. High on adrenalin and eager to prove my mettle, I won at 154 pounds, pinning my opponent in 3:46. Following two days of practice, Conrad faced William Penn on a Wednesday night and I won an 11-6 decision, although Conrad lost its first meet 24-15.

Bob said he'd pick me up at Conrad Friday night after practice. He wanted to have a chat with Mom and me about my predicament: while team members breezed through practice round-robins, pushups, sit-ups, and wind sprints, I was grimacing and groaning from exhaustion and headaches. The headaches, crushing me like a vise, had become unbearable during the middle of our practices. It got so bad I almost cried. The pain always faded away with cool, after-practice showers and rarely bothered me during class or at home. None of this seemed normal.

I had just showered and returned to my locker when I heard the coach yell, "Hey Dixon, your ride's here!" I turned around and there stood Bob, right in the center of the aisle, with two wet and naked wrestlers trying to squeeze by him. He had surprised me, because I thought he was meeting me outside in front of the school, not in the locker room.

In control, and en route to a 3:46 pin during a home match.

"Oh, hi Bob," I muttered nervously. "Coach, I'd like you to meet Bob, a good friend. Bob, this is my coach, Mr. Baker." The two men greeted each other and shook hands.

The coach said, "Tom, rest well tonight, and I'll see you at tomorrow's meet. Nice to have met you, Bob."

The coach returned to his office and I rushed to get dressed. Some of my teammates were a little uncomfortable seeing a strange, older man standing around in the locker room. I considered telling Bob that it would have been better if he'd waited for me outside, but no harm had been done and I was sure he meant well.

Back at home, Mom said, "Well, Bob, what do you think is causing Tommy's headaches?"

"Myrtle, I have some suspicions, but I'm sure we can eliminate carbon monoxide or some other toxin at school."

"Yeah, you're right Bob," I said. "If that were the case, all the wrestlers would be getting headaches, wouldn't they? So it's got to be something with me, right?"

I kept wondering: is the exhaustion causing my headaches or vice versa. Mom, Bob, and I agreed that it was time to see our family physician.

Conrad's fifth meet was against Brandywine, on Saturday, January 23. Conrad won 32-10 and my match went well—until the last two minutes, that is, when my headache returned with a vengeance. Moreover, a burning sore throat didn't help matters. After losing a tough match (5-3), I collapsed in tears on one of the warm-up mats. I'm not sure what the coaches and spectators may have thought, but they had no way of knowing what I was going through.

Reversing the cliché, I added injury to insult on Sunday morning when I rolled out of bed with a searing pain just below my solar plexus, a delayed injury from my match. It wasn't a constant pain; it mostly hurt when I twisted or turned a certain way. I went to school on Monday morning and, for insurance purposes, reported to the nurse's office. She called Doctor Hershon and reported my injury, and I was given an appointment for that afternoon. During classes I gave Coach Baker the bad news. He said, "I want you at practice anyway. Let's give it a light workout to see how bad it is."

"I can't, coach, it hurts real bad. Besides, I have to see the doctor right after school." The coach seemed disappointed that I would even consider missing practice over a little rib pain.

I met with the doctor, who proceeded to poke and prod at the point where my ribs met the sternum. He asked me to breathe in and out deeply, and to bend and twist in various painful ways. Then he said, "Tom, I don't think we need to take X-rays. It looks like you have a common but mildly severe sports injury."

"What's that?"

"You've separated the cartilage at your rib cage."

"Oh. Is it that bad? Can I still wrestle?"

"I'm afraid this is a pretty serious injury, Tom. It's going to take two to three weeks for this to heal. That means no wrestling for at least two weeks."

I was stunned. This could kill my chances for a state championship. About to walk out of the examining room, I remembered to ask the doctor about my sore throat, my headaches, and the stamina problem. After examining my eyes, ears, nose, and throat, he said that my throat and sinuses were inflamed, indicating a sinus infection and/or a mild case of strep throat. He gave me the name of an over-the-counter decongestant and told me to take one dose an hour before engaging in any strenuous activity, and another before bed. To me, that meant one hour before wrestling practices and matches. He also gave me a prescription for an antibiotic, and said that if my condition didn't improve after ten days, come and see him, he might have to reconsider my medications.

Before sending me on my way, Doctor Hershon made a point of reminding me that wrestling was one of the most physically demanding of sports and therefore requires proper nourishment. The doctor knew our family was on welfare and didn't have the healthiest of diets, so he said I should increase my caloric intake, drink plenty of fluids, eat lots of fruits and vegetables, and start taking a good vitamin supplement, all of which required money that we didn't have. Mom and I discussed our options that night after dinner. With my older siblings pitching in a little more, I began implementing the doctor's suggestions.

Tuesday morning I saw the coach and showed him the doctor's written excuse. Again, he asked me to attend practice anyway. I said, "I didn't bring my stuff." He seemed irritated. In spite of Dr. Hershon's warning, I found myself compromising with the coach: I would nurse my injury that night at home, sit out the match with Concord on Wednesday, and return to practice on Thursday. But somehow, I knew that this return was too soon and not advisable.

I watched Conrad defeat Concord (26-14) that Wednesday. On Thursday my sternum felt tight, quite tender to the touch, and hurt when I moved. Not encouraging. I remained cautious as I went through the usual warm-up and stretching exercises. Pretty soon, just twisting and turning became dreadfully uncomfortable. When I tried to please the coach by wrestling a little, the pain was excruciating, like a red hot poker, and I worried that the cartilage had ripped further. I said, "Mr. Baker, it hurts too much. The doctor said I should give it a rest, and that's what I'm going to do."

"Tom," he said, "I wrestled through a torn cartilage during college. You should be able to work through it, too. You just have to grit your teeth and bear it."

I said, "I'll be back to practice in a week or so, coach," and headed for the lockers.

"Go ahead then," he shouted after me, "I can't force you to do something against the doctor's orders."

It was too early to catch a ride, so I walked the two miles home on a cold mid-twenties night. No matter; I had a thick jacket, heavy-duty anxiety, and the coach's attitude to keep me warm. The man seemed to have so little concern for my injury and well-being. No one could ever say that Coach Baker pampered his grapplers. Pampered or not, though, my once solid respect for the man had withered.

I rested my ribs the rest of that week and enthusiastically supported my teammates, cheering them on from the bleachers as they defeated Christiana (39-10) on Saturday, January 30.

Shenanigans

Mom loved her children. I knew it way back at age ten or eleven, but twelve seasons of living at Schoolhouse Lane and Rodman Road really drove the point home. She really doted on David and me. Before rushing off to her mushroom picking job, she would fix us breakfast, pack our lunches, and send us out the door in time to catch our bus. I hated to see her looking so tired and drained at the end of the day. She never complained; she just kept washing those dirty clothes (and sweaty jock straps).

I needed little encouragement to do my homework assignments, but Mom threw in constant reminders anyway.

"Tommy, don't you and David have homework to do?"

"I was getting ready to do it, Mom."

I remember one evening as though it were yesterday. David and I were sitting at the kitchen table doing our homework. I had just completed a series of complicated math problems and may have been feeling pretty proud of myself.

I poked David to get his attention. "Watch this," I said. "Hey Mom, can I see you for a minute? I have a question."

Mom joined me at the table. "What is it?"

"I can't get this one," I said, pointing to one of the math problems, "can you help me?"

She smacked me hard on the shoulder. "Tommy, you know I don't know how to do that."

David and I both laughed, fully enjoying Mom's reaction.

Before my injury I had started an exercise regimen—fifty push-ups after rolling out of bed in the morning and one hundred sit-ups before bedtime. My hope was to regain my wrestling edge. Mom always stood by, offering encouragement.

She'd say, "Tommy, don't forget to do your sit-ups."

I'd say, "Oh, okay. Thanks, Mom."

Or she'd ask, "Tommy, did you do your push-ups this morning?"

She definitely had a bit of drill instructor in her.

* * * * *

I returned to practice on Monday, February 1, just ten days after my injury. I had gained three pounds (well within my weight class limit) and felt like a new person. Although I still had a slight tenderness, I managed to go through two days of practice at eighty percent effort. I didn't wrestle in the February 3 meet against Claymont, which we won 29-16. The coach said I hadn't "sufficiently" recovered for a wrestle-off. I thought that rather strange, considering how much he wanted me to "wrestle through" my injury. Then the coach surprised the hell out of me when he invited me to dinner at his house after Thursday's practice. I thought it would be rude to turn down his invitation. "Not only will it help us get to know each other better," he said, "it'll also give you a chance to savor my wife's great cooking."

I felt a little uneasy that night sitting at the coach's dining room table, consuming his wife's delicious, home cooked meal, and answering so many personal questions. It took me back to Mrs. Jester's sixth grade class. Except this time it wasn't good-ole Doug Snitch peppering me with questions; the coach and his wife were doing a bang-up job.

"Tom, what are your plans for college? Are your parents working? Did you say Bob was your uncle, or a friend? How many of your brothers and sisters are living at home? Where's your father living now? What does your friend Bob do for a living?" And on and on.

I eagerly filled in the gaps, but arrived home that night feeling like I had been set up. *Why all this now? After all, he's been coaching me for almost three years. Hum, maybe I told him too much. What's he going to do with all that personal information he's gleaned from me*?

After two more practices, I felt more than a hundred percent ready. I was out-wrestling everyone, breezing through the round-robins and wind sprints—and doing it without the headaches. It was amazing. The doctor's recommendations (rest, antibiotics, fruits, vitamins, etc.) seemed to be working. I sat on the sidelines at Friday's practice watching Coach Baker officiate the team wrestle-offs for our next-to-last meet the following day, Saturday, February 6, when he again skipped over me. I said, "Mr. Baker, what about me?"

He said, "I'm going to allow you a few more days to get in shape."

"But I'm ready now!"

"I'm sorry, Tom, I don't think you are," and walked away.

Talk about being pissed. I thought, *is he playing games with me because I didn't do exactly what he wanted—wrestle through my injury*? I sat in the bleachers again that weekend, trying to be enthusiastic while cheering on my teammates, but I was seething inside. I had missed four meets, the last two because the coach wouldn't give me a chance to defeat my teammate and earn the right to wrestle in the match. *The coach is flushing my hopes down the tubes.*

That final meet was two weeks before Delaware's Blue Hen Conference tournament and three weeks before the state tournament (referred to as "the States"). I made sure the coaches saw my renewed strength and endurance, and I still expected a wrestle-off with Paul or Bill. A successful elimination bout would allow me to wrestle in the final meet of the season on Saturday, February 13, against Dickinson. It would also give me four varsity matches, the same as my team competitors, and enough (so I thought) to qualify for the tournaments.

After two days of practice, the coach pulled me aside. "Tom, you're looking good, but I can't allow you to wrestle in the tournaments."

"Why not?" I complained, in shock.

"It wouldn't even matter if you won your eliminations today. You haven't wrestled enough matches to qualify."

"What? You're kidding!"

"No, Tom, I'm not kidding. Those are the rules."

"I didn't know that. Why didn't you tell me earlier?"

"There wasn't any point in it, Tom. I'm sorry."

I felt like punching him.

I showered with the team for the last time that night, and I let some teammates know what I thought of the coach's decision: "I only missed three matches because of my injury—and this happens. He's screwing with me!" A few wrestlers were surprised that the coach wouldn't allow me a wrestle-off. Some agreed with him, but just as many thought the best wrestler in each weight class should go to the States. Like me, they thought I should have been allowed a wrestle-off, considering it was an injury that had sidelined me earlier and not my grades or some juvenile behavior.

I refused to participate in the final practices. And I didn't support the team with my presence during the state tournament. Basically, I had given up. I could hardly look Mr. Baker in the eye when I passed him in the halls; the man disgusted me so much. I had wrestled for six years and my sights had always been set on a high school state championship. No athlete could ever overcome a coach hell-bent on a personal crusade. It wasn't my injuries that held me back, because I overcame them. Yes, I think it was all about Coach Baker, and it was spiteful and deliberate.

I moved on as best I could, although every now and then I wondered: *Could I have successfully eliminated my teammate for the States? Was I good enough to finish first at the States?*

Because of Coach Baker's shenanigans, I'll always wonder.

* * * * *

The Easter holiday came and went and class studies were occupying my mind, as well as thoughts of a June graduation day. The first time I really, really noticed Joyce was in the hallway between classes, as she stood by her locker chatting with a group of girls. I had seen her in class before, but this time there seemed to be something special about her. For some strange reason, my silent approach seemed to draw her attention away from her friends. Our eyes met and she smiled.

"Hi Smiley," I said. "Is that smile for me?"

"If you want," she said. "But, I have to warn you, I smile at everyone like that."

"You do? Smiley, you've hurt my feelings. I thought that smile was mine."

"Well, maybe it was," she said, in a sudden flirtatious tone.

"Good," I said, "see you in class."

Walking to my next class, I had a renewed confidence in my ability to strike up a conversation and flirt with the girls. I guess Pete, way back in Texas, would have been proud of me; that is, if I really cared. Lying in bed that night, I wondered if I had started something way over my head. *Am I mature enough and prepared emotionally to begin a new relationship*? Thinking about meeting Joyce in class the following day made me nervous. *What am I going to say*?

I don't know how it happened. Maybe it was our chemistry. Or could it have been the fact that Joyce had just broken up with her boyfriend, and I had been without a steady girlfriend for several months? I learned that she lived near me. We would have been riding the same bus to school, were she not accepting rides from a friend or two. So, our first date, a school bus ride home together, provided a great way to talk and get to know each other.

The spring flowers were blossoming, right there with our mutual attraction. During the last weeks of April I met Joyce's family, invited her to my apartment, and introduced her to Mom and David. During our romantic walks through the parks I told her about my plans for college. I had decided to attend Wesley Junior College in Dover, Delaware, and would be working that summer for Bud and his boss, R.C. Crown, serving as a helper at the Crown Estate in Andover, Massachusetts. I let Joyce know about my alcoholic father, and a little about how and why the family moved to Delaware. And then, when the distressing news arrived, I told her that too: Gary had been arrested and sentenced to nine months in a Delaware prison. He and one of his so-called friends had been caught in a burglary attempt. Gary proclaimed his innocence and insisted he was taking the rap for someone else. Again, family members were left shaking their heads and wondering: what next?

Three weeks into our courtship, as I was walking Joyce home from the bus stop, she stopped abruptly, turned, looked at me, and said, "Tom, there's something I have to tell you."

"What's that?" I said, smiling and gazing into her twinkling eyes.

"We can't see each other anymore."

My stomach felt like it had been punched.

"Why not?" I cried.

"I'm engaged now. Robbie has asked me to marry him, and I said yes."

There's no better word to describe how I felt: dumped. I knew Joyce had made up her mind and there was no use trying to talk her out of it. After all, I had nothing to offer her and no good reason to tell her not to go with her heart.

"Is it something I did or said?"

"No, Tom. That's not it. It's just that…well…I think I've always loved Robbie."

I struggled to compose myself. She gave me a big hug and a kiss, saying, "I know you'll do well in college, and I'm sure you'll meet lots of girls there." She took a step back and looked me square in the eyes. "Goodbye, Tom." Turning away, she said, "I'll see you back in class."

"Bye Joyce!"

I could not watch her leave, so I quickly turned away. Had she sensed my pain? Like other times when I'd been rejected, I didn't want her to know how much it hurt.

I had little time to think about the latest break-up. However, it tortured me having to see her in class twice a week. I tried to avoid her. One way was by making sure she left the classroom well ahead of me. The method worked, and by the end of May I gathered enough courage to say, "How are things going, Joyce?"

"Oh, fine," she said, fiddling with her engagement ring, "everything's just fine."

* * * * *

During the month of May, Bob and my school guidance counselor, Mr. Capodanno, had been working on securing state tuition scholarship funds for my freshman and sophomore years. Oh, by the way, I had finally made up my mind as to what I wanted to be when I grew up. Loving the country, woods, and mountains the way I did (and still do), I decided that a career in Forestry or Wildlife Management would be my ticket to salvation and eternal bliss while here on earth. Before I could be awarded the funds, however, I had to take a barrage of tests offered through the mental health clinic. Bob had initially referred me to Mr. Alexander at the clinic in Newark, and after one consultation he referred me to Mrs. Hultsch in Wilmington for psychological and academic evaluation. I started to worry about these exams. Would they think I was too flaky for college or might drop out? Looking back, I see this as normal teenage angst. I really didn't have much to worry about.

Between studying for finals and all that goes with it, I sort of forgot about setting up an appointment for the psychological exam. Fortunately, Mr. Capodanno called me to his office on June 1 and told me that Mrs. Hultsch from the state mental health clinic had been trying to locate me. The phone number she had didn't connect, and she had to finally call the school. I called her back between classes using the office phone. Her name was Catharine, and she seemed very nice and friendly over the phone. I made an appointment for the following afternoon.

We met in her office, a room filled wall-to-wall with paintings and stacks of boxes and scattered papers. I sat in a large leather-upholstered captain's chair next to her desk. Mrs. Hultsch cordially asked me how I was doing and seemed impressed when I told her that my brother and I had driven by the place the previous afternoon, to make sure of the location and to ensure that we'd be on time. I may have scored some points with that one.

The evaluative categories included appearance, attitude, behavior, family background, health, schooling, employment history, vocational plans, interests, hobbies, mental ability, school achievements, personality features, and more. The three-hour session seemed almost as stressful as the SAT exams. I walked away thinking I had done well enough to secure some college funds, and soon learned that I had been granted a two-year state scholarship. I never expected to see those test results, but I learned about them three decades later and found them amusing. Who wouldn't, after all those years?

I stayed busy the rest of my senior year, what with tests and schoolwork. I breezed through all my finals. Like most students, I spent a good part of the last day signing yearbooks and offering up mine for signatures. A favorite was the comment written by my cocky, longtime wrestling buddy, Ed Janvier. He wrote: "Tom, good luck in the future. Never forget the times in wrestling. But, I must admit, I am tired of looking at your mug through the years, 7, 8, 9, 10, 11, 12." Uh-huh. I could not have said it better, Ed.

They scheduled the graduation ceremony more than a week away, but a summer job with a heap of grass cutting awaited me in Andover. Bud said, "The estate's grass is growing high and the weeds need hoeing, so get your ass up here now. You can fly back for graduation later." I hadn't even reported to work, and he was already behaving like a pain-in-the-ass boss.

A day or two later, Bob bought me a roundtrip ticket to Boston on Allegheny Airlines and watched me board my flight at the Wilmington Airport in New Castle. Sitting there on the plane, I knew that another grand adventure awaited me—another chapter in my early life saga.

V

College Days

1971-1973

One of many proud Henry C. Conrad graduates, class of 1971.

Leaving Home

Every two weeks I got paid. I collected my first paycheck from the Crown payroll office, down the street from Bud's apartment. I walked across Main Street to the Bank of Andover and opened my first savings account. Those days I paid cash for everything, so I saw no point in opening a checking account.

I flew back to Delaware for my high school graduation during the second week of June. The warm, sunny weather was perfect for the outdoor ceremony conducted on the Conrad track and football field. I loved how that square mortarboard cap kept the sun off my face. Perfect! More than four hundred graduating students and many more parents and family members were in attendance. Representing my family were Donna (now nine months pregnant) and my mother. After the ceremonies, Donna reminded me that I'd just become the second of our lot to have graduated from high school. As if I didn't know that.

I sincerely hoped that I wouldn't be the last. At nineteen, all I had to do was look to my siblings, four older and one younger, for proof of the importance of a high school education. Although many high school dropouts were finding well-paid jobs (Wesley making a career in the military, Ronnie working in auto manufacturing, Paul and Gary gaining employment thanks to skills they learned through the Job Corps), those kinds of opportunities were steadily decreasing. More and more poor or low-income high school graduates like me were taking advantage of state and federal grants to earn a college education.

Donna took several pictures of me in cap and gown standing by my school locker and alongside Mom. I couldn't tell which of us looked the proudest.

While at home I received some good news. First, Wesley and Kay were the proud parents of a son, Anthony (Tony) Wayne, born in May at the Fort Dix hospital. After two girls, they welcomed a healthy son. Second, Mom was allowing Debbie to live with her and David at the apartment in Elsmere as a "test" or temporary arrangement until the state could place her in a foster home. Mom didn't want to resume permanent custody. The pain and distrust she felt (and maybe some stubbornness) ran too deep.

Our landlord said he didn't want more than three occupants residing in the apartment. Mom and I understood his rule, as the apartment was already tight with Mom, David, and me. But with me away for the summer and living in a college dorm the rest of the year, Debbie could stay with Mom for a time and the state wouldn't be under pressure to find her a home.

Two days before boarding my flight back to Boston, I had a long chat with my one and only younger sister. David, Debbie, and I had finished a late breakfast and were lounging around the living room while Mom straightened up the kitchen.

I said, "Debbie, you seem a little troubled today."

"Yeah, I have a lot on my mind, Tommy."

"Really? Girl, you're too young to be having all these problems. It wouldn't have anything to do with boys, now, would it?"

"Maybe, but I don't want to talk about it here."

"Okay, how about we take a walk in the park and talk about it?"

She looked at me with those big hazel eyes of hers, as if to say: "You, you of all people, want to take a walk and chat with me, your little sister, the troublemaker?"

But I was sincere about it. For years I had been focused on my own issues (school, Deanna, wrestling, college) and had pretty much failed at spending quality time with family, especially my little sister.

I told Mom that Debbie and I were taking a walk in the park.

"That's nice. You be careful out there now. Watch out for strangers—you know, creeps and perverts lurking about."

Debbie said, "Oh, Mommy," and snickered.

I laughed. "Sure, Mom, but don't worry, we won't be long."

Debbie and I walked two blocks south on Rodman Road, where we picked up the footpath to Canby Park West.

"So Debbie, what is it you wanted to talk about?"

"I don't know where to start."

"Then let's start with the boys. Do you have a boyfriend?"

"Sort of. His name is Bobby. He lives in The Park."

"Oh, that's not good. It must be pretty tough to see him, you know, with you being in a girls' home and all that. How do you plan on having a steady boyfriend while being in foster care?"

"Well, it's making my life pretty miserable," she said, raising her voice. "That's one of my biggest problems. How can I have a life living like this?"

After crossing the Penn Central Railroad tracks, we joined the walking trail at Canby Park East.

"I know it can seem tough at your age, Debbie, but all of us go through this kind of stuff. Heck, did you know Deanna and I broke up last summer?"

"No! Did you, really?"

"Yep. We'd been going steady for over a year."

"Wow, I thought you two might get married."

"Don't count us out yet, Debbie. Deanna and I are still friends, and we never know what life has in store for us, now do we?"

"No. I guess not."

"Isn't that the point, though? Debbie, we're both still young. We've got a lot of time to get really serious about girls and boys after we complete our education and get jobs."

"Yeah, you're right. I really should forget all about boys. They only want one thing, anyway."

"Oh, and what's that?"

"You know what I'm talking about, Tommy."

"Really? You really think that's all they want?"

"I don't think it, Tommy, I know it. They're always trying to get into my pants."

"Well, I have to admit it, you do have a point. I've been just as guilty as some of the boys you're talking about. But I've done some growing up the last couple of years. Debbie, you should forget about those kinds of boys. Look more for the mature ones, the ones that respect girls. Maybe, as a girl, you should see the situation as a responsibility. You know, like a boy's goal might be to worm his way into a girl's pants, while your responsibility is to fight him off. When the pest gets the message, he'll stop. If he don't, then it's time for the girl to punch him or dump him."

Debbie laughed.

"Maybe both, huh?" I grinned. "Then you can refocus on more important things, like finishing high school."

"Humph. That's fine for you to say, Mr. Brainy. You made good grades. You're a jock, too, and now you're going to college."

"You can still get your high school diploma, Debbie. That should be your main focus for the next three or four years." I grabbed her arm and turned her around to face me. "By the way," I said, looking into her eyes, "can you forgive me for smacking you with the belt?"

She hesitated. "Sure. I forgive you, Tommy." Turning away, she said, "I know you were only doing what Mommy told you to do."

"Thanks Debbie."

Tommy, Ginny, Debbie, and Gary. quieter times at #5 Rodman Rd.

Debbie and I returned from our walk about an hour later, leaving me unsure as to how much I had gotten through to her.

Three days later I was back working at the estate. Donna had given birth to little Cynthia, and Wesley and Kay had decided to welcome Debbie into their growing family of five. The plan—and we all know how often plans go awry—was for her to spend the summer with them at Fort Dix and begin ninth grade there in the fall. Debbie had wasted two earlier chances, both due to her lack of discipline. Ginny and Charles took Debbie in at 14. Paul and Linda gave it a try when she turned 15. That whole summer I kept thinking my little sister had no ambition, that boys, marriage (maybe one of those shotgun types), and kids, most likely, were her priorities. Then, just like her mother, her only job in life would be to raise a family. Some of us were hoping that Wesley's military style of discipline would improve her attitude. Anyway, it would mean serious adjustments for all involved.

At the same time, Mom and David moved from the Elsmere apartment into Paul and Linda's trailer at the Glasgow Trailer Park. Having finished sixth grade at Oak Grove in Elsmere, David entered the seventh grade at Glasgow Junior High.

* * * * *

Living in Andover and working at the estate was a blast. I felt truly free for the first time in my life. The key? Well, it sure wasn't hanging out with Bud, although he certainly made my stay interesting at times. The real key had to be my meeting Beth, that special someone I'd been yearning for ever since I'd become interested in the opposite sex. Our candle burned so brightly that summer that I couldn't imagine anything extinguishing it, not even time itself.

When it comes to romance, I learned that time and distance work both ways. I hooked up with an old sweetheart before driving to Dover for my first semester. Driving Donna's Plymouth, I picked up Deanna at her apartment and drove to a local park for a picnic. The date felt strange and awkward, knowing I already had a new girlfriend. That's probably why I was satisfied with the way we parted: as friends, not knowing when, if, or even why we'd ever get back together. Time has a way of sorting out these things.

The two-month "growth" experience in Andover, however, seemed lacking compared to the next two years at college. It was amazing how much crap two years of classes, together with a dormitory existence, could throw at your typical college student. And, since I wasn't your typical student, you can bet some things didn't just roll off my back like water off a duck's. Instead, I seemed to have caught much of it directly in the face. I did manage to fine tune my study habits and acquire new friends. Some actually became "good" friends. In other words, someone I could count on—at least for a while. Much better, would have been the rare and honest "true" friend, someone we continue to see years down the road, someone who is there for us as much as we are there for them. Maybe that's what I was looking for: not the lite version, or good friend, but the true one. Many of us need to grow up before we meet those, or even know it when we have them.

Brenda and Sammy were my friends too. Back then I considered them "special" friends. Yep, you got it. Call it young love, if you please. Looking back, I now see each of these young women entering my life at just the right moment and for just the right reason: mutual growth and support. We helped each other move on to something (and maybe someone) more permanent.

* * * * *

After surviving my first semester of college, spending Christmas with my sister and brothers provided a welcome break. But first I needed to clean up some unfinished business in Andover. Now, I ask you, who in their right mind would shell out hard-earned cash for a roundtrip ticket to Boston just to say, "Goodbye, I've fallen in love with someone else." Well, I did. My conscience would have slowly eaten a hole in me if I had simply provided Beth with the news over the phone. Well intentioned as I was, saying goodbye in person did not make it any easier. Beth and I said our tearful goodbyes, basking in the warmth of Bud's apartment that day. Outside, layers and layers of ice blanketed the streets and sidewalks of Andover.

I spent parts of Christmas Eve and all of Christmas with Donna and John in Woodcrest, helping Ronnie and Charles (Ginny's husband) install shingles on two houses. On the last day our fingers got so cold that we had to stop working three times to warm ourselves in the car. That was the coldest I've ever been. We knocked off early and, in the process of thawing out, I did something I had not done since childhood. I curled into the fetal position and fell asleep on Ronnie's living room floor, no doubt suffering from a mild case of hypothermia. Paul and I spent the better part of a day squirrel hunting near Blackbird State Forrest. We bagged two, and Mom prepped and cooked them for us, just like the old days.

Someone shuffled me over to Wesley's place at Fort Dix for three days during the first week of the New Year. Wesley marched me onto the base one day and introduced me to some of his troops, just as he'd done in the summer of 1964 at Fort Hood, Texas. Fortunately, this time the men were fully dressed, and I saw no one strutting about singing in the nude. On one of those days I sat in the bleachers with a hundred or more troops and watched my big brother give a live demonstration of the M72 LAW (Light Antitank Weapon), the shoulder mounted replacement for the old bazooka we knew as kids. It fired a 66mm rocket at 475 feet per second; capable of penetrating eight inches of steel, or two feet of reinforced concrete, or six feet of soil, all at a distance of 200 meters. That's more than two football fields. It was frightening! Here's a tip: don't stand anywhere near the back blast from this weapon.

I also had a chance to spend more time with Debbie during my brief stay at Wesley's. Everything seemed to be working out fine. However, several weeks later, soon after Debbie's sixteenth birthday, Kay and Wesley were ready to bail out. Debbie's position when it came to studying, dating, curfews, and boys—especially boys in the house—created a lot of friction. So much so, that Wesley and Kay drove her back to Delaware and dropped her off at Donna's. A few weeks later, the state resumed custody. Now, almost sixteen, she would be looking for another foster home to take her in. I wish I could have done something or said something to get through to her. But so many people had already spoken so many words, and none of them seemed to be helping. Debbie was running out of options.

Mother's Choice

After working most of my second summer at the Andover estate, I phoned my college roommate Karl from the YMCA in Lawrence, Massachusetts. He asked me what I was doing at the YMCA. Too embarrassed to give him the gritty details, I told him that Bud and I had a disagreement and he kicked me out of the Andover apartment. During our chat, Karl wanted to know if he could sign me up to work with him on the Wesley College orientation committee. We were going to remain roommates our sophomore year, and he wanted me to join him in welcoming the new freshmen class. I didn't hesitate; I gave him all the information he needed to fill out the form and submit it.

When I called Paul to gather the latest news about the family, he said, "Oh, haven't you heard?"

"No, heard what?"

He told me that Dad had collapsed from lung failure two weeks earlier and was in critical condition at the Bluefield Sanitarium Hospital, suffering from emphysema and black lung disease. This should have been sad news, but I wasn't surprised at how little it bothered me. What he said next, however, shocked the hell out of me.

"Mom's down there with him right now."

"What! You're kidding!"

"No, Ginny and Charles drove her down last week."

"Oh, no. Why would she do that?"

"Yeah, I know what you mean, Tommy. I asked myself the same question. I think Wesley and Daisy talked her into it."

Facing death, Dad had begged Mom to come back to him. He told her he loved her and would give up alcohol and behave himself. At the urging of Daisy, Wesley, and Kay, Mom agreed to move back to Boissevain to live with and take care of him. My emotions went from surprise, to shock, to horror. But I knew my mother. Once she made up her mind, there was no turning back. Was love motivating my mother or a warped sense of duty? Had time mended old wounds, even the most glaring?

I couldn't talk to Paul for more than a few minutes, since long distance calls were expensive. I rode the elevator to my room trying to imagine why my mother would take such a risk, not only for herself but for David as well. I could do little with me living and working so far away. I thanked God for giving me a good summer job to keep my body tired and my mind occupied; otherwise, I think I would have gone mad.

After two days with Karl at his parents' place in Bridgeport, Connecticut, they drove us to Delaware, dropping me off at Donna's place in Boxwood before journeying on to Dover and checking into a motel for the night.

It took me several hours at Donna's to pack up notebooks, papers, extra clothes, and my all-important stereo system and record albums. While there, she informed me that Dad had been discharged from the hospital and back living with Mom on Boissevain Mountain. Mom was taking good care of him and making plans for David to join them as soon as possible. I shivered; the news disturbed me so much. I just couldn't believe it. After all Mom and our family had suffered, after all the years of living in Delaware with the modern conveniences she had grown used to, how could she return to our mean, alcoholic father and an impoverished life on Boissevain Mountain? *Crazy*!

The next morning Donna hauled me and my belongings back to Wesley College.

* * * * *

As usual when visiting home, I divided my time between my siblings and their families. One or two nights with Paul and Linda, and one or two with Ronnie and Charlene, was the usual routine. At Donna and John's, my home base, I enjoyed a delicious Thanksgiving dinner with all the trimmings. I called Mom long distance for a brief chat, happy to find out that they could afford a telephone in the house, a first for my mother and father.

"So, how are you doing, Mom?"

"I'm okay, Tommy."

"How's Dad?"

"Glad to be alive. He's regained most of his strength and he's behaving himself."

She was happy to be taking care of Dad and living on Boissevain Mountain. A near brush with the Grim Reaper had apparently been a wake-up call for Dad.

"Why'd you move back with him, Mom?"

"Oh, I don't know, Tommy. One reason was my job, I guess. The jobs the state of Delaware assigned us were wearing me out."

"There's got to be more to it than that, Mom."

"Let's just leave it at that, Tommy. I think I'll be more useful here in Boissevain. You know, taking care of your father and seeing that David graduates from high school."

In a way, I think Mom felt important there. She was wanted. Someone needed her. Maybe in Delaware she felt less valued, living under the same roof as her grown children.

I also spoke with David.

"How are things going down there?"

"I don't like it here, Tommy. I don't like it a bit."

"Why, what's going on?"

"I feel out of place. These people don't even speak the same language."

I chuckled. "Give it time. You'll get used to it," I said, trying to cheer him up.

I didn't believe my own words. I knew I'd never get used to living there again. So how could my little brother? It had to be a huge adjustment—no running water, an outhouse out back, wood to chop, coal to carry, chickens to feed, and chicken coops to maintain. There was little doubt in my mind that David would rather be living with Paul and Linda and attending school in Delaware.

David went on to say that he felt out of place entering the eighth grade at Pocahontas High. He was fearful of the repercussions of living near relatives and other people who knew his brother, his father, and the things they had done or rumored to have done. David had attended school for less than a month when a couple of kids began picking on him. He held his ground by being a tough and sometimes funny type of kid. Eventually the bullies learned about the family background and either through fear or sympathy decided to leave him alone. Still, David thought no good would come from Mom's decision to start all over with his father. David was barely six years old when the family left Dad behind. That essentially made his father a stranger. All he knew about him he'd heard from his siblings—not encouraging, to say the least.

Around the time Dad first got sick, Debbie had just been released from the girls' home in Wilmington when she heard that Mom and David had packed up and moved to Boissevain. This upset her and made her feel as if she had again been deserted. Having first worn out her welcome with her mother, then with Ginny, followed by Paul and Wesley, Debbie sighed with relief when Daisy and Chester said they'd give her a chance.

Graduation ceremonies at Wesley Junior College took place the third weekend of May. Considering the many distractions that year, I was happy to have finally made the dean's list with a respectable 3.25 GPA. Donna, Bob, and my girl Sammy were there for me. Then Bob insisted on stopping at the Blue Coat Inn at Silver Lake, a popular restaurant on North State Street, a bit north of the college. Of course it was his treat. After dining, Donna drove home alone while Sammy and I joined Bob for a toast at his apartment in New Castle. He took several pictures of the two of us there, and we gave Sammy a ride home around sunset.

VI

DESTINY'S DOORSTEP

1973-1974

I'm celebrating my graduation from Wesley Junior College at Dr. Bob's apartment, May 1973.

Stepping Stones

Rest assured that whenever Mom noticed one of her children procrastinating or acting in a lazy manner, she'd say, "Time stands still for no one." A direct order usually followed these well-worn words of wisdom. Something like, "Now get your butt in gear and…"

Yes, the summer of '73 had arrived, and I had no job, no money, and no clue as to where or how I would complete my education. The good news? I had a $1,500 grant from the state of Delaware for a year's tuition at the in-state institution of my choice—if, that is, I could find one that would have me. My advisor at Wesley had told me that my ambition of having a career in forestry or wildlife management was a bit unrealistic. "Tom, I hate to tell you this," he said, "but nepotism runs rampant in those fields. Unless there's someone in your family already working the trees and cataloguing wild critters, you had better be rich or famous or know someone with special influence. Otherwise, you're unlikely to land a job there." The man didn't mince words. I had spoken with my advisor twice in two years, and all he provided was discouragement.

So, as I set about redefining (once again) my career goals, I got a letter of acceptance from the University of Delaware, inviting me into their agriculture program. Believe it or not, I actually felt disappointed. My first thought was a negative one: *Damn, I don't want to be a freakin' farmer!* The university informed me that if I didn't choose to enroll that fall, I could reapply the following year. In the meantime, I lived free of charge at Donna's, taking up space in her upstairs bedroom and eating food my brother-in-law paid for by sweating and toiling on the Chrysler production line. Donna, like my college advisor, didn't hold back. She put it to me straight, telling me exactly what I already knew: "Tommy, you need to get a job, at least for the summer, until you know what you're going to do about college."

Although Bud and Mr. Crown said they'd be happy to have me work another summer at the estate, I'd have to be a masochist to work for Bud again or spend another summer at the Y. And since I wasn't a masochist, I began to search out the local job environment. A week later I stood in front of a mirror, admiring the uniform I would wear as an Allstate Insurance security guard, patrolling the fenced in grounds of a trucking company at night and keying clocks at different times and stations. Boring! I hated it. Having never worked a night shift—or alone—it was no surprise when I began having problems staying alert.

Somehow Allstate's management astutely decided that warehouse night patrol wasn't my forte. Four days into the security guard job, management transferred me to day work at Almart, a department store at the Concord Mall, on Route 202 northeast of Wilmington. Whoopee! I felt like I'd been let out of prison. I was one of three security guards assigned to prevent theft by inspecting and securing all customer bags and packages. My tools were my eyes, a roll of labels, my trusty staple gun, and a fresh can of Mace to handle the would-be troublemakers.

I couldn't have landed a more perfect summer job. Working the three entrances and exits at Almart provided plenty of opportunities to meet young women and, in some cases, even get to know them. And so did the patrolling (or should I say trolling?) at the mall's shops and restaurants on my breaks and lunch periods.

Eventually I spotted Sarah, a young lady working the sandwich bar at Lonni's Luncheonette near the middle of the mall. Blonde, cute, and curvy, Sarah communicated availability. To make sure I wasn't imagining things, I kept dropping by each day for a sandwich, a drink, and some idle chitchat. My sister accused me of flirting. "Whatever," I replied. "I was paying for it, wasn't I?"

Two weeks earlier, riding around with Bob, I noticed a car for sale. We pulled off Route 40 onto the gravel parking lot of an old warehouse to take a look. At first glance, the white Ford Galaxy 500 looked great and the sign said "ONLY $350," and so we found the owner and took it for a test drive. The interior was in excellent shape and the paint job looked good. The engine purred and it seemed to drive well enough. I saw only one problem—the front right side of the car's frame sat a bit low to the ground. The owner said the car had been damaged when he hit a traffic barrier a few months back. It seemed like an awful lot of damage from one little barrier.

"I can't pay full price knowing that," I said. "I'll give you $250."

"No, I've already lowered the price with that in mind. But I'll let you have it for $300."

I hesitated, never having bargained for anything. I walked around the car again, checking it out some more. I really wanted that car. I had always liked the profile of the '66 Galaxy 500, and except for the front right corner this one looked great. *Oh, what the hell*, I thought, *handicapped cars need a home too.*

"Well, mister, you've got yourself a buyer!"

So with a small loan from Donna, a bigger loan from Bob, and some cash of my own, I bought my first car.

* * * * *

Standing guard at the store entrances would often get a little boring. But just when my attention began to fade, a chunk of eye candy would saunter by, raising my blood pressure and sometimes throwing me into a panic state. And no eye candy caught my attention more than Rita and Genia, two slender and curvaceous cashiers who—just like me—rotated to and from the various doors and checkout counters in the store.

They were two hot-looking chili peppers! Rita was a tall, well-built brunette—definitely model material. She carried herself in a somewhat aloof manner that said: "I'm taken!" I didn't think I could ever reach first base with her, even if she were available. Genia didn't seem to offer much better odds, or so I thought. Friendlier than most, she conveyed oodles of confidence. But I couldn't figure her out; she was the only employee who flirted with me, winking and blowing kisses when she thought no one else was looking. I thought she could be older, maybe 24 or 25, and I further assumed that she, like Rita, was also taken. Why else would she behave the way she did? I had the feeling she regarded me as cute, while teasing me, and dismissing me as young and immature. How little I knew.

But what could I do? I couldn't ask all three women for a date. Heck, I was feeling pinched for money. Knowing my luck, they'd all accept my offer. Then what would I do? *No, I'll take my time. I won't rush it. I'll be friendly and get to know them before spending money I don't have.*

With my attitude adjusted, I developed extra spring in my step—and quite noticeably, too—especially when I stopped by Lonni's Luncheonette. Sarah, so cute and sweet, joined me for lunch a couple of times. So I asked her out for dinner and a movie. She jumped at the chance.

Wouldn't you know it? Two days before my big date with Sarah, I was stationed at the mall entrance when Genia strolled past, pushing a shopping cart loaded with items to be returned to the shelves. I almost didn't recognize her; she had changed her hairdo. I learned later that a wig had added to her allure.

She winked at me, made a quick left turn in front of me military style, and marched down the aisle.

Decked out in two-inch high heels, nylon stockings, and a short hip-hugging skirt, she not only gained my attention, but also the full attention of every male in the area—the custodian behind me; Joe, the sporting goods manager, standing to my left; and Mr. Fox, my boss, who just happened to be walking by. Yeah, right. I think you could say the old fart was "tailing" her.

As she strolled down the aisle, I quickly noticed her well-defined calf muscles and slender thighs. *Wow, does she look great!* I promised myself, right then and there, that I would overcome my shyness, confront her, and get to know the woman who carried all that sparkle and glitter. The most she could do: tell me to get lost. But it would be better to make my move on another day, maybe when she wasn't looking so hot and the wolves weren't hunting in pack formation.

I bit awestruck, I guided my early model Ford, slightly listing to starboard, over to Sarah's house that Saturday afternoon. Her neighborhood looked great. I knew by her address that she lived in an upper-class suburban development off Concord Pike near Talleyville. Her father greeted me at the door and treated me to a cold cola, while Sarah did her last minute preparations. I told him I had just graduated from Wesley Junior College and was trying to decide what to do about further education. Both parents projected a professional presence. I pictured Sarah's father as a successful businessman, a DuPont chemist, or maybe a physician.

Sarah and I enjoyed each other's company that night. She told me that she wanted to become a corporate secretary and was planning to attend Goldey-Beacom College. She seemed like a very sweet, happy-go-lucky girl, a giggler, sometimes silly, and I could tell she had old-fashioned values. She seemed to enjoy the way I opened doors for her. She never offered to pay for anything, not even the tip. That didn't bother me a bit, but I did take note of it. I kissed her on the lips that first night, thinking about how much I had enjoyed her company and how much I wanted to get to know her better. It had all gone smoothly.

The following week I began making small talk with Genia during a lunch break. That's when I knew I had misjudged her. She was only nineteen, two years younger than me. She had just graduated high school, with zero plans for college. She had thoughts of going into the banking business, maybe starting as a teller and working her way up the ladder. She liked to watch old movies, play tennis, shop (window shop, that is), and save money. She drove a recently purchased 1968 Ford Mustang fastback, a dark blue muscle car that didn't fit my image of her. Since I also enjoyed tennis, we made a date to play the following Saturday morning. Maybe we'd have lunch afterwards.

Come Saturday, I drove to Genia's house and met her parents, a nice Polish couple. From there she drove us in her Mustang to her high school tennis courts, gliding through the gears like a pro. *Impressive*! Her car purchase made sense when she told me she bought it as an investment, a steal from an 80-year-old gentleman. She planned to resell it in a few years for a handsome profit. I was impressed all over again. *This young woman has a business head on her shoulders.* She said she liked tennis, but she didn't possess the skills I'd imagined. I held back, taking it easy on her. We enjoyed lunch together afterward, and I got to know more about her.

Genia's parents, Theodore and Agnes Rucinski, had adopted "Eugenia" from a Polish orphanage in April 1964 at the tender age of 10. In many ways, the harsh conditions her family endured in Poland could have mirrored those of my own here in the United States. She spoke of living in an environment where, nearby, chickens scratched for their food. Even I, a child of Appalachia, found that hard to believe.

Everyone remembers the fairy tale of the old woman who lived in a shoe: "She had so many children she didn't know what to do." Well, somehow Genia's biological mother was forced to give up at least one of her children for adoption, even after losing three of six to untimely deaths. A remarkable story indeed, and I leaned into every word of it.

Two years before Ted and Agnes adopted Genia, they had adopted Wentzel from the same orphanage. So when Genia arrived in the good-ole U.S.A., she had a ready-made Polish family awaiting her—a mom, a dad, and a brother, two years older. Learning to speak English became the most daunting of challenges for the two orphans. Two years after adoption they were speaking English so well that they could barely form a complete sentence in Polish. Now that's assimilation!

Over the next three weeks I had a second and third date with Sarah. She was a swell girl, but after having dated Genia twice, and having had dinner with her and her parents, I found that I just couldn't be myself around Sarah. I felt more comfortable with Genia and, besides, dating two girls at the same time cost money. Should I mention the stress? I'd heard of guys juggling three and four girls, but those games weren't for me. I was having conniptions trying to hold the interest of two young women. I felt I had to choose one or go broke. In August I ended my relationship with Sarah, telling her I'd decided to date someone else exclusively. I have no idea how hard it hit her, or if it hit her at all. The fact that Genia insisted on going Dutch certainly helped me make up my mind.

Not since Deanna, the girl from my early teens, had I shared someone so much with family and friends. Now that I had a car, a job, and a steady date, Donna began to offer me hints, hints like I should start looking for my own place. I knew that was coming. George, my coworker, reminded me of the three-bedroom apartment in Newark he shared with two other college students. He said they had room for another renter since one would be leaving soon. I accepted, and made a quick and easy move out of Donna's place.

The new apartment living room contained a TV, a coffee table, and nothing else. The student I replaced had taken the sofa, the sofa chair, and end tables. George and I quickly set up my entertainment system in the living room. I bought two pine planks, stained them red chestnut, and strung them across several fancy masonry blocks. We were so proud of the results. We even had enough shelf room to store several of our college textbooks. I secured an old twin bed and dresser, and an even older chest of drawers that jammed and screeched like a hawk every time I opened them. I purchased a new alarm clock and lamp, and placed both on the pine nightstand I'd made way back in Mr. Emmel's junior high woodshop class, feeling good about having my own bedroom and sharing an apartment, although my roommates spent very little time there.

I also let the girls know I was quitting my security guard job to work for Kaiser Aluminum at their Boulden Boulevard location near Wilmington Manor. Jim Rouch, a Kaiser employee and good family friend, had encouraged me to apply, saying he would put in a good word for me. It worked and I started as a laborer in a 20-acre yard, stacking, strapping, and bundling "to fill" orders for aluminum drainage pipes. The pluses: two dollars more per hour and a shorter commute. The negatives: no more air conditioning and working outside in all weather.

The Hard Way

Genia and I dated at least two or three times a week during August and September. During that time she met most of my family, and she was with me in September when I said farewell to Ginny, Charles, and the kids, who were moving to Abbs Valley, Virginia. Yes, back to where our family story began. It felt strange, knowing they were returning to a place that harbored some pretty unpleasant memories—especially for Ginny. Her decision to move may have been eased by the fact that Mom and Dad were already there and she would be living just three miles away. I guess they also figured that Charles's new job took precedence. I'm sure the place also held a few good memories for them, and they were dwelling on those and not the bad ones.

After a full day at work, I was barreling down I-95 south listening to music on the radio:

"Doo doo doo doo doo doo doo doo.
Jesus is just alright with me,
Jesus is just alright, oh yeah…"

What group is this? I dug that funky beat, bobbing my head, doing 60 mph—pretty good, considering that my car looked and handled like a handicapped Sherman tank. I waited anxiously for the song to end so I could find out who was responsible for this fantastic piece of art.

"Well, listeners, you have just heard *The Doobie Brothers'* version of 'Jesus is Just Alright' from *Toulouse Street*, their latest (Nov. 15, 1972) album."

Wow! I don't believe I've ever heard the group!

Trying to imprint the song in my memory, I kept repeating the title. That weekend I dashed to the neighborhood record store and bought the album.

Minutes later I had it spinning on my turntable, using my headphones so I wouldn't disturb my roommates. I was deep into the groove of "Rockin' Down the Highway" when George tapped my shoulder to get my attention. Removing my headphones, I sat up.

"Tom," he said, pointing to the doorway, "someone's here to see you."

I looked toward the door and there stood Genia, smiling one of her mischievous grins. "I hope I haven't come at a bad time," she said.

"Genia! It's good to see you," I said, dashing over to greet her. "Don't tell me you drove all the way over here just to see me?"

"Well, I did."

"Hey! I asked you not to tell me that—just kidding," I said, smiling. "Why didn't you call to say you were coming?"

"I wanted to surprise you."

"Ahh, that's nice." I smothered her with one of my best hugs.

"Did you have any trouble getting here?"

"Nope, only one wrong turn, that's all. It really wasn't bad."

Genia couldn't have arrived at a better time. I introduced her to my roommates, and of course she already knew George. We ordered pizza and began listening to *The Doobie Brothers*. I kissed her goodbye that evening and watched her rush away in her 1968 Mustang—a 2-door fastback, all presidential blue, boasting a boss-sounding 302 cubic-inch V8 engine (the term "Boss" was actually first applied to the 302's in the '69 and '70 model years), fueled by a gas-guzzling 4-barrell carburetor. Truly worried about her safety during such a long drive in traffic, I asked her to call me the moment she arrived home.

About an hour after sunset I still hadn't heard from her, so I called her at home.

"Hey, you didn't call me. I was worried."

"Oh, I'm sorry, Tom. I would have called, except my mother was on the phone long distance with my brother Wentzel in Germany. Things were a little hectic around here."

"Oh?"

"Yes. He's going to be home on leave from the Army next week. I'd like for you to meet him."

"No problem. I'm looking forward to it."

I must have slept better than usual that night, but not before I did some thinking. I thought back to the few relationships I'd had, romantic and otherwise. They were all wonderful people, each special in his or her own way. Some had been there for me when I needed them, and I hoped I had been there for them, too.

But I thought again about the long distance aspect of many of my relationships, especially the romantic ones. *Did they ever work? Could they work for me? They hadn't so far. I hadn't seen or heard from Deanna since I started college. Odds are she's married with a kid, and another on the way. I could see Beth married to that paratrooper by now. Brenda could be sharing (smoking) roaches with a new roommate, attending a fresh four-year university. And Sammy? God only knows, considering all we went through. I just hope she hadn't dropped out of college.*

The last time Sammy and I had spoken was long distance. I told her about my security job at the mall, how I had become interested in Genia but was afraid to approach her. Sammy said, "Don't be such a scaredy-cat, Tom. Ask her out!" Sammy was getting a great tan spending the summer at her family's beach house and looking forward to returning to Wesley for her second year. I thanked her for the encouragement and wished her a happy summer.

Although I had wheels and could come and go as I pleased, I worried that my car would break down at any time. *It would be nice to have a long-term relationship with someone in a convenient location. Maybe someone, say, within a 25-mile radius. Would it be Genia? Or would it be someone else?*

God, there were so many questions! And worst of all, I couldn't make up my mind about going back to college. Then, as I was about to fall asleep, I thought of Genia. She had gone out of her way to drive from Talleyville to Newark, a considerable distance for her, to see me and surprise me, not even knowing whether I'd be home or not. The girl I considered too old, too taken, too good looking, and too far out of reach, had come all that way—just to see me.

Not long after I started the Kaiser job, other people were also making changes. Genia had secured new employment as a cash clerk, counting money in the back room at Mitchell's Trains, Toys & Hobbies, a five-and-dime department store that specialized in electric trains. She also moved out of the house she had shared with her family for the past nine years. Her friend Jeannette had recently filed for divorce, and as soon as her husband moved out of their apartment in Wilmington Manor, she asked Genia if she wanted to split the rent. Genia jumped at the chance to establish her independence.

George had stopped working security, too. He was now preparing for a busy class schedule two miles away at the University of Delaware.

My new job was brutal at times. Young male workers would come and then go, unable to endure the heat and physical demands. Were it not for my youth and above average physical conditioning, I would have also quit. But I didn't give up easily, especially when faced with a challenge. I held tight and endured, knowing that the cooler fall season was only a few weeks away.

By September I began to change my tune. Quitting didn't seem such a dirty word anymore. My right forearm ached and my right hand went numb whenever I used the handheld metal banding tool. The pain and numbness grew worse by the day, and just when I thought I would have to quit the job, three of us were offered a chance to try out for the available forklift driver position. It offered more pay, less walking, and an escape from possible nerve damage due to heavy use of the banding tool.

My "audition" came second, so I had to wait a week. Time passed quickly, and on a Monday morning in late September I began day one of forklift training.

I was looking great, zipping about the yard picking up pipes for an order, when I had an encounter with Barry, our most experienced forklift operator. Somewhat of a loner, Barry made little effort to get to know the yard workers, communicating only when necessary. He had been working at Kaiser for one or two years and had developed a good rapport with management, as I wanted to do. He was a short, slim fella, about 30 years old, with a full head of straight, dark brown hair and long sideburns that flared out toward the chin line. He wore green or blue work slacks and white t-shirts, with a pack of Camels tucked away in a rolled-up sleeve, just like the greasers from the 1950s. *I'll bet he's lost more than one pack of cigarettes carrying them around that way,* I thought. *But what do I know? I'm just a nonsmoker.*

I hadn't had any problems with Barry, but this day I caught him sitting on his forklift taking a smoke break and blocking access to a pipe on my list. I sat silently for a minute, watching him savor every drag. *Doesn't he know I'm here?* I thought perhaps he hadn't seen me, so I blew my horn. No reaction. I blew my horn longer and louder. Still nothing.

"Hey," I shouted, "how about moving out of the way!"

Barry turned and stared at me with a frown. "Go around!" he shouted, waving his hand and turning his back on me.

I sat motionless, staring at Barry's cold shoulder and feeling my blood pressure soaring higher and higher. *What do I do? Who the hell does he think he is?* I was not about to ignore such blatant and disrespectful behavior. Going around him would take me an extra ten or fifteen minutes to secure my pipe—and that didn't include the time it would take to transport it back to the rack. *Dammit! This isn't fair! But what can I do?*

At that point it hit me—I had a plan.

I drove forward, guiding my forklift blades beneath the rear of Barry's lift. Then I slowly raised the blades. Once I had the rear of his forklift elevated to about eight inches off the ground—I let it go. *Whump!* That got his attention.

"Hey!" he screamed. "Dixon, I told you to go around!" Again he turned his back on me.

Now I was really pissed. Had I been the type of fella who turned the other cheek, I would have been on my way back to my strapping rack, with my load delivered. But I wasn't that kind of fella. So, all rational thinking aside, I backed my blades out from under his lift, raised them to the height of his shoulders, and moved forward. I slowly closed the distance: three feet…two feet…one foot. Finally, from inches away, I poked the blade into Barry's shoulder. He winced as heavy steel met flesh-n-bone, and I knew instantly that I had screwed up.

"Cut it out!" he screamed, and I backed away.

"Then move the hell out of the way!"

"You'd better stop fooling around, Dixon! If you don't get back to work, I'm going to report your ass!"

At that point, I realized he had me. By letting my temper get the best of me, I had lost the high road. With no other recourse available, I took the detour—exactly what I should have done in the first place. Later that day I caught up with him and gave him a rare, but sincere apology.

"Barry, I'm sorry for poking you with the forklift. It was stupid. I bet it hurt, too, didn't it?"

"You bet your ass it hurt."

"So, you accept my apology? No hard feelings?"

"Apology accepted. Just don't ever pull another stunt like that again, Dixon!"

"You don't have to worry about that, I've learned my lesson."

The following Monday was the first day of October. I'll never forget it. Mr. Johnson, our supervisor, called me into his office. Jim Rouch and Barry were already there. Boy, were they sportin' some sour looks, and no face looked sourer than Jim's. Mr. Johnson went straight to the point.

"Tom, did you hit Barry with the forklift last week?"

"Uh, I didn't hit him, but I did poke him in the shoulder with it."

"Deliberately?"

"Yes sir."

"Why in the world would you do such a crazy thing?"

"He pissed me off."

"That's it? He pissed you off?"

"He wouldn't move. He just sat there, smoking a cigarette and blocking my way."

"I see," he said, glancing at Barry. "Well, you should have gone around him. You could have told us later that Barry was slowing you down."

"Yeah, I know that now. I apologized to him right after I did it."

"Tom, I think you've learned something from this. Unfortunately, we can't allow you to operate a forklift after pulling such a stunt. You're lucky we aren't firing you. Because you're such a hard worker—and we need you—we're going to give you another chance. You'll be on probation for a month. You can thank Jim for that. If it wasn't for him, I might be firing you right now."

I turned to Jim. "Thanks, Jim."

"It's okay, Tom. Now, get on out there and keep up the good work."

I walked back to my old workstation out in the yard, emotionally upset, almost in tears. My coworker greeted me there.

"Well, did you get the job?"

I could hardly speak. In all my life, I had never felt so distraught and angry at the same time.

"No…ahumm…I didn't."

"You didn't! Why not? I thought you did a great job with the forklift."

I would have rolled up into a ball like one of those wooly caterpillars and hid, were it not for my coworker staring at me. With my voice breaking at regular intervals, I told him how I had screwed up and how Mr. Johnson had almost fired me.

The worst part was Barry's squealing on me after my apology. He had accepted no blame. In his mind, it had been all my doing, my mess, my mistake. I guess he was right, in a cold, cruel sort of way.

I tried to put all these thoughts aside and concentrate on my job, but couldn't. I walked back into the office and asked the boss to let me take the rest of the day off.

"I can't believe you," he said. "We almost fire your ass, and you have the nerve to ask for the rest of the day off. No! I can't spare you! We're way too swamped with orders."

"I'm in no condition to work today, boss. I'm taking the day off anyway."

"I'll fire you if you do."

My mind started racing. I couldn't continue to work that day. I couldn't see returning the next day either, not with losing the forklift job, not with the pain and numbness I experienced every day with the banding tool, the use of which was a critical part of my job.

"Well, then, you won't have to—I quit!"

As the boss sat there, seemingly stunned, I stomped over to the time clock, punched my card, and stormed out of the office. On the way to my car, I told at least three coworkers that I had quit. They said they were sorry to see me go.

* * * * *

The next day I began a frantic search through the help wanted ads of the two Wilmington newspapers. As if things weren't bad enough, two of my roommates had moved into a dorm at the U. of Delaware, leaving George and me with double the rent. Desperate, with time and money running low, I applied for a forklift job at a warehouse in New Castle and another as a printing press operator at Delaware Bag, a textile company on the banks of the Christina River in Stanton. Both jobs said "No Experience Necessary—Will Train." With urging from my brother-in-law John, I also applied that Thursday for a lab assistant position with the DuPont Company in Wilmington. John said, "The job's right up your alley, Tom." Considering all the biology and chemistry courses I had taken at Wesley, he was surprised that I hadn't thought of it earlier. So was I.

My hopes were running high as I rode the elevator up several floors in the DuPont building. When I told the secretary I wanted to apply for a lab technician position, she said, "Oh, you're in the wrong place. You should be applying over at the Main Gate of the Experimental Station."

"Really? Where's that?"

I felt a bit dumb. I had lived in the Wilmington area for more than nine years without knowing where, or exactly what, the DuPont Experimental Station was.

She gave me some papers with directions and sent me on my way. At the Experimental Station I placed my application and promised to return the following Monday morning for a four-hour series of aptitude tests. Meanwhile, Delaware Bag called and asked if I could report for an interview on Tuesday morning.

That Friday I stopped by Kaiser and picked up my final paycheck. While there, I thanked Jim for getting me the job and apologized for having disappointed him. I also let him know about my injured hand and arm, saying I might have nerve damage and that it was probably for the best that I quit. He seemed to understand.

Two years of college courses had left me well prepped for the Monday morning aptitude tests at DuPont. I expected high marks in the math and mechanical sections, not so high on the verbal. On Tuesday I interviewed for the printing press job at Delaware Bag and, after a short test, they offered me the job on the spot. I accepted and was set to start my training the very next day.

That night, while I visited with Genia and Jeanette at their apartment, her mother called.

"Eugenia, are you sitting down?"

"No. Why? Why do you want me to sit down, Mom?"

Hearing her say that grabbed my attention.

"Well, you need to sit. I have some bad news."

I watched Genia pull a chair from the dining room table and take a seat next to the phone.

"Okay, I'm sitting. What is it, Mom?"

Earlier that week, an ocean away in Germany, Genia's adopted brother had been killed. Wentzel had apparently been run over by a truck while hitching a ride to his military base. The news must have hit Agnes and Ted like a sledgehammer. Fortunately, Jeanette and I were there to console Genia. Her mother said she would call again, after she gathered more information.

I started press training Wednesday with thoughts of Wentzel's demise haunting me. I had met him only once. Genia had introduced us a few weeks earlier while standing in her parents' driveway. He was on leave for two weeks, and we'd spoken fewer than a dozen words. *I wish I could have had more time to get to know him. I guess it was God's will—but why? He was only 21. Like Genia, me, and so many others, Wentzel had his whole life ahead of him.*

* * * * *

Learning to operate the printing press would have been a lot easier if it didn't break down so often. But with every problem, there's usually a new lesson to be learned. Two presses and dozens of heavy-duty industrial sewing machines were located on the second floor of a large 1920s-style factory building. Each floor measured about 3,000 sq. ft. Up to thirty women (and an odd male or two) operated the machines, sewing sections of burlap together to form a bag. The bags were stacked two feet high on a cart and then fed one bag at a time through one of the printing presses. The final product had the familiar red and white-checkered Purina pattern (as in Purina Cat Chow) emblazoned on one side. That is, if everything went according to plan.

I finished my second day on Thursday, wondering what the hell I'd gotten myself into. *Did I go to college for this?* First, the work area wasn't really air-conditioned; instead, fans sucked air through one end of the building and forced it out the other. Second, I went home reeking, the place stunk so bad—even with the forced air. Third, some of the women continually teased me, often in a suggestive fashion. I didn't know how to take it. Oddly enough, the women old enough to be my mother were the worst. I think I got my first real dose of on-the-job sexual harassment from some of the women at Delaware Bag. Finally, operating and repairing the press was a tedious and messy job. Since the machine jammed every hour or so, I spent a lot of time dealing with ink stains, rags, and solvents. Moreover, the outgoing operator was a lousy trainer, and at the end of the day he left me more confused than the day before. I began to question whether I had the right stuff for this job.

My pain and frustration ended on a Thursday night, when my roommate informed me that someone from the DuPont Company had called, offering me a job and telling me I should report to work the following Monday if I was interested. I called Delaware Bag Friday morning and gave them the bad news, and on Monday, the 15th of October, I reported to the Training Lab at the DuPont Experimental Station.

Kaiser was the first job I ever quit. Delaware Bag wasn't the last, but it was the easiest. Until then, I would have considered myself one of the most loyal employees a company could ever have. But I wasn't *that* stupid. Loyal, yes. Stupid, no. As long as my employer and boss were fair, ethical, and respectful in their treatment of employees and customers, I took great pride in always giving 110%. That included remaining a loyal employee, sometimes to my own detriment.

The next day I drove to Wentzel's funeral services, held just off Maryland Avenue in the Browntown section of Wilmington. My new employer gave me time off—without pay, of course. Sporting my one and only coat and tie, I met more of Genia's family, delivered my condolences, and forced myself to face someone I once met, someone I had high hopes of getting to know better, someone no longer of this world. I was 21 years old, stumbling through my first viewing. How sad that someone so young and so vital could skip out of this world so suddenly—and tragically. Wentzel was a budding mechanic. He loved to work on cars and rarely hesitated to bust a knuckle for a friend in need. A nonsmoker and serious weightlifter, he struck an impressive pose and was a shining example of health to all those around him. Later on I attended the funeral at All Saints Cemetery.

And so, no sooner had I turned from those somber reflections to more personal and immediate concerns, than the Organization (of Arab) Petroleum Exporting Countries (OAPEC) imposed an oil embargo on the United States. All this came about as a consequence of the U.S. having supplied the Israelis with weapons in the ongoing Arab-Israeli War (Oct. 6-26). By the end of that week, gas stations were limiting purchases to no more than ten gallons. The price of gasoline, which averaged 30 cents a gallon at the time, began to skyrocket, forcing me (and many Americans) to consider dumping my gas guzzling Ford Galaxy 500 for a newer, more economical vehicle.

A Touch of Reality

It was early November. After spending less than the expected two weeks in the training lab, I moved to a lab of my own, working under Dr. Michael Delmorro and Dr. George Sorenson, two top-notch Dupont chemists. Along with my job, the social and romantic aspects of my life were improving dramatically every day, and I wanted to tell somebody.

So I called on my old friend Sammy, eager to learn how her first semester at Wesley was going (without me there to add unnecessary excitement) and to let her know how things were going with me. I told her about my stimulating and challenging new job, and how much I enjoyed going to work and earning such good pay. I also let her know about Genia. She congratulated me, saying, "I told you, all you had to do was ask her out." I inquired about how things were going at the college and whether or not she had seen any of the "troublemakers" of old. She had. Hearing some of the students from my old dorm describe the ways I had treated them as dorm monitor, had caused her considerable embarrassment. She said, "They said you were a narc, a rat, and a jerk, Tom."

"Oh, I'm not surprised they felt that way," I said. "You know what a bunch of babies they were. I was just doing my job."

"Tom, I think they have a point. It really wasn't fair the way you treated them. They were only trying to have a good time."

That really hurt. I couldn't believe my own ears. They were only trying to have a good time? Sure, but at whose expense? Sammy had been there with me. She had seen every crooked stunt and prank those college "kids" had thrown at me, and at other people, and she had stood by and supported me as I reported some—but not all—of their dirty deeds. And now that I lived miles away, in flesh and spirit, she was exhibiting a surprising, 180-degree change in attitude. My parting words were: "Sammy, you just don't get it. I'm really sorry you feel that way. Good luck at Wesley." Then I hung up. I had never done that to anyone—ever.

I had been working as a lab assistant for about five weeks when my sole remaining roommate told me around Thanksgiving that he was giving up the lease to the apartment. When he asked me if I wanted to sign a new lease, I needed a couple of days to think it over.

And that's what I was doing while driving into work the next morning. I also fiddled with the radio, trying to find a good station and a good song with a good beat, something like *The Doobie Brothers*. I found one and settled back into my seat to enjoy it. The song: "Rockin' Roll Baby" by *The Stylistics*. I had heard the song once or twice before, but hadn't paid much attention to the lyrics. For the first time, I really heard the words: "He was born in a theater in Bluefield, West Virginia…" *Hey, what did he say?* Hardly believing what I had just heard, I continued to listen, and there it was again: "He was born in a theater in Bluefield, West Virginia…"

"Wow! They're singing about my hometown."

And the song, a Top 20 pop hit, came in at #14 on the charts. *The Stylistics* were one of the most successful soul-singing groups ever, with other hits like "Betcha by Golly, Wow" (#3), "I'm Stone in Love with You," "Break Up to Make Up" (#5), and "You Make Me Feel Brand New."

At work I told my bosses and a couple of coworkers about the song's lyrics. One boss said, "Cool." One of my coworkers said, "Big deal." Another said, "So?" I'm surprised one of them didn't add: "What do you want—a metal?" I didn't understand their lack of enthusiasm. Who wouldn't be excited and proud to have their hometown mentioned in a song by a famous group?

You can bet it was the first thing out of my mouth when I called Genia that night. Like my coworkers, she wasn't excited either, just happy for me. I also spoke to her about my option to lease the apartment, hoping she might want to move in with me. I didn't have time to pose the question. Instead, Genia and Jeannette invited me—out of the blue like—to room with them. Imagine that. Commuting from their New Castle apartment would cut my gasoline bill in half, at a time when gas was still being rationed. We all relished the thought of splitting the rent three ways. That meant less than $40 per month each, a real good deal.

I moved in with the girls, feeling on top of the world. I couldn't imagine how things could get any better. The three of us got along so well. I used most of the college tuition money from my savings account to buy a new bedroom set. Genia and I were tickled pink the night they delivered the furniture, exulting in our newfound freedom and the opportunity to share our own, brand new double bed.

That special glow fizzled a few days later, when Genia told her parents that the three of us were sharing the apartment. That little tidbit of news did not go over too well. Staunchly Catholic and old-fashioned, they didn't approve of us "living in sin" and demanded we separate; if we didn't, they vowed never to speak to Genia again.

That threat forced the two of us to step back and reevaluate our relationship. I had special feelings for Genia, much different than the feelings I had for the other women I dated. I thought that it might be serious this time, but I still wasn't totally sure what true love was. In any case, I was at least hoping this was it—the real deal. I'm pretty sure Genia hoped for the same. I guess you could say we thought we were in love and were committed to living together. For both of us, but especially for her, having our independence and doing what we wanted was more important than pleasing (kowtowing to) her parents. Many months would pass before Genia spoke again to either of them.

Jeanette moved out of the apartment in the spring of 1974. She left her sofa and end tables as going away presents. By this time Genia had secured a teller position working at Delaware Trust Company, one of the biggest banks in the state. Her branch office was located just three blocks down the street from the apartment.

* * * * *

October 1974 marked my one-year anniversary with DuPont. "Tom, you're doing a super job," my boss said, as he handed me a 3.5" x 8.5" slip of paper.

"What's this?" I asked.

"It's your last wage roll adjustment. If you look closely, you'll see that you've been promoted from lab assistant to lab technician. You're a salaried employee now, Tom. Congratulations!"

Yes! I couldn't wait to get home and give Genia the good news.

After that initial boost, I received regular cost of living and performance-based salary adjustments. I was beginning to love my job; I enjoyed all the benefits and challenges the position offered—flexible lunchtimes, weekly lunch outings with coworkers, monthly safety meetings, setting up and running experiments, collecting and analyzing dozens of samples every week, and, most of all, maintaining my very own research notebook. That's where I got the chance to record exactly what I did, along with the experimental results. Good notebook records were often critical when seeking future research patents. I learned something worthwhile almost every day, and I took pride in working hard and diligently, with near-perfect attendance.

I played hard, too. I was making friends at work, and I had just finished the summer playing on one of the teams from The Station Intramural Softball League. George, Mike, and I were teammates. They were super intelligent, kind, fair, and considerate bosses. Indeed, chemical research continued to grow into a challenging and stimulating occupation. So much so, that my ambition to finish college began to wane. My boss George asked me one day if I had considered taking night courses in chemistry. I said, "What for? I'm making a good salary here, and I love what I'm doing."

"You mean you don't want to finish school and earn your bachelor's in chemistry?"

"Why? I don't want to be a chemist. I like what I'm doing."

I've had many years to regret not acquiring a degree in chemistry. But, to this day, 40 years later, I still have no regrets. I just couldn't identify with a position that seemed such a far cry from working with my hands, building and creating something. It wasn't that I was lazy, or totally disinterested. On the contrary, I recall hitting the books many times to brush up on my chemistry. Mainly it was just that a chemistry degree wasn't a requirement, or necessary, to be a topnotch lab technician at that time. Lab technicians were the doers, the performers, the hands-on executants and installers. As a chemist, I'd be in an elevated position with more responsibility—managing subordinates, my own projects, a higher budget, and a significantly higher salary. I'd spend more time behind a desk balancing equations and drawing mechanisms that could lead to major discoveries, multiple patents and, hopefully, no loss of life should an equation not balance out. Yes, a few lab technicians and chemical operators had been seriously injured and even killed while on the job. I did not want to be responsible for someone else to that degree.

George dropped the subject that day, and I don't believe either of my bosses ever asked me again. Oh, and in addition to saving money, I had already paid back my student loan. Again, life was good.

Nonetheless, I was still concerned about my mother and little brother living with my father and making do in Boissevain. I thought I needed to be there and make sure things were okay. Some of my older siblings had reported that things were fine: "You know Dad, he's not much of a threat anymore. Mom and David can deal with him."

Genia and I decided to drive down to Virginia and visit the family over the Thanksgiving holiday. I wanted to see the situation with my own eyes and get the scoop straight from Mom and David.

EPILOGUE

Mom and Paul pose by the wood pile on Tank Hill Rd., July 1974.

Coming Home

Somehow my life in Delaware kept improving every day—I had a car, a job, a girlfriend, a roof over my head—while life for Mom and David in Boissevain seemed to be gradually worsening. I thought and worried about them often.

No sooner had Mom nursed Dad back to health than he started smoking and chewing tobacco again. Not smart for a man in his condition, but Mom and David chose not to make an issue of it. If those two vices helped keep him calm and happy, so be it! But they didn't suffice—not for Sleepy Dixon.

A year earlier, sometime in the spring of '73, Dad acquired a bottle of whiskey and started drinking again. And with the alcohol came verbal abuse and threats. When a man in such poor health threatened you, you can bet he didn't have a boxing match in mind.

Dad still kept a loaded .22 pistol and a .22 gauge bolt-action, single-shot rifle in the house. And amazingly, my mother allowed it.

David could hardly stand to be around his father, and the August try-outs for the Pocahontas High School football team gave him the perfect excuse to avoid his father's corrosive behavior. He was looking forward to impressing the coaches with his strength, speed, and overall athletic abilities.

It was scorching hot on the second day of practice, and David's exposed legs and arms still sizzled from the nasty sunburn he'd acquired the previous day. To top it off, Sleepy Dixon showed up. And he didn't just park his Ford Falcon in a designated area and watch his son from a distance like any normal father. No, he drove the car completely onto the practice field.

"Who the hell is that!" the coach shouted.

"It's my dad, coach," David said. "I'll go see what he wants."

"Yeah, you do that, Dixon. And tell him to get that car off the field and keep it off before I call the sheriff."

Dad had stopped the car almost in the middle of the field. The windows were rolled completely down, and David noticed that his father's long and lanky arm had scraped dirt from the door, like a windshield wiper blade, as he sucked on a nearly exhausted cigarette.

"Dad, what are you doing here? Cars aren't allowed on the field."

"How long is this game gonna take?"

"It's practice, Dad, not a game. Why?"

"I just wanted to make sure you were home in time to feed the chickens. You know they can't feed themselves."

"Don't worry. I'll be home in time to feed the chickens. Now, could you get the car off the field before the coach gets upset?"

"Oh, I'm not afraid of him."

"Dad! Would you please leave before you get me in trouble?"

"Uh…alright then, but I want your ass home within the hour."

David backed away and watched his father slowly maneuver the car off the field. As the Falcon disappeared from view, he returned to his coach and teammates, overcome with embarrassment.

Two days later, Dad drove the car onto the field again. This time he was drunk, and the coach and players knew it. David quit the team that day, without getting a chance to play in a single football game. Such humiliation rushed upon him in waves, even days later, and he began to wonder how much more of Sleepy Dixon he could endure.

Throughout that fall and again come springtime, Dad forced David to "earn his keep" by helping him strip parts from abandoned vehicles that littered the gullies and roadsides around Boissevain and Pocahontas. David worked all day at this, while his father gave orders and directions. All he received in return for his busted and bleeding knuckles was a hotdog and soda.

Looking back, I believe Dad thought that whatever he did was for the good of the family. In his own mind, he was always right. On the rare occasion that he "fessed up" to making a mistake, he usually blamed it on circumstances; or alcohol, a handy, all too convenient scapegoat. When conniving and manipulation failed to achieve his desired results, Dad would often resort to threats to get David (or Mom, for that matter) to do something.

Dad often insisted that David tag along when he wanted to get drunk at a Pocahontas bar or restaurant. David stood by, ready and available to drive him home, although he hadn't yet obtained a driver's license. Dad wasn't about to lose his license to a DUI; he would rather have his son take the heat. If the authorities were to find him passed out in the car with his son driving, he assumed that he could escape the consequences.

On one bitter cold and snowy night, David was driving home with his father drunk and passed out in the passenger seat without his seatbelt fastened. Out of the blue he thought of abandoning the car with his father inside, then watch it make a 30-foot drop to the railroad tracks below. Of course he didn't follow through with the plan. He wisely concluded that he didn't want such a murderous deed to haunt him the rest of his life. But he sure did think about it a lot.

* * * * *

Genia and I had a fantastic driving experience on our way to Boissevain to visit the family. Before the trip we thought about driving her Mustang with its extra wide mag wheels. We'd look so cool. But gas was now 55 cents a gallon and the trip involved some serious mountain climbing. Genia said, "Why don't you want to take your Galaxy, Tom?"

"Its gas mileage isn't much better than your Mustang's, Genia. Plus, I don't think it will survive a one thousand mile round trip. The odometer already shows 120,000 miles. Don't you want a pleasant trip without any hassles?"

Well, after taking all things into consideration, I decided to sell the Ford Galaxy to my brother for $100. It was a good deal for both of us, since Ronnie wanted to drop the engine into another, nicer looking Galaxy 500, one that didn't list to starboard like a sinking ship. Then, after signing for my very first auto loan, Genia drove me to Van's Chevrolet on DuPont Highway where I bought a used aqua green, four-door, 1970 Chevy Nova. It had an inline, slant six, 230 cu. in. engine. Thanks to the Air Quality Act of 1967, it also utilized a few rather crude pollution control devices that hampered its performance. No matter, I wanted economy; if I had wanted speed and power, I would have taken the Mustang. I thought the Nova was the all-around perfect answer for our traveling jitters, but I had a few things to learn.

After ten hours of laughter, sightseeing, and rock-n-roll, the two of us arrived on Boissevain Mountain much later than expected, mostly due to the Nova's poor mountain climbing abilities. Fortunately, there were no breakdowns. The first sight of the house amazed me. I would never have imagined my family members living there with my father, in the very same house "the old colored lady" had lived in, barely a hundred feet downhill from Mama's old place, which had been demolished, by the way. Mom, David, and Dad seemed so happy to see us, and Mom was especially happy to meet Genia for the first time. David gave us an enthusiastic tour of his little farmlet on the hill, boasting about how he had practically rebuilt the chicken house all by himself, "with nothing but lip from Dad." David introduced us to a new litter of puppies, which startled me. *Wow, Dad has not only allowed a dog in the house, but a female with puppies, too. He sure has mellowed out.*

Following the tour, Mom cooked dinner: baked chicken, green beans, mashed potatoes and gravy, and homemade biscuits. Not unusual fare in the least, but oh so much better than the fast food and TV dinners Genia and I had been consuming. After dinner we played cards and watched television, sitting on a sofa by the wood stove, while Mom and Dad relaxed on their bed over in the corner. A smoker herself, Genia grew nauseated watching Dad's manners. Smoking rolled cigarettes was one thing, but chewing and spitting tobacco into a pot on the floor was a bit too much, especially when he missed—which was often.

When the sun goes down in the mountains the temperature drops fast, and a bedtime walk to the outhouse happens to be a good test for braving the elements. I managed to talk Genia into the trip.

"Genia, you don't have any choice up here on the mountain. The closest public restroom is miles away." Her only other choice was the chamber pot in the bedroom.

She quickly relented, but only after insisting I keep her company on the walk. Mom and David's exaggerated tales of early morning confrontations with black bears had put her on edge.

A sheet, two blankets, and a thick quilt helped us stay warm and toasty in our bed. When nature called early the next morning, the temperature had dropped to the mid-40s inside the bedroom. The chamber pot didn't give me pause; I quickly did my business and hopped back into the warm bed. But during the night Genia realized that she couldn't keep ignoring Mother Nature. About three o'clock in the morning she had her first visit to the chamber pot, another milestone.

During the final day of our visit Genia helped Mom in the kitchen, while David and I repaired the roof on the chicken house. Later, David and I made kindling out of a dead apple tree we'd felled in the front yard. Just before sundown, Dad loaned us his revolver and some ammunition for target practice. While he watched from a rocking chair on the back porch, David, Genia, and I practiced shooting cans on a stump about twenty yards away. In the middle of all this, we were startled by a strange commotion to our left. It was my father shimmying up one of the porch support columns, like a linesman climbing a utility pole but minus the boots and spikes.

I said, "Dad, what the hell are you doing?"

Dad's beady eyes stared down at us from the top of the pole. "I'll bet…betcha you didn't think your old man could do this," he grunted, straining to maintain his grip, "now—did-ja?"

I said, "I don't know, Dad. I never really thought about it before."

Red in the face and still holding on, he said, "I still got some piss-n-vinegar left in me."

David says, "Yeah, Dad, we know you're full of it. Now you better get down from there before you mess your pants." Genia and I burst into loud laughter, as Dad slid slowly back down to the porch floor.

I said, "Okay, Dad, you fooled me. I didn't think you had it in ya." Breathing heavily, Dad just smiled and took a seat in his rocker. We put in five more minutes of target practice, and then Mom called us in for our final dinner.

Before leaving, David took me aside and told me that Dad had been on his best behavior while we were there. He also informed me that our father had begun drinking again, making him nervous and apprehensive, not only about his safety, but especially for his mother's safety. David had been locking his bedroom door at night and placing a baseball bat near his bed. If Dad tried to break into his room at night, David was prepared to greet his father with a wood-splintered kiss. With this plan in place, David found that he could study and complete most of his homework assignments in his bedroom, while ensuring that he could handle his father's potential violent interruptions.

Driving back to Delaware the next morning, I told Genia that I believed David's fears and reservations were real, and that Mom wasn't being honest when I asked her how things were "really" going. Genia said, "Oh, your father didn't seem so bad. Maybe he has changed. I thought he was funny, although in a disgusting kind of way."

"I don't know. You know, it's almost 1975, Genia. Fewer and fewer people are living such an antiquated life. It's one thing for Dad to want to live like that, but Mom doesn't have to. I think she's taking on too much. And it's hard on David."

"It's her decision, Tom. There's nothing we can do about it at this point. Sooner or later these things will all work out, and probably for the best."

"Yeah, I sure hope you're right."

Commitments

Sometime between Thanksgiving and Christmas, Genia gave me an ultimatum: "Marry me, or hit the road, buddy." It was a not-so-subtle reminder that the test drive period had ended; I would have to buy this car or turn it in. We both knew and accepted each other's shortcomings. She couldn't cook and had a temper. I couldn't tune a car and had an even worse temper. We both were products of a dysfunctional family, etcetera, etcetera, and etcetera. I knew she was serious, and it forced me to admit that I loved her too much to lose her. I said, "Genia, I'm a much better person with you by my side." Plus, I had experienced enough relationships. I didn't want any more playing the field, and I thought this might be the real deal. Alone, in our apartment one evening, I dropped to my knee and formally asked her to marry me. She said yes, and we set a date for the following spring, April 26, 1975.

* * * * *

I had just celebrated my twenty-third birthday in late January when we got the news from one of my siblings. Mom and Dad had a big blowout argument, so big that they called the sheriff to break it up. It all started with Dad's unrelenting, false accusations that Mom had been "fooling around" with other men while living and raising us kids in Delaware. It was all utter trash-talk. I had never seen Mom share a cup of coffee with another man, let alone date one. For her, sleeping with another man would have been total anathema, even though all her children felt she deserved a good one and encouraged her to keep her options open.

No one knows or remembers exactly what Dad said or did to Mom that day, but something snapped. First, she got good-n-drunk after belting down half of Dad's whiskey stash. Then, while David stood guard in his upstairs bedroom with a loaded rifle, she snatched the pistol from Dad and yelled, "Now, you dirty bastard, I dare you to get up from that bed!"

"You ain't doing shit with that gun," he said, making a move toward Mom.

Mom fired. *Pow! Pow!* Two bullets struck the wall inches from Dad's head. Mom had Dad on his knees, in bed, cowering in the corner.

"Aaaeee, David!" he screamed, "get down here and stop your mother before she kills me! David! Help! David!"

Mom had just fired another round close to Dad's head when David walked into the living room.

"David, take that gun from your mother before she shoots me."

David took a good look at his humbled father cowering in the corner, ready to pee himself. He thought, Dad, you made your damn bed. Now you're gonna hafta lie in it. Seeing that Mom had everything under control, David said, "I'm not getting involved in this," and returned to his room, where he locked the door. Unable to concentrate, he put aside his homework. Twenty minutes later, with Dad still being held at bay, loud banging and shouting rattled the front door.

"Sleepy! Sleepy Dixon! This is the sheriff! Are you in there?" Someone had heard the gunshots and called the law.

"Help! Sheriff! Help me! My old lady's gonna shoot me!"

Mom said, "Go away, sheriff, this is between Harold and me!"

"Mrs. Dixon, somebody better open this door, or I'm gonna break it down!"

Hearing this, David thought it was best that he answer the door.

Dad told the sheriff that Mom had fired the gun at him. Three fresh bullet holes in the living room wall seemed like good enough evidence. And, of course, she admitted to firing the shots. Dad told the sheriff he wasn't going to put up with his "old lady" shooting at him. Can you imagine that; after the way he treated her for years? Dad said, "I want to press charges against her." With that, the sheriff had no choice but to haul Mom into jail.

Wesley flew all the way to Roanoke from Fort Greely, Alaska. Then he hopped a Greyhound bus to be at Mom's court hearing in Tazewell, Virginia. Ronnie and Linda drove down from Delaware. They all, including Dad, sat in court waiting their turn with the judge, who happened to be Judge Peery, the same one who had sentenced Dad so many times before.

They watched and listened as the judge worked the case before theirs, where a woman had fired a weapon at several co-workers for some crazy reason. Everyone watched Judge Peery practically throw the book at the woman. Wesley said, "Oh shit. This don't look good for Mom." Linda began to cry, thinking about her sweet, gentle mother-in-law, who was about to do some serious jail time.

When the court called our family's case, Wesley took it upon himself to approach the judge. He had something special he wanted to say, something he'd practiced over and over during the long trip by plane and bus.

"Judge, I want to present my mother's case from the position of a child, a child suffering from years of abuse at the hands of a mean and miserable old bastard, a man living his last days with nothing but his vices—which are many—and a biting and nasty tongue to keep him company. Your honor, since I am the oldest son, I know for a fact that my father has been in your court more times than I can count. That's why I'm hoping you will take all of this into consideration before you sentence our mother."

The Judge turned from Wesley and looked at Mom. "Mrs. Dixon, I've read your case. When I hadn't seen or heard from you after five years, I thought you had finally rid yourself of this lousy, no-count husband of yours. It's been ten years. I never expected to see you standing here in front of me. Not like this. What do you have to say for yourself?"

"Your honor, I was a fool to think Harold had changed."

Wesley said, "Judge, Mom needs some peace-n-quiet. She needs to go home to Delaware."

"Myrtle, do you have a place to stay in Delaware?"

"Yes, your honor, I do."

Judge Peery fined Mom a small amount plus court costs and sent her on her way. He also set down a condition; Mom had to promise she'd "never—ever—see her husband again."

Once outside the courthouse, they all relaxed a bit. "Come on, Mom," Wesley said, grabbing her arm, "let's go pack your stuff."

"No you don't," Dad complained, "if that woman puts a foot on my property again, I'll shoot her."

Wesley stared close-up and deep into his father's eyes.

"Well, you'd better get a good head start, cause I'm comin', and I'm comin' armed."

All bluff, Dad backed down. He stayed away from the house most of the day, allowing Mom time to pack her belongings and leave in peace. She moved back to Delaware and began living with Donna and John in Woodcrest.

* * * * *

David finished the tenth grade at Pocahontas High while living with Ginny and family in Abbs Valley. In June he returned to Delaware to live with Paul and Linda in Cheswold. He entered the eleventh grade at Dover High School in September, 1975.

Debbie was working and sharing an apartment with a girlfriend in Wilmington. A couple of years earlier, on September 20, 1973, she had received official notification of her discharge from the custody of Juvenile Corrections, a division of the Delaware Department of Health and Social Services. She was seventeen-and-a-half years old.

Harold "Sleepy" Dixon, sittin'-n-spittin,' on Tank Hill Road, c. 1974.

The letter stated:

"Dear Deborah...Such discharge from legal custody terminates all legal aftercare responsibility of the staff in your case... If you have not passed your eighteenth (18th) birthday, your legal custody returns to your legal parents or legal guardians unless otherwise awarded by court action."

Having officially "aged out" of foster care, Debbie caught a Greyhound bus to Ayer, Massachusetts and began living with Daisy and her family. She worked her first job in an apple factory, packing apples. Three months after she turned 18, she quit her job and caught a Greyhound back to Delaware. Thereafter, Debbie was on her own.

Gary was partying hard and working hard, off and on—but mostly off—at various carpentry and roofing jobs, and trying to stay out of trouble while living with his girlfriend's family in New Castle, Delaware. The rest of my siblings were married and focused on their jobs, raising families, and becoming productive citizens of this great country.

Genia and I were married as planned on April 26. We enjoyed a small, informal ceremony at The Little Wedding Chapel in Elkton, Maryland where several family members and close friends attended. A smaller, rather raucous, reception followed at our apartment in Wilmington Manor. About half of the family attended. We felt especially happy when Genia's mother showed up at the wedding and stopped by the reception briefly to congratulate us and wish us the best. Her father remained stubborn. Having both our mothers present was the real icing on the cake. We spent the first week of May on our honeymoon at Disney World in Orlando, Florida.

* * * * *

Thomas and Eugenia, wed, April 26, 1975.

In December 1975, Dad was overcome with complications related to emphysema and black lung disease, made worse by the fact that he wouldn't give up drinking and smoking. Also, without someone like Mom or Blanch to nurture and take care of him, he hadn't eaten properly or paid any attention to health issues. He spent several days in the Bluefield hospital, gasping for every breath, before expiring on January 10, 1976, two months shy of his fifty-seventh birthday.

My parents' marriage may not have been the worst ever, but—damn—was it bad, or what! My mother and father were like oil and water. They were as opposite as white and black, good and evil. Unfortunately, in this case, they were also like magnets: Mom was the (+) and Dad was the (-), and, far too often, the two seemed to work their way together. Much of my mother's struggle took place in an era and geographical location where many people ignored brutal spousal treatment, and some folks downright condoned casual spousal abuse. Mom stuck with our father for many (30 plus) years out of fear for our safety. Yet, we know it wasn't fear that prompted her behavior that last time; it was anger and frustration. Alcohol, as it so often does, provided the spark for conflagration. I'd like to believe it was a combination of divine intervention, plain old luck, and an innate goodness lurking deep within my father's soul that allowed us all to survive him. If our father had really wanted to do deadly harm to his family, he would have done so. He had so many opportunities.

A month or two after Mom and Dad's final split-up, Dad paid a visit to his (so-called) favorite daughter, in Abb's Valley, Virginia. Ginny's youngest, little Wanda, was about a year old. "Ginny," Dad shouted down the hallway, "the baby just spit up! She needs to be changed, too!" For a second she thought, What's he doing in the bedroom with Wanda, anyway? Then she realized that Dad had gone to the room to play and bond with his newest granddaughter. Ginny found it rather touching.

Normally a robust and proud woman, Mom would often set aside her pride if it helped support and protect her children. Nevertheless, little could undermine her strong moral character. Neither Mom nor Dad had a need or desire to get a divorce, let alone remarry. Dad shared company with other women. Mom, on the other hand, never divorced our father and for a reason—she simply had no desire for another man. She, unlike her husband, never dated.

I'll always recall a remark she made a time or two. The first time was shortly after leaving Dad the last time. She was almost 53 years old, and someone said, "Mom, you need a good man in your life."

Mom replied, "Oh no. I'll never have another one of those dirty son-of-a-bitches."

True to her word, she never did.

Sources of Reference

- The *Evening Journal* and The *Morning News,* two precursors (1989) to The *News Journal,* the Wilmington, DE newspaper.
- The *Bluefield Daily Telegraph*, the Bluefield, WV newspaper.
- Delaware Historical Society, Wilmington, DE
- Delaware Public Archives, Dover, DE
- The Killeen Area Heritage Association, Killeen, TX
- Mercer County Circuit Court, Records, Princeton, WV
- Tazewell County Circuit Court, Records, Tazewell, VA
- Family, friends, pertinent others, and a lifetime of interviews

Thomas, at home, March 2014.

ABOUT THE AUTHOR

THOMAS DIXON has kept himself busy most of his life, sweating his way through hot summer jobs as a young man, participating in numerous sports, several organizations, and serving his country in the Delaware Air National Guard. He worked in the chemical research field for more than 30 years before retiring in 2008. Five weeks later, his mother's death spurred him to collect notes and memories for a long overdue family history. He finally found something he truly enjoyed—writing about his life. After a lot of work and much consideration, he decided to publish his stories as a series of memoirs, feeling there's much to be learned from reading the highlights of anyone's life, not just the rich or famous.

TOMMY MACK: An Appalachian Childhood is his first memoir, and *TOMMY MACK: Unsettled Years* is the sequel. He has grown more ambitious and plans, not one, but two more books based primarily on the evolution of his life with much smaller bits and pieces of the Dixon family. Tom also enjoys puttering around the house, taking his time with handyman projects, and sharing precious moments with family, especially his two daughters and three granddaughters. At this publishing, he resides in Newark, Delaware with his wife Mildred.

PHOTO DIRECTORY

No.	Name	Page(s)
1	David	17
2	Debbie	18, 184, 267
3	Gary	17, 184, 267
4	Tom 19, 96, 201, 214, 236, 246, 262, 267,	278, 322, 326
5	Donna	17, 50
6	Paul	17, 96, 308
7	Ginny	267
8	Ronnie	96, 120, 214
9	Wesley	80
10	Daisy	48
11	Myrtle (Mom)	308
12	Harold (Dad)	320
13	Newport aerials: 1932, 1962, 1966	xvi, 70, 71
14	Newport: old bridge, Wroten's Hardware	56, 98
15	Newport: Krebs School, Conrad High	64, 156
16	Killeen: '64 aerial, Ave. D at Gray St. '74	29, 30-31
17	Killeen: off-base housing & '62 Pontiac	39
18	Boissevain Company Store and P.O., VA	138
19	Jenkinjones Company Store and P.O., WV	142
20	Jenkinjones, Trestle Hollow Road, WV	143
21	Richardson Park at Aunt Kitty's old place	2
22	Elsmere at # 5 Rodman Road	216

NOTES

CPSIA information can be obtained at www.ICGtesting.com
Printed in the USA
BVOW07s1228131114

374980BV00001B/48/P